## CHRISTIANITY AND MARKET REGULATION

Historically, the Christian tradition has played an influential role in Western economic thought concerning the regulation of markets, but, with the fracturing of the Christian tradition following the Reformation, the decline of Christian influence in academia, and the increasing specialization of economic analysis, that influence has become increasingly opaque. This volume brings together an interdisciplinary team of prominent academic experts on market regulation from four different continents and various faith traditions to reconsider the impact of Christianity on market regulation. Drawing on law, economics, history, theology, philosophy, and political theory, the authors consider both general questions of market regulation and particular regulatory fields such as bankruptcy, corporate law, and antitrust from a Christian perspective.

DANIEL A. CRANE is the Frederick Paul Furth, Sr. Professor of Law at the University of Michigan and counsel at Paul, Weiss, Rifkind, Wharton & Garrison LLP. His scholarship focuses primarily on antitrust and economic history. He is the author of many books and articles on antitrust and competition policy, including *The Institutional Structure of Antitrust Enforcement* (2011).

SAMUEL GREGG is Research Director at the Acton Institute. He is the author of many books including *Reason, Faith, and the Struggle of Western Civilization* (2019), *For God and Profit: How Banking and Finance Serve the Common Good* (2016), *Becoming Europe* (2013), and *Wilhelm Röpke's Political Economy* (2010). He is a Fellow of the Royal Historical Society.

## Law and Christianity



The Law and Christianity series publishes cutting-edge work on Catholic, Protestant, and Orthodox Christian contributions to public, private, penal, and procedural law and legal theory. The series aims to promote deep Christian reflection by leading scholars on the fundamentals of law and politics, to build further ecumenical legal understanding across Christian denominations, and to link and amplify the diverse and sometimes isolated Christian legal voices and visions at work in the academy. Works collected by the series include groundbreaking monographs, historical and thematic anthologies, and translations by leading scholars around the globe.

### Books in the series

*Christianity and the Laws of Conscience: An Introduction* Helen M. Alvaré and Jeffrey B. Hammond

*Infidels and Empires in a New World Order: Early Modern Spanish Contributions to International Legal Thought* David Lantigua

*The Possibility of Religious Freedom: Early Natural Law and the Abrahamic Faiths* Karen Taliaferro

*Catholic Social Teaching: A Volume of Scholarly Essays* edited by Gerard Bradley and E. Christian Brugger

*The Immortal Commonwealth: Covenant, Community, and Political Resistance in Early Reformed Thought* David P. Henreckson

*Great Christian Jurists in American History* edited by Daniel L. Dreisbach and Mark David Hall

*Great Christian Jurists and Legal Collections in the First Millennium* Philip L. Reynolds

*English Ecclesiastical Lawyers: A History of Their Life and Work* R. H. Helmholz

*Law, Love and Freedom: From the Sacred to the Secular* Joshua Neoh

*Great Christian Jurists in French History* Olivier Descamps and Rafael Domingo

*Church Law in Modernity: Toward a Theory of Canon Law Between Nature and Culture* Judith Hahn

*Common Law and Natural Law in America: From the Puritans to the Legal Realists* Andrew Forsyth

*Care for the World: Laudato Si' and Catholic Social Thought in an Era of Climate Crisis* edited by Frank Pasquale

*Church, State, and Family: Reconciling Traditional Teachings and Modern Liberties* John Witte, Jr.

*Great Christian Jurists in Spanish History* Rafael Domingo and Javier Martínez-Torrón

*Under Caesar's Sword: How Christians Respond to Persecution* edited by Daniel Philpott and Timothy Samuel Shah

*God and the Illegal Alien* Robert W. Heimburger

*Christianity and Family Law* John Witte, Jr. and Gary S. Hauk

*Christianity and Natural Law* Norman Doe

*Great Christian Jurists in English History* edited by Mark Hill, QC and R. H. Helmholz

*Agape, Justice, and Law* edited by Robert F. Cochran, Jr. and Zachary R. Calo

*Calvin's Political Theology and the Public Engagement of the Church* Matthew J. Tuininga

*God and the Secular Legal System* Rafael Domingo

*How Marriage Became One of the Sacraments* Philip L. Reynolds

*Christianity and Freedom (Volume I: Historical Perspectives, Volume II: Contemporary Perspectives)* edited by Timothy Samuel Shah and Allen D. Hertzke

*The Western Case for Monogamy Over Polygamy* John Witte, Jr.

*The Distinctiveness of Religion in American Law* Kathleen A. Brady

*Pope Benedict XVI's Legal Thought* Marta Cartabia and Andrea Simoncini

# Christianity and Market Regulation

AN INTRODUCTION

*Edited by*
DANIEL A. CRANE
University of Michigan

SAMUEL GREGG
Acton Institute

CAMBRIDGE
UNIVERSITY PRESS

**CAMBRIDGE**
**UNIVERSITY PRESS**

University Printing House, Cambridge CB2 8BS, United Kingdom

One Liberty Plaza, 20th Floor, New York, NY 10006, USA

477 Williamstown Road, Port Melbourne, VIC 3207, Australia

314–321, 3rd Floor, Plot 3, Splendor Forum, Jasola District Centre, New Delhi – 110025, India

79 Anson Road, #06–04/06, Singapore 079906

Cambridge University Press is part of the University of Cambridge.

It furthers the University's mission by disseminating knowledge in the pursuit of education, learning, and research at the highest international levels of excellence.

www.cambridge.org
Information on this title: www.cambridge.org/9781108495103
DOI: 10.1017/9781108860932



First published 2021

*A catalogue record for this publication is available from the British Library.*

*Library of Congress Cataloging-in-Publication Data*
NAMES: Crane, Daniel A., editor. | Gregg, Samuel, 1969– editor.
TITLE: Christianity and market regulation : an introduction / edited by Daniel A. Crane, University of Michigan, Ann Arbor; Samuel Gregg, Acton Institute.
DESCRIPTION: Cambridge, United Kingdom ; New York, NY : Cambridge University Press, 2021. | Series: Law and Christianity | Includes index. Provided by publisher.
IDENTIFIERS: LCCN 2020045370 (print) | LCCN 2020045371 (ebook) | ISBN 9781108495103 (hardback) | ISBN 9781108816939 (paperback) | ISBN 9781108860932 (epub)
SUBJECTS: LCSH: Capital market–Law and legislation. | Capital market–Religious aspects–Christianity. | Capital market–Deregulation. | Corporation law. | Antitrust law. | Subsidiarity.
CLASSIFICATION: LCC K1114 .C47 2021 (print) | LCC K1114 (ebook) | DDC 346/.09–DC23
LC record available at https://lccn.loc.gov/2020045370
LC ebook record available at https://lccn.loc.gov/2020045371s

ISBN 978-1-108-49510-3 Hardback

# Contents

# Contributors

**André Azevedo Alves** is Associate Professor at the Catholic University of Portugal's Institute for Political Studies and Reader in Economics, Political Economy, and Public Policy, and member of the Benedict XVI Centre for the Study of Religion and Society at St. Mary's University, London. He is coauthor of the book *The Salamanca School* (Bloomsbury, 2013).

**Margo A. Bagley** is Asa Griggs Candler Professor at the Emory University School of Law and previously held the Hardy Cross Dillard chair at the University of Virginia School of Law. Her publications include the coauthored books *International Patent Law and Policy* (2013) and *Patent Law in Global Perspective* (2014). A member of the National Academies Committee on Advancing Commercialization from the Federal Laboratories, she is an expert advisor to the African Union, and has been a consultant to WIPO, the FAO, and the CBD.

**Stephen M. Bainbridge** is William D. Warren Distinguished Professor of Law. He has written over 100 law review articles and 19 books, including 7 in multiple editions. According to Gregory Sisk and Brian Leiter's rankings of law professors by scholarly impact, Bainbridge was the third most frequently cited scholar in corporate law for the period 2013–2017.

**Philip Booth** is Professor of Finance, Public Policy, and Ethics at St. Mary's University, Twickenham and Director of the Vinson Centre for the Public Understanding of Economics and Entrepreneurship at the University of Buckingham. Philip has also worked at the Bank of England and has honorary positions at the University of Kent and Notre Dame University, Australia. He blogs at and edits the www.catholicsocialthought.org.uk website.

**Kenneth G. Elzinga** is Robert C. Taylor Professor of Economics at the University of Virginia. His specialty is antitrust economics and he was the economic expert in three Supreme Court cases. Elzinga has written four mystery novels and his Principles of Economics course at UVA attracts 1,000 students each year.

**Andrew Godley** is Professor of Business History and Management at Henley Business School. He cofounded the Henley Centre for Entrepreneurship, one of the leading university entrepreneurship centers in the world, and he is Chair of the Department of Leadership, Organizations, and Behaviour as well as the Associate Dean International. He has published many articles in the discipline of business history, with a particular focus on understanding the role and impact of context on entrepreneurial behavior through time.

**Inês Gregório** is a research assistant at the Catholic University of Portugal's Institute for Political Studies, where she is also a teaching assistant in BA in Political Science and International Relations. Her work is mainly related with public policies on education.

**Ian Harper** is Dean and Director of Melbourne Business School at the University of Melbourne and a member of the governing board of Australia's central bank. He is a professional economist best known for his work in public policy, and has worked with governments, banks, corporates, and leading professional services firms at the highest level.

**Danielle C. Lloyd** is a 2021 Master of Divinity graduate from the Candler School of Theology and a 2011 Master of Leadership & Public Policy graduate from the Batten School at the University of Virginia, is an Atlanta-based project manager and community engagement professional. A former Emory University School of law research assistant, her research and practical interests involve using public policy and community engagement to address issues of affordable housing, economic inequality, and the effects of racial injustice from a Christian perspective.

**Carroll Rios de Rodríguez** is cofounder and president of Instituto Fe y Libertad, op-ed columnist for *Prensa Libre*, a trustee and professor at Francisco Marroquín University, and board member of Centro de Estudios Económico-Sociales in Guatemala. She is also a member of The Mont Pelerin Society and The Philadelphia Society.

**Brian Rosner** is the principal of Ridley College, Melbourne, Australia, having previously taught at Moore Theological College and the University of

Aberdeen in Scotland. He is the author or editor of more than a dozen books and a New Testament scholar of international standing with expertise in biblical ethics.

**David Skeel** is S. Samuel Arsht Professor of Corporate Law at the University of Pennsylvania Law School. He is the author of *True Paradox: How Christianity Makes Sense of Our Complex World* (InterVarsity, 2014); *The New Financial Deal: Understanding the Dodd-Frank Act and Its (Unintended) Consequences* (Wiley, 2011); *Icarus in the Boardroom* (Oxford, 2005); *Debt's Dominion: A History of Bankruptcy Law in America* (Princeton, 2001); and numerous articles on bankruptcy, corporate law, financial regulation, Christianity and law, and other topics. Professor Skeel has also written commentaries for the New York Times, Wall Street Journal, Books & Culture, The Weekly Standard, and other publications. He has received the Harvey Levin award three times for outstanding teaching, as selected by a vote of the graduating class, the Robert A. Gorman award for excellence in upper level course teaching, and the University's Lindback Award for distinguished teaching.

# Acknowledgments

The editors gratefully acknowledge the excellent research assistance on this volume of Jesse Schupack and Brian Weber.

# Introduction

DANIEL A. CRANE AND SAMUEL GREGG

The regulation of economic life, whether through law or politics, has been a fixture of daily life from time immemorial. Formal regulation occurs through a variety of formal devices, the efficacy of which is argued about by legal scholars, economists, policymakers, legislators, and governments. Even expressions like "to regulate" or "to deregulate" carry a range of political and even moral connotations, depending on who is using the phrase and how they are deploying it.

Different historical periods are marked by greater and lesser degrees of regulation. Much of Adam Smith's *Wealth of Nations* amounts to a critique of the extensive regulation of trade and commerce that was part and parcel of the mercantile system. The nineteenth century witnessed efforts to diminish regulations and broader laws in many Western countries that had allowed the hundreds – if not thousands – of guilds to control the entry of individuals into various professions, the prices charged to customers by those in different occupations, etc., for several hundred years. Re-regulation of considerable portions of economic life had, however, begun by the beginning of the twentieth century and accelerated after World War I and the Great Depression. From the mid-1970s, a significant amount of deregulation occurred in many Western economies. Following the Great Recession of 2008, there was a swing back toward regulation, especially with regard to the financial sector.

The reasons for these developments varied. They have included ongoing concerns about the emergence of potentially anticompetitive behavior, the belief that the state must have a role in ensuring health and safety in the workplace and the making and selling of products and services, and, in some cases, the desire on the part of governments and legislators to be seen to be "doing something" in the wake of a major economic scandal or severe economic downturn that is deemed to be the result of inadequate regulation.

One reason that the topic of regulation evokes considerable argument is that it is inseparable from issues of the extent and character of state power. Regulation is, after all, the requirements that the state enacts and enforces on private and collective economic actors in order to realize specific ends. This can be further broken down in to the type of regulation that defines who can create a business or profession as well as the prices that they charge, and the type of regulation that governs how individuals and companies act in order to address what are often considered market failures.[1]

On one level, regulation does touch on issues of utility and efficiency. Much economic literature, for instance, focuses on whether a given regulation will contribute (or not) to the smooth workings of the economy, or whether it will end up distorting incentives. At the same time, the topic of regulation cannot be separated from questions of liberty, justice, and the common good. Regulation not only seeks to shape the ways in which market actors operate. To some extent, it is concerned with what people owe each other as a matter of commutative, distributive, and legal justice, and is directed (at least ostensibly) toward helping to realize what is often called "the common good": that sum of conditions that help people to pursue the types of goods that are central to the flourishing of all individuals and groups in a given community.[2]

There is, however, another way of thinking about regulation. Law, legislation, and the state are formal ways of shaping economic action and are accompanied by legal coercion. But there are other elements that can guide our free choices and actions from without and that operate separately from government. What was called, for example, the *lex mercatoria* that regulated much international trade and commerce throughout the medieval and early-modern period was, for the most part, something that emerged from below rather than being imposed from above.[3]

Though it was often adjudicated by what were effectively private arbitrators and occasionally enforced by public courts, the *lex mercatoria* consisted primarily of customs and practices adhered to, at least initially, on a voluntary basis and very much influenced by the experiences of merchants rather than governments and political leaders. The *lex mercatoria* also embodied a certain degree of self-regulation by merchants. Awareness that breaking informal rules

1 See Robert Litan, "Regulation," Library of Economics and Liberty, www.econlib.org/library/Enc/Regulation.html

2 See John Finnis, *Natural Law and Natural Rights* (Oxford: Clarendon Press, 1980), pp. 154–156.

3 See Leon E. Trakman, *The Law Merchant: The Evolution of Commercial Law* (Littleton, CO: F.B. Rothman, 1983).

may lead other merchants and customers to mistrust you can be a very effective deterrent to unethical and unreasonable actions.

The very idea of self-regulation causes us to ask what might be some of the other sources of norms and principles that encourage marketplace actors to do X rather than Y. In this regard, one can look to specific ethical and philosophical systems, ranging from Aristotelianism to Kantianism. There is little question that a major source of such values and guidelines that influence the free choices of individuals and businesses is religion.

Christianity is a faith that has always taken liberty very seriously. This theme of free will is clearly summarized in the Book of Ecclesiasticus, written by the Jewish scribe Ben Sira of Jerusalem sometime in the second century BC.

> It was he who created man in the beginning, and he left him in the power of his own inclination. If you will, you can keep the commandments, and to act faithfully is a matter of your own choice. He has placed before you fire and water: stretch out your hand for whichever you wish. Before a man are life and death, and whichever he chooses will be given to him.
>
> (Ecclesiastes 15:11–12)

The Decalogue gives human beings very clear direction for right action, especially the second tablet that specifies the negative commandments such as don't steal, don't lie, don't kill, don't be envious, etc. But while Christianity is not a religion that accords a central importance to law and legality as, for instance, most expressions of Islamic faith, it has a great deal to say about the content of freedom and justice. Over the centuries, the Christian church has also developed an ever-growing body of guidance for how to live a life marked by the pursuit of good and the avoidance of evil in the conditions of the world of supply and demand, as well as principles for how we should think about the role played by law, legislation, and state authorities in the regulation of such economic activities so that they contribute to the realization and maintenance of the common good.

It was our understanding of the importance of this body of knowledge, but also questions about how Christianity can help believers and nonbelievers alike to think about the question of the nature, extent, and goals of regulation, that led us to commission the essays contained in this volume. In some cases, it was the first time that some of our authors have consciously reflected upon the meaning of Christian faith and morality for areas such as corporate law, antitrust legislation, price controls, and financial regulation.

When, however, we see that one feature of Christianity is that it articulates a distinct view of human beings and human nature, we see that it *must* have implications for Christians and those who live in societies and cultures shaped by the Christian faith and culture. Christianity speaks long and eloquently about the nature and ends of human liberty, but it also underscores the truth that humans are flawed, make mistakes, and, while redeemed, cannot escape the effects of human sin. Likewise, Christianity stresses that humans are both individual and social beings as well as capable of being creative in their use of their talents and the material world with which they have, Christianity teaches, been entrusted with dominion and stewardship.

This conception of human beings and the world in which they live has powerful implications for that which regulation seeks to direct: i.e., the economy. The first chapter in this collection, "Christianity and the Morality of Markets," seeks to outline "a Christian view of the central *moral* assumptions of the market economy, so as to elucidate how a Christian might think about a mode of economic life in which millions of Christians and non-Christians live out their lives." That entails clarifying (1) what is meant by "the market economy"; (2) underscoring the fact that there is considerable room for Christians to disagree about what they consider to be the most optimal policies concerning different dimensions of economic life; (3) the complicated relationship between commerce and Christianity over the centuries; (4) Christianity's view of the person and society; (5) the manner in which Christianity addresses the vexed issue of self-interest; (6) the unexpected ways in which Christianity affirms key institutions and protocols of the market; and (7) specific moral, spiritual, and material challenges that arise in market economies to which Christianity has given considerable thought over many centuries.

All these topics have implications for the limits and use of government power in the marketplace, much of which is manifested through regulation. Using the idea of the common good – one that arises from Greek and Roman thought but considerably infused with Christian theological and philosophical meaning – Ian Harper and Brian Rosner outline what they regard as the parameters of government activity with regard to the economy. In "The Common Good and the Role of Government in Regulating Markets," they show the specific ways in which Christianity invests the idea of "common" and "good" with particular meaning that could not be obtained from other sources. They then illustrate how markets contribute to the realization of these goods through facilitating exchange and promoting a type of material welfare, but also the limits of markets in these areas. The issue of market failure features significantly here and the manner in which government is understood as an agency that attempts to prevent or resolve subsequent problems. Harper and Rosner then place all this in the context of what Christianity has to say about the good, the character and effects of economic activity, and the ends and limits of state power. Economics and Christian theology approach some of the questions from different angles; they stress and offer often quite varying perspectives. They maintain, however, that there are areas in which economics and Christian thought can mutually contribute to a better understanding of the nature and limits of regulation in the marketplace, despite their very different starting points.

Economics also teaches us that there are many unintended consequences of our choices in the marketplace as well the policies adopted by government. One school of economic thought that has devoted much reflection to this subject is called "public choice theory." Carroll Rios de Rodríguez seeks to illustrate how "the claims made by public choice scholars regarding the political acts of individuals and groups correspond with the behavior of some historical figures featured in the Bible and with Christian thought more broadly." In Chapter 3, entitled "Public Choice Theory and Interest Group Capture," she outlines the building blocks of public choice theory, and shows how its attention to the ways in which regulation and regulatory bodies can be captured by interest groups (and thus diverted from their proper focus on the common good) is a phenomenon that Christian sources and thinkers have been very aware of. She concludes by demonstrating that Christian thought about the nature of governance and its implications for constitutional order may be one way to address the rent-seeking behavior that regulation can often encourage.

Chapter 4, "Christianity and Antitrust: A Nexus" takes readers in a different direction. The attention of Kenneth G. Elzinga and Daniel A. Crane is upon antitrust institutions, understood as regulatory agencies that play a major role in seeking to address questions ranging from anticompetitive practices to the development of cartels. They ask if "the Christian faith has a nexus with the institution of antitrust," to which their answer is yes and no. Through carefully distinguishing between the economics and morality of antitrust law and institutions, Elzinga and Crane show some of the expected connections between the logic of antitrust and the insights of Christian faith into reality. The latter, they hold, is particularly well-equipped to give direction and deeper purpose to the workings of antitrust so that it gives effect to Christian emphases such as stewardship and justice in ways that help us to comprehend the inefficiency and morally problematic nature of practices such as price-fixing and monopolies.

Much of the target of antitrust law and regulation more generally in our time is the modern corporation. In Chapter 5, "Christianity and Corporate Purpose," Stephen M. Bainbridge begins by demonstrating that Christians have expressed mixed views of businesses and corporations, with some stressing the economic prosperity and efficiency that they have engendered, while others argue that they have engaged in morally and economically questionable behavior. For Bainbridge, this raises the question of what the Christian faith might say about the goals of corporations and business, and the role of the state in regulating organizations toward these ends. He is especially attentive to what Christian sources suggest about questions such as corporate social responsibility, the place of profit, the issue of externalities, and the role of law and regulation in shaping the ways in which business understands itself.

Part of the "business" of business is entrepreneurship and the discovery of new ways to create wealth. In Chapter 6, "Entrepreneurship and Market Structure," Andrew Godley "aims to be a catalyst in stimulating informed and constructive debate on the relationship between Christianity and enterprise." A considerable body of Christian opinion, both in the past and present, entertains neutral to outright hostile views of wealth-creation via entrepreneurship and free enterprise, something that, he believes, flows from the fact that Christianity and the social science of economics prioritize different ethical principles. This in turn leads to different conclusions about the nature and effects of policymaking and regulation. But it also allows us to imagine how a Christian-informed ethics might shape how we think about regulation and the goals that it seeks to realize in an economy that stresses the principles of liberty and autonomy.

Few areas of modern market economies are considered to be in need of more regulation than the financial sector, especially since the Great Recession of 2008. It is also an area that has sparked increasing reflection from Christians since that time. In Chapter 7, "Subsidiarity and the Role of Regulation in the Financial Sector," Philip Booth shows how many Christian leaders and thinkers have placed a premium on state regulation as the optimal way to address what they regard various problems associated with the functioning of markets, especially financial markets and innovation. At the same time, they are unaware of the ways in which state regulation and excessive intervention can have counterproductive effects. Booth uses the principle of subsidiarity, much developed in official Catholic social teaching and which has strong echoes in the Reform tradition, to delineate how Christians can approach the very complicated area of financial regulation. He also, however, echoes a theme much stressed by other authors in this volume – that Christianity has a very realist comprehension of human nature (thanks to its consciousness of the element of sin), and that this should shape Christian reflection on the efficacy of different types of regulation in the financial sector but also the economy more generally.

In many ways, modern finance is concerned with the issue of the use and leveraging of debt. At the same time, debt is often something that leads to the insolvency and bankruptcy of individuals and companies. A fact of life in the economy is that many businesses and enterprises fail. This is one area in which there is considerable unanimity that regulation is necessary, both to expedite matters relatively quickly but also to meet the demands of commutative and distributive justice. In Chapter 8, "Christianity and Bankruptcy," David Skeel notes that while the word "bankruptcy" is not to be found in the Hebrew and Christian Scriptures, Christianity has a great deal to say about the topic of debt. Much bankruptcy law concerns trying to resolve issues of debt, and Skeel explores the question of the extent to which developments in bankruptcy law over the past century represent the working-out of Christian thinking about debt, whether at the level of individuals or countries, and what a Christian vision of bankruptcy law might look like.

For many Christians, it may seem crass, inhumane, and materialistic to think about necessities of life in market-based terms. Should health care really be created and allocated on the basis of profit-based incentives and economic competition? In Chapter 9, "Patents, Access to Health Technologies, and Christianity," Margo Bagley and Danielle Lloyd consider the relationship between markets and health care from a Biblical perspective. Focusing particularly on pharmaceutical patents, they show that Christian teaching requires respect for the economic enterprise of the pharmaceutical industry, but also suggests limits on the exploitation of patents in order to promote the Christian virtue of healing.

Our collection of essays ends, in a way, where it began – the observation that much regulation has traditionally been focused on the issue of prices, indirectly or directly. In Chapter 10, "Price Controls and Market Economies," André Azevedo and Inês Gregório examine the long history of price controls, something that predate the Christian era, and engage in detailed analysis of the ways in which Christian thinkers ranging from Thomas Aquinas to prominent Protestant thinkers, including Martin Luther, approached the matter. On this basis, they also attempt "to synthesize (at least to the extent common ground can be found) a general Christian position on price controls and market economies." In doing so, they show the influence of the idea of the just price in shaping Christian thinking on this subject, and the questions that it raises about the efficacy and morality of regulating such an important part of the operations of the market economy.

Regulation will remain, for the foreseeable future, part and parcel of life in the market economy. Christians and others will continue to disagree about its benefits and limitations as well as the manner in which many believe different types of regulations have unintended and often negative consequences. The authors of the chapters in this book, however, provide a comprehensive overview of how Christians can approach issues of market regulation according to the lights of their faith, the long tradition of Christian thought about the origins and ends of government power, and an appreciation of the Biblical mandate to act economically in the world. Believers, we hold, will certainly benefit, but so too will those with a strong interest in how religion can affect human thought, choice, and action in the most unexpected of areas.

# 1

# Christianity and the Morality of the Market

SAMUEL GREGG

It is no exaggeration to say that, now and in the past, many Christians have maintained very critical – if not hostile – views of the world of commerce. At the same time, there are Christians who have a positive view of business but nonetheless are skeptical about the market economy. Commerce can and has, after all, operated in conditions that are not reflective of a market economy, ranging from the heavily slave-based economies of the worlds of Greece and Rome to the mercantilist economies that characterized many European nation-states and their colonies from roughly the late fifteenth century until the late eighteenth century.

Every day, millions of Christians across the globe engage in the free exchange of goods and services. Yet some Christians insist that there are deep tensions between actions, protocols, and institutions associated with the market economy and the demands of the Christian faith. Some Christians insist, for example, that market economic orders facilitate materialistic cultures. These kinds of Christian unease with the market are often associated with concerns about what is often called "individualism." Individualism, in this context, tends to be defined primarily as an attitude characterized by self-idolatry and a tendency to ignore what Christianity identifies as clear moral obligations on the part of each person to others.

Such factors suggest that many Christians believe there are aspects of the market economy that are particularly problematic. That, in turn, indicates that articulating a Christian critique or defense of the market economy is not the same thing as a Christian critique or defense of business or commerce more generally. Throughout the twentieth century, the proposed remedies of some Christians to these perceived problems ranged from advocacy of a mixed economy to proposals that are recognizably socialist in design and ends.

Further complicating matters is the way that, throughout history, the market economy has assumed different forms in different societies and cultures. There are Anglo-American, East Asian, and continental Western European versions of market economies, all of which differ significantly from each other. The market economy in Hong Kong differs from the form it assumes in the United States, which in turn is not precisely the same character of the market economy in Australia or Canada. In all these cases, the role of the state in the economy, including government regulation of economic affairs, has taken on somewhat different characters.

Yet another complicating element is that, philosophically speaking, market economies are also associated with "liberalism" (itself a very ambiguous expression that means very different things to different people) – and not just any form of liberalism, but the liberalism associated with the Scottish Enlightenment. Christianity has viewed aspects of the liberal order as compatible with the Christian faith (not least because features of such orders, such as constitutionalism, have deep Christian toots) while questioning some of the theological and philosophical assumptions underlying a range of liberal philosophical positions. At the same time, it should be noted that market economies and economic liberalization policies have been promoted by many "non-liberals." These include the founder of modern conservativism, Edmund Burke, but also center-left governments of countries like Australia and New Zealand in the 1980s or the Social Democrat–Green coalition that held office in Germany in the early 2000s.

The purpose of this chapter is not to enter into the details of these particular discussions, especially insofar as they touch upon questions of how Christians should view specific economic policies or the role of the state in market economies. Nor is it to ponder whether Christians would regard one particular expression of the market economy as more congenial to Christianity than others. Rather, it is to articulate a Christian view of the central *moral* assumptions of the market economy, so as to elucidate how a Christian might think about a mode of economic life in which millions of Christians and non-Christians live out their lives.

## 1.1 SOME QUALIFICATIONS

Before, however, examining these matters, some qualifications need to be made, not least among which is what we mean by *market economy*.

One way to define markets is in terms of where one sees the locus of decision-making about economic questions. From this standpoint, a market economy means an economic system that responds to the problem of scarcity from the "bottom-up." In market or free economies, the decisions regarding (1) the creation, production, and distribution of wealth and (2) the allocation of capital and labor are mediated through the process of supply and demand, which is (3) reflected through the free price mechanism. The market economy is thus the opposite of an economy that is directed by top-down planning: i.e., that which determines the allocation of goods and services in advance via a plan, usually implemented by a government, that covers all economic activity in a given territory.

Especially since Communism's collapse in the former Soviet Union and Eastern Europe, planned economies in the sense of command economies have become scarce. Nonetheless, virtually all economies today reflect some degree of planning. This can take various forms, ranging from central banks determining interest rates that are tracked closely by the allocators of private capital to regulations applied to different parts of the economy and levels of government spending in different segments of the economy. Most economies today thus embrace aspects of a "pure market" economy overlaid with different forms of intervention by the state into that market.

A second qualification to note is that any discussion of a Christian view of the morality of the market economy should begin by noting that there is significant room among Christians for prudential disagreement about the optimal set of economic arrangements for any one society. There is nothing in the Gospels or Christian tradition that mandates any one economic system. Certainly, principles of Christian ethics may indicate that some economic systems, such as the command economy, so deeply denigrate human dignity that supporting them is difficult to reconcile with the Gospel. Nonetheless, Christians cannot equate matters such as belief in Christ's Divinity or the prohibition against intentional killing of human beings with questions such as whether the state should control 20 or 30 percent of a nation's gross domestic product, or whether antitrust law is an optimal solution to the problem of cartels and monopolies.[1]

Why, then, is there considerable room for Christians to prudentially disagree about these matters? The answer is that on many economic issues, the choice is between not only good and bad options, but also a range of good options. Some of these options may be incompatible with one another but nonetheless compatible with Christian teaching. In many cases, the discernment of *how* a modern society attains a good end in the realm of economics and economic policy may depend upon empirical and prudential judgments reasonably in dispute among people equally well-informed by principles of Christian teaching.

[1] See Chapter 4: Kenneth G. Elzinga and Daniel A. Crane, "Christianity and Antitrust: A Nexus."

Having surveyed the available evidence and informed themselves of the relevant Christian principles, some Christians may conclude that something like universal health care is best realized by a predominantly state-funded system. Other Christians, having examined the available evidence and informed themselves of the same principles, may conclude that private health insurance – with the state providing a safety net – is the best approach. This illustrates how there are many economic policies that Christians can advocate in order to realize particular goals in the setting of a mostly market economy (or a highly regulated economy) while remaining in good standing with the Christian community.

But having made these qualifications, the question remains: Is it possible for "the market economy" to be reconciled with the Creed professed by those who believe that Jesus Christ is the Way, the Truth, and the Life? The answer is: it depends. No Christian is likely to claim, for example, that people have no responsibilities to others beyond contractual obligations. At the same time, Christianity has always affirmed the essential legitimacy of private contracts as an expression of free association, and takes the requirements of commutative justice very seriously.

Another factor requiring consideration is the fact that Christians and Christian churches have lived "inside" market-like economic arrangements for centuries. Once we look beyond the myth of the Middle Ages as a time of ignorance and misery, we see that the first major expansion of commerce and market exchange in the West occurred during a period of history in which Christianity was regnant throughout Europe. In the high Middle Ages, trading towns became a more regular feature of the European landscape. These commercial centers varied in size from the great Italian and Flemish cities to numerous small towns of Germania. They also differed between those focused upon long-distance trade, such as Venice, Lübeck, and Genoa, those producing for export, especially of cloth (Florence, Cologne, and Amsterdam) and metal (Augsburg), and the great majority of smaller towns engaged in local trade. The commercial population typically included small retailers, independent craftsmen, merchant-entrepreneurs, bankers, producers of luxury goods, as well as many living off the profits of rents.[2]

For the great majority of Christians, these social changes were not problematic. Indeed, in developing Christian teaching on the subject of usury, medieval and early-modern scholastic thinkers (which include a considerable number of Protestant Christian thinkers from the Reformation onward)

[2] See A. Hibbert, "The Economic Policies of Towns," in *Cambridge Economic History*, vol. 3 (Cambridge: Cambridge University Press, 1963), pp. 157–229; F. Rörig, *The Medieval Town*, trans. D. Byrant (London: Penguin, 1967).

contributed significantly to expanding the amount of capital available for investment.[3] The fact that most marketplaces were located near churches – typified by the enormous square outside medieval Milan's cathedral – indicated that neither merchants nor clergy found anything theologically incongruous about commerce. Nor was the Church blind to the benefits flowing from the growth of market exchange, such as the emergence of town constitutions, criminal codes, the minting of currency, as well as the associated suppression of lawless nobles and the practice of vendetta. Moreover, trade expansion did not lessen the attention of Christians to the needs of the poor. Merchants and traders became major contributors to church almshouses and hospitals, not least because of the greater availability of capital resources generated by the spread and growth of commerce.

There is, however, another side to this story. In the same Middle Ages, for example, there were sporadic explosions of violence against merchants, traders, and private property holders. These often contained a specifically religious impetus, with wild itinerant preachers, often from Franciscan backgrounds, denouncing trade and property ownership as sinful. These episodes sometimes resulted in temporary collapses of order, mass pillaging, and the murder of nobles, merchants, clergy, and peasants alike. It goes without saying that the suppression of such uprisings was equally brutal.[4]

This background is important because it underscores a relationship between markets, commerce, and Christianity that is generally favorable but not without its shadows. More generally, any reflection upon Christianity and the morality of the market does not occur within a historical void and any discussion of this subject needs to be attentive to that reality.

But having made these qualifications, the question remains: Is it possible for the market economy to be reconciled with the Creed and the moral beliefs professed by those who believe that Jesus Christ is the Way, the Truth, and the Life? One starting point for this discussion is the Christian vision of who human persons are – that is, anthropology.

## 1.2 A CHRISTIAN ANTHROPOLOGY

An indispensable reference point for a Christian anthropology of human beings is the Genesis account of Creation. This defines humans in terms of

[3] See John T. Noonan, *The Scholastic Analysis of Usury* (Cambridge, MA: Harvard University Press, 1957); Thomas Divine, S.J., *Interest: A Historical and Analytical Study in Economics and Modern Ethics* (Milwaukee: Marquette University Press, 1959), pp. 3–116.

[4] See Margery Reeves, *The Influence of Prophecy in the Later Middle Ages: A Study in Joachimism* (Oxford: Clarendon Press, 1969), pp. 10–70.

our most fundamental relationship to God – the relation of image and likeness. "Let us make man in our own image, in the likeness of ourselves" (Genesis 1:26). The creation of the first man is announced with an emphasis that is absent from the creation of other creatures. The essential difference between humans and all the other creatures is reinforced when God makes humanity the steward of all other creatures. This call to stewardship is not based primarily on the physicality of the man or the characteristics that he shares with the rest of the visible world. Rather, it is based upon the human being's specific likeness to God, and the life and light that are breathed into the first man.

This being the case, God's call to humans to assume stewardship over the earth is not a call to sheer power and domination. "God saw that it was good" (Genesis 1:10, 12, 18, 21, 25). This divine "seeing" is in every way primary, because it creates being and good. Human seeing and human doing are thus always secondary because they always encounter pre-constituted value. For while humans are called "to fill the earth and subdue it" (Genesis 1:28), their task of dominion is defined in terms of a conditional superintendence (cf. Genesis 2:15) – it must be used in accordance with the original intention of God. This is why, after investing humans with the dominion of stewardship, God warns the man and the woman not to eat "of the tree of knowledge of good and evil" (Genesis 2:17). Human stewardship is not therefore to be understood as absolute sovereignty; it does not give people the authority to use other persons or creatures according to arbitrary human preference. Instead, humans should freely act in accordance with God's law. "The human mind plans the way, but the Lord directs the steps" (Prov 16:9).

Christians also believe that humanity's knowledge of their special dignity only receives its final Revelation in the Person of Jesus of Nazareth. In Jesus Christ, God entered human affairs in an unrepeatable way, becoming one of the multitude of actors in human history but at the same time unique. The Incarnation reminds us that nothing, except God, surpasses the dignity of humans. Each human person is made in the image of *the* Image that God gives us of himself – his own Son: He who is "the image of the invisible God" (Colossians 1:15). The life of Christ also reminds us of the profound significance of human action, reason, and will. Through the Incarnation, people rediscover the deep esteem that all should have for each human person in their totality – body, intellect, and will. They also learn that these qualities enable people not only to enter into a relationship with God, but to act as stewards of God's creation: something that has obvious economic implications as people decide how best to use the natural world to meet, first, their needs, and then their wider aspirations.

Note here that this understanding of human beings points to the importance of the *freedom* that is intrinsic to humans as creatures who possess reason and the ability to make choices: features shared by no other being. Without these individual qualities, humans would not be able to act as stewards. This aspect of Christian anthropology is accompanied by an emphasis upon the person's social dimension. Revelation makes clear the full significance of the human person's social character. Genesis stresses that God did not leave humans as solitary creatures. If people are to know themselves, they must encounter other human persons. From the beginning "male and female he created them" (Genesis 1:27). The man instantly recognized this essential unity with another human: "This at last is bone of my bones, flesh of my flesh" (Genesis 2:23).

This companionship of man and woman produces the primary form of interpersonal communion. Man and woman were made for each other, to be in communion so that each is "helpmate" to the other. Though different, they are equal in dignity and *interdependent* because they are unable to fulfill themselves as *isolated* individuals. There is a certain resemblance here between what Christians understand as the unity of the Trinity, and the communion that Christians believe that people should establish between themselves. The Trinity is not reducible to its members considered in their distinction from one another. The divine persons, united in their mutual communion, are God, and God is perfectly one in his reality, goodness, and love. Yet the three divine persons really are distinct individuals, not merely parts of a larger whole.

Given that the person is social by nature, it follows that the good of each individual person is related to what Christianity understands to be the *common good*: a common good that in turn can only be defined with reference to the individual person. For Christians, the phrase "common good" does not mean collectivism or socialism. Rather, it is the sum total of social conditions that allow people, either as groups or as individuals, to reach their fulfillment more fully and more easily.[5] It follows that advancing the common good involves each human person and human community supporting others as they seek, through free choice and action, to do good and avoid evil and thus flourish, but also providing others with the necessary liberty that they need to make such choices as individuals and communities.

[5] See Second Vatican Council, Pastoral Constitution on the Church in the Modern World *Gaudium et Spes*, December 7, 1965, paras. 26, 74, in A. Flannery, O. P., gen. ed., *Vatican Council II: The Conciliar and Post Conciliar Documents*, vol. 1, rev. ed. (Leominster: Fowler Wright Books, Ltd., 1988).

All this, however, is complicated by another aspect of human nature underscored by Christian anthropology that is deeply relevant for political and economic life. Although God created all, and it was good, the description of the Fall in Genesis also reminds us of the *mysterium iniquitatis*: the deep interior rupture that sin creates within human beings. From the beginning, Christianity has proclaimed that, although humans were made by God in a state of holiness, humans abused their liberty from the onset. As Genesis indicates, it was not God who withdrew from humanity, but humanity from God. The man and the woman committed the error of attempting to seize for themselves the knowledge of the tree of good and evil (cf. Genesis 2:3:1–24) – of seeking the power of deciding for themselves what is good and what is evil.

In sinning, humans made a claim to complete moral independence from God by refusing to recognize their status as created beings and seeking instead to become the Creator. Thus, as Augustine wrote, sin is "love of oneself even to contempt of God."[6] Christianity acknowledges that psychological, social, and cultural factors can condition the manner in which individual persons make their choices for good or evil. Yet while they can limit moral responsibility and constrain freedom, these influences should not be understood in ways that obscure the deeper reality – that sin is an integral part of the truth about humans because the human person is a free moral actor. To acknowledge the reality of sin is thus, paradoxically, to acknowledge the reality of freedom. This truth cannot be disregarded in order to place the blame for individuals' sins on external factors such as structures, systems, or other people. This would be to deny the person's freedom, which is also manifested – though in a negative way – in each individual's responsibility for the sins that he commits.

## 1.3 CHRISTIAN ANTHROPOLOGY AND THE MARKET

All these staples of Christian anthropological truths have profound implications for Christian reflection about the morality of the market. An economy that involves the systematic suppression of human freedom in the economy is deeply problematic from a Christian standpoint. In short, economic life needs to reflect a deep respect for human freedom and initiative. Likewise, an economy that acknowledges that certain things are owed to human beings because of their unique dignity will be radically dissimilar to one that regards human dignity as a polite fiction.

6 St. Augustine, *Concerning the City of God against the Pagans* (London: Penguin, 1984), Bk. xiv, chapter 28.

Applying these Christians insights to economic life tells us some important things about the morality of markets. Consider, for instance, the way in which Pope John Paul II in his 1991 social encyclical, *Centesimus Annus* reflected upon the reality of sin and then linked it to the issue of self-interest and its relevance for the economic order:

> [M]an, who was created for freedom, bears within himself the wound of original sin, which constantly draws him towards evil and puts him in need of redemption. Not only is this doctrine an integral part of Christian revelation; it also has great hermeneutical value insofar as it helps one to understand human reality. Man tends towards good, but he is also capable of evil. He can transcend his immediate interest and still remain bound to it. The social order will be all the more stable, the more it takes this fact into account and does not place in opposition personal interest and the interests of society as a whole, but rather seeks ways to bring them into fruitful harmony.[7]

The Christian language and logic deployed here bears more than a passing resemblance to the ways in which Adam Smith wrote about self-interest in his *Wealth of Nations*. Certainly, the parallel is not exact, not least because Smith's outlook is that of a Deist rather than a Christian. Yet the shared point in common made by the pope and the philosopher is that trying to wish away the reality of human fallibility and the truth that people *do* ask themselves what is in their self-interest is a mistake, especially when it comes to economic life. Markets, according to Smith, help direct the pursuit of self-interest in ways that benefit society, even when that is clearly not the intention of those creating goods and services and engaging in economic exchanges in the marketplace. Pope John Paul's point is that human sin underscores the truth that there is no utopia. Hence, part of the challenge for Christians is think about how to harmonize the common good with the pursuit of self-interest. To the extent that markets can harmonize these things, Christians should consider them positively.

In this regard, it is very important to distinguish greed from self-interest. Greed implies a desire to possess something – power, wealth, sex, position – at virtually *any* cost and beyond what each of us reasonably might need. Greed, like covetousness and avarice more generally, is thus the sin of excess. It perverts, for instance, the principle of ownership into a principle of egoism, whereby I prioritize my possession of things over my family, church, and even my own flourishing. It changes the business leader from someone who

[7] John Paul II, *Encyclical Letter* Centesimus Annus (Boston: St Paul Publications, 1991), para. 25 (hereafter CA).

contributes to the material and moral well-being of himself and others through his work, into a selfish monopolist who preserves his possessions by enlisting government power to deter potential competitors.

The pursuit of *rational* self-interest is, however, quite different. Playing off Adam Smith, the theologian Michael Novak explained this idea in the following way:

> We imagine that self-interest sets man against man, and flights individuals apart in centrifugal directions. We forget that human action is full of intelligence. Action is not random, wholly undirected. Free persons are intelligent and self-correcting. They have an interest in order.... What actually moves them is their own practical intelligence.[8]

No less a theologian than Thomas Aquinas insisted that there *is* a reasonable love of self. That was how he understood the Second Commandment, which instructs one to love our neighbor *as oneself*. This, Aquinas suggested, meant that people should be *reasonably* concerned for their self-preservation and their own participation in the good.[9] Indeed, the theologian Germain Grisez stresses that "Faith in Jesus is in human persons' ultimate self-interest," because "it holds out the hope of everlasting joy in heaven."[10]

These words remind us that much of the Christian assessment of self-interest and its place in economic life depends on *what* the "self" is interested in and *why* that self is interested in it. I may, for instance, be interested in acquiring wealth because I simply want to possess more stuff for the sake of possessing more stuff. Not only is that greed, it cannot be reconciled with the negative Christian view of materialism (whereby we are no longer stewards but rather slaves of the material world). Another person, however, may want to acquire wealth because his or her intention is to fulfill their responsibility to take care of their family's needs. Yet another individual may be anxious to trade, barter, and enter into free exchanges with others because he or she wants to build some of the material resources that they and others may need if they are going to be able to participate in any number of non-material goods. In these cases, the "interest" of the "self" cannot be classified as greed.

At this point, however, we need to ask: If the market economy reflects, in part, the workings of each individual's self-interest, does this not implicitly restrict the capacity of people to build the authentic communities of love

[8] Michael Novak, *Free Persons and the Common Good* (Lanham: Madison Books, 1989), p. 78.

[9] See Thomas Aquinas, *Summa Theologiae*, ed. T. Gilby, O.P. (London: Blackfriars, 1963), I–II, q. 26, a.4 and I–II, q. 94, a.2.

[10] Germain Grisez, *The Way of the Lord Jesus*, Vol. 2: *Living a Christian Life* (Quincy: Franciscan Press, 1993), p. 37.

demanded by Christianity? Does the market economy not therefore run the risk of distracting people from establishing those conditions that assist others in fulfilling themselves that Christians call the common good?

The answer is Yes and No. The pursuit of self-interest and market competition suggests that commercial activity cannot be expected to mirror, for example, the life of that first *communio personarum* that we call the family. To this extent, commercial relations tend not to embrace the degree of self-giving that occurs, for example, in family life.

Christianity, however, recognizes that different forms of communities have naturally different purposes. It is therefore unreasonable to expect them all to be like the family or the nation-state. The philosopher John Finnis distinguishes a variety of relationships such as "business," "play," and "friendship," all of which are embodied, to varying degrees, in any form of community.[11] The relative strength of these relationships within any one form of community makes all associations naturally conducive to certain activities and outcomes, and less conducive to others.

At the same time, the market economy does promote many material and social developments that contribute to the noneconomic dimension of the common good. Leaving aside their effective provision of the material basis required by any group of humans for existence, market economic orders do allow individuals to serve each other – albeit often indirectly – through the process of exchange. It also brings people from very different backgrounds into contact, while simultaneously reducing the potential for conflict by softening the intensity of political life. As Alexis de Tocqueville – a man who struggled all his life with the claims of the Christian faith – pointed out in an echo of Montesquieu:

> Trade is the natural enemy of all violent passions. Trade loves moderation, delights in compromise, and is most careful to avoid anger. It is patient, supple, and insinuating, only resorting to extreme means in cases of absolute necessity. Trade makes men independent of one another . . . it leads them to want to manage their own affairs and teaches them how to succeed therein. Hence it makes them inclined to liberty but disinclined to revolution.[12]

Another aspect of Christian anthropology that takes one in the direction of affirming, in principle, a market economic order is the way in which it allows

[11] See John Finnis, *Natural Law and Natural Rights* (Oxford: Clarendon Press, 1980), pp. 134–160.

[12] Alexis de Tocqueville, *Democracy in America*, vol. 2, ed. J. P. Mayer, trans. G. Lawrence (New York: Perennial, 2000), p. 637.

human beings to live out their freedom and use their reason and capacity for choice in economic life in ways that are less obvious in other economic systems. The market economic order is, after all, incomprehensible without its emphasis upon individual choice in the production and purchase of material goods and services. In much economic reflection, this reality is sometimes obscured by a tendency to speak of the "market" as if it were an anonymous conglomerate that exerts its own will.

Certainly, there is an "abstract" dimension to market economies in the sense that they are premised upon widespread acceptance of certain rules and institutions. These rules include the law of contract, while the institutions are exemplified by private property rights and the idea of rule of law more generally. But though essential, these rules and institutions remain ancillary to what is truly central to market exchanges: human persons, human choices, and human acts. If one accepts as a matter of Christian belief that God created each person to choose the truth freely, and that the human person ought therefore to be free, then a free economic order – a market – is surely *part* (and obviously not all) of the order of human freedom. As observed by the Catholic philosopher, Rocco Buttiglione:

> The smallest element of the free market is a contract, the encounter of the free will of two human beings. They must both be free, for if they are not there can be no contract, and thus no free market. In this way, the law on contracts that stands at the very basis of a free-market economy is a law that presupposes human freedom.[13]

Note how Buttiglione justifies the market not primarily by the fact that it is the most efficient system for allocating scarce resources, but rather because it is a moral requirement of a social order that takes the idea of freedom seriously by allowing people to assume responsibility for themselves in the economic sphere. Through contracts, we freely make ourselves the author of particular obligations and acquire responsibilities. We thus freely place limits upon our own tendency to act on whim in order to realize mutually beneficial goals.

Similar arguments were made by the *ordo liberal* economist and Lutheran, Wilhelm Röpke. History illustrated, he insisted, that only a market economic order had proved able to give individuals the necessary scope for free choice in the material realm, which is theirs by reason of who they are. Hence, we should not be surprised to see Röpke explaining in 1953 – at the height of Keynesian programs in the West and statism in the Communist world – that

[13] Rocco Buttiglione, *The Moral Mandate for Freedom: Reflections on "Centesimus Annus"* (Grand Rapids, MI: Acton Institute, 1997), p. 7.

"my opposition on technical grounds is that socialism, in its enthusiasm for organization, centralization, and efficiency, is committed to means that simply are not compatible with freedom."[14] Röpke also argued that, to the extent that choice in the economic realm remained free, it helped to limit the subsuming of individual persons into artificial collectives.[15] "My fundamental opposition to socialism," Röpke wrote, "is to an ideology that, in spite of all its 'liberal' phraseology, gives too little to man, his freedom, and his personality; and too much to society."[16]

Röpke later went further in underscoring how Christianity's attention to human individuality led him to support the market economy – again, not primarily because of the way it helps to solve economic problems, but because of Christianity's concern for human freedom:

> My picture of man is fashioned by the spiritual heritage of classical and Christian tradition. I see in man the likeness of God; I am profoundly convinced that it is an appalling sin to reduce man to a means (even in the name of high-sounding phrases) and that each man's soul is something unique, irreplaceable, priceless, in comparison with which all other things are as naught. I am attached to a humanism which is rooted in these convictions and which regards man as the child and image of God, but not as God himself, to be idolized as he is by the hubris of a false and atheist humanism. These, I believe, are the reasons why I so greatly distrust all forms of collectivism.

Neither Buttiglione nor Röpke believe that the market is in itself sufficient for human freedom. Their case, however, for an essential compatibility between the market economic order and the Christian vision of man is further strengthened once we take into account the anthropological truth than human beings are not God. It follows that human beings are incapable of knowing everything or possessing the knowledge of the constantly changing state of human economic preferences and the never-ending changes in terms of what products and services are available at any one point in time.

Market economies do, however, take into account the fact that humans are not God because they are attentive to this knowledge problem. And the manner in which markets address this problem is through the free price system. In this highly decentralized system, prices are determined not via state

14 Wilhelm Röpke, "The Economic Necessity of Freedom," *Modern Age*, vol. 3 (Summer 1959), p. 230.

15 See Wilhelm Röpke, *The Social Crisis of Our Time* (New Brunswick, NJ: Transaction Publishers, 1942/1992), p. 105.

16 Röpke, "Economic Necessity," p. 230.

fiat but rather by the *asking* prices of thousands of producers and sellers corresponding with the *bid* prices of millions of consumers, all of which reflect each consumer's subjective valuation of what they need and want in light of what is being offered by sellers. The resulting *price signals* allow producers and buyers to mutually adjust their respective prices relative to the urgency of millions of ever-changing wants and in light of limited resources. This constant and unending interchange establishes the *market price* of goods and services and allows producers and consumers to rethink what they want and need as well as how they allocate their resources.

In this connection, it is noteworthy that Christian minds ranging from Augustine to Aquinas held that, in most circumstances, the economic value of a good or service is reflected in its price, and price is determined by *what people are willing to pay* for a good or service in the settings of a free and open market – or so concluded Aquinas long ago.[17] In short, the just price is *normally* the market price, provided that the market is indeed free.

## 1.4 A MARKET SOCIETY?

For all the moral and material benefits that market transactions as well as their associated rules and institutions bring to the social order, Christian ethics does not consider the market economy in itself to be a sufficient basis for a society that is conducive to people's efforts to live in truth and pursue their particular vocations. The contractual justice that is embodied in commutative justice is important. But, for Christians, it is only one species of justice. Christianity also upholds other modes of justice such as legal justice and distributive justice. All these modes of justice imply different responsibilities on the part of individuals, communities, and even the state, many of which may involve some regulation of different forms of commercial and market activity. Even commutative justice implies that binding decisions need to be made by the law in adjudicating disputes about the various responsibilities freely agreed upon by parties to a contract, or even authoritatively deciding in a definitive way the precise meaning of different clauses of a given contractual agreement.

But even beyond the demands of justice – all of which, for the Christian, are summed up in the Commandment to love God and love our neighbor as ourselves – the morality of the market for Christians is ultimately determined by the degree to which a given set of market economic arrangements permits people to live out their Christian life – including the obligation to help the

[17] See Aquinas, *Summa Theologiae*, II–II, q. 61, a. 4c and II–II, q.77, a. 1, a. 4c, and ad. 2.

poor – and the extent to which the market can distract Christians from this primary goal.

Free markets are, for instance, unparalleled in their ability to reduce poverty over sustained periods of time. But this also depends upon the extent to which a market economy is embedded in particular cultural and institutional conditions. These can range from the extent to which rule of law exists in a given society to whether or not private entrepreneurship is seen as an essentially positive or negative occupation. Given, however, the Christian imperative to love and care for the poor, the market economy's ability to diminish material poverty systematically over time would, it seems, be something valued and even to be promoted by Christians.

On the other hand, the material prosperity generated by markets comes with its own challenges to which Christians should be especially attentive. One such challenge is consumerism and materialism.

Without the substantial and regular creation of material things and services, it is difficult to take people out of poverty, and keep them out of material distress. But even beyond enabling Christians to serve the materially poor, participation in market economies via the process of creating and refining goods and services, people can shape not just the world around us, but also give honor to God through living out the Genesis mandate to be creative. It is very easy, however, for people to imagine that possessing things is somehow fulfilling in itself: that I become "more" of a person because I possess more cars, more jewelry, more whatever.

By "consumerism," we do not mean the raw fact that whatever the economic system, everyone is a consumer of goods and services. Nor, from the Christian standpoint, is consumerism really about "how much stuff" is created and exchanged in the economy. Instead, consumerism primarily concerns the *attitude* we adopt toward material goods, the importance we ascribe to goods that are means rather than an end that Christians should pursue for its own sake, and what Christianity regards as the deep error of thinking that human happiness can be realized through using and possessing goods, which are limited and finite by nature.

From a Christian standpoint, there is something profoundly irrational about thinking that while some is good, more is always better. Central to the problem of consumerism is old-fashioned materialism: the notion that the more one has, the happier one is, or when we start to identify ourselves in terms of what we possess. Such materialism is deeply disfiguring of human character. It undermines human flourishing in the sense that the possession of things becomes central to people's identity and a culture develops in which the only ideal is "more."

How then should Christians think about this? The first contribution is surely to offer perspective. On the one hand, Christianity views the wealth that markets are especially good at creating in whatever form it comes – property, monetary capital, shares and stocks, etc. – as an instrumental good. It is not fulfilling to the deeper moral and spiritual needs of the human person. On the other hand, the Christian's legitimate concerns about consumerism and materialism should not cause them to trivialize or romanticize the material privation that business, the free market, and economic growth have helped millions of people to escape. Historically speaking, the age of prosperity is relatively recent. The type of consumerism that manifests itself in market economies partly reflects the fact that such economies *enable* increasing numbers of people to partake of goods and services that were once the preserve of relatively few people. The costs of such things are constantly lowered by competition; the spectrum of products of which more and more people can partake is widening in a regular basis; and the relative availability of cheap credit has brought goods and services within the realm of possibility for millions for whom it would have been previously beyond their means.

These facts are not reasons for Christians to lower their guard in the face of the temptation of consumerism. Consumerism is, however, a problem that often comes with prosperity, and generally speaking, prosperity is to be preferred to poverty. Why, otherwise, would Christians bother trying to help people escape poverty?

A second point that Christians should make is that the market itself is not the source of the problem. The temptation to engage in undignified, irrational behavior manifests itself whenever people possessing weak moral compasses become intoxicated with the acquisition of material goods and status symbols. Market economies do not exist in a social vacuum. They are influenced by the cultural configurations in which they exist. And while culture certainly consists of traditions, customs, and laws that influence human choices, they are ultimately shaped by past and present human choices and actions: including economic choices made in the context of a market economy. As Pope Benedict XVI once wrote with reference to free markets, "It is man's darkened reason that produces [harmful] consequences, not the instrument per se." It follows that people, rather than markets in themselves, are responsible for the harm.[18]

Features of life in a market economy, such as incessant advertising, which may appeal to our baser instincts, exacerbate the problem. But consumerism – we should reiterate – is essentially an attitude of practical materialism, and

[18] Benedict XVI Encyclical, *Caritas in Veritate* (Boston: St Paul Publications, 2009), para. 36.

practical materialism can easily manifest itself in societies in which there is a lack of sufficient material possessions. The failure of command economies to provide sufficient goods and services contributed to people living under Communist regimes focusing what would otherwise be regarded as excessive attention upon the acquisition and possession of material things.

Consumerism is not a moral problem that the market itself is capable of resolving. But Christianity does have much to offer in terms of restraining consumerism and putting material goods in their proper perspective. This involves not only reminding people of the Scriptural admonition against making an idol of material things and the folly associated with, as Saint Paul states, the love of money. Great Christian minds have also written at length about how human flourishing can be facilitated within conditions of material prosperity. It is not true that the only safe route for Christians to live out their individual calling as a child of God is to retreat to a monastery or convent or to live in isolation from others. Many Christians writing on questions ranging from moral theology to spirituality have provided extensive guidance about how to live the Christian life of detachment from material goods in conditions of economic well-being. One prominent example of this is Francis de Sales' classic, *Introduction to the Devout Life*, which provides counsel about how to cultivate the life of prayer and the degree of detachment that helps people to live in the midst of considerable material comfort while not allowing their thought and activity to be consumed by the conditions around them.

This emphasis upon detachment from material goods that Christianity encourages in any set of economic conditions, including those of a market, does not mean that Christianity sees no role here for the state. Law and government can certainly do some things, but largely on the margins. Examples might include prosecuting those peddling manifestly fraudulent schemes, or those who prey on the impressionable, or engage in activities that really do reduce humans to the level of objects (such as human trafficking and prostitution). There is, however, always the risk that governments can easily slip into a type of Puritanism that sees little good in material well-being.

But more generally, families and churches are usually better placed than government officials to teach their children how to value material goods, use mass media, and apply their minds critically to what they see and hear so that they can make critical judgments about what they are being told in advertising.

## 1.5 CONCLUSION

Historically speaking, Christianity has a great deal to say about the use and possession of material goods. This is especially true of its approach to questions of the distribution of wealth. The growth and spread of market economies since the mid-nineteenth century has not diminished Christianity's attention to the distribution issue. But it has meant that Christians have needed to think about the other side of the economic equation: the *creation of wealth*. Indeed, it is arguable, as Michael Novak stated in his classic *The Spirit of Democratic Capitalism*, that Christians have been historically much slower to grasp the moral good that can be potentially realized in the process of creating wealth.

What, for example, does Christianity have to say about real or apparent monopolies within the settings of a market? It may be that an effective monopoly is generating wealth in a market economy, but is it just that such a monopoly exists in the first place, and if not, then how should Christians respond to it? The extension of the market beyond national boundaries allows, as Adam Smith underscored, a greater division of labor, more opportunity for individuals and groups to identify and pursue their comparative advantage, and thus generate more wealth. But what does Christian ethics teach us about how to address the greater turmoil introduced into many people's lives by the liberalization of international trade and flows of capital? Or consider the fact that there are many people who seek to cheat others in the conditions of a market. Does this mean that Christians need to think about new ways to protect consumers? Is the question of usury, long a subject for reflection by Christians of all confessions, something that requires reexamination in the conditions of highly sophisticated capital markets?[19]

These and other questions are addressed in other chapters of this book. Yet these are necessarily shaped by the broader and deeper themes that Christian ethics has always considered from the very beginning of the Christian church. In that sense, the most fundamental moral questions posed by market economies for Christians are the same questions posed by the fact that God has created human persons and placed them in a material world over which they exercise dominion that is mediated by stewardship. This is a truth that Christians should not lose sight of, if they want to address many of the specific moral issues they encounter in the market economy in ways consistent with the Gospel of Jesus Christ.

[19] See Chapter 8: David Skeel, "Christianity and Bankruptcy."

# 2

# The Common Good and the Role of Government in Regulating Markets

IAN HARPER AND BRIAN ROSNER

## 2.1 INTRODUCTION

*The common good* is a term used in different ways in different contexts and, depending on the context, can be defined *aggregatively* or *holistically*. In economics, notably welfare economics, the common good is typically defined aggregatively. That is, the whole or common good of a group of people is determined by aggregating the good enjoyed by each of its individual members. In this conception, the common good can be represented by a *social welfare function* specifying how the economic welfare of a society is comprised of the levels of economic welfare enjoyed by its constituent individuals. This device is utilitarian in concept and indicates how social welfare rises or falls with increases or decreases in the welfare of individual consumers, where welfare is defined in its narrow economic sense to depend exclusively on the consumption of material goods and services.[1] For the economist, then, the relationship between the common good and government regulation of markets consists in identifying circumstances in which government regulation alters the economic welfare of individual consumers in ways that raise social welfare as measured by the social welfare function.

The authors gratefully acknowledge comments and suggestions on an earlier version of this chapter provided by delegates to the Colloquium on Economics and Theology held at the Australian Centre for Christianity and Culture in Canberra on October 13 and 14, 2017. They also wish to thank Richard R. Glover for research assistance on the subject of the common good in the history of Christian thought.

1 Strictly speaking, individual welfare need not depend exclusively on the consumption of material goods and services. People can be thought of as better off if they find themselves in circumstances they prefer, whether or not this involves higher levels of material well-being. For present purposes, though, however people count improvements in their individual circumstances, the social welfare function aggregates those improvements into a measured improvement in the circumstances of the group, thereby raising the common good.

In Christian theology and ethics, on the other hand, the common good is defined holistically. Against a utilitarian conception of the common good, Christian articulations generally hold that the good of any given thing is discovered precisely in its being common to the members of a community – that is, how it is shared. Goods point beyond themselves to the community in which they find their value and, ultimately, to the universal common good of human communion with the Creator. The common good is not understood aggregatively – as the sum total of the welfare of individuals – but as the way in which those individuals find their welfare in the context of community or social life. In other words, what matters for the common good is the quality of the relationships enjoyed by members of a group rather than individual levels of well-being.

The key Christian contribution to discussion of the common good is to deepen the concepts of both "common" and "good" beyond the utilitarian notion that prevails in modern political and economic discourse.[2] For the Christian ethicist, the relationship between the common good and government regulation of markets consists in identifying how market exchange and its regulation by government are either "community-building or exploitative,"[3] that is, how they affect the quality of relationships among people.

The remainder of this chapter proceeds as follows: Section 2.2 presents the standard economist's view of the welfare-enhancing properties of market exchange. Section 2.3 advances reasons why economists believe markets might fail to enhance social welfare and why government intervention might or might not ameliorate market failure. Section 2.4 explores in greater depth Christian ethical notions of the common good. Section 2.5 follows Oliver O'Donovan in presenting *koinonia* or "communication" as the standard by which Christian ethics assesses the common good of market exchange and government attempts to regulate it. And, finally, Section 2.6 compares the two approaches, concluding that government regulation of markets is more likely to secure the common good according to an economist's conception than according to a Christian ethicist's conception, the latter holding both markets and their regulation by government to a higher standard.

## 2.2 MARKET EXCHANGE AND ECONOMIC WELFARE

Markets exist to solve what economists describe as the "economic problem" – namely, *what* to produce, *how* to produce, and *for whom*. The presumption is

[2] Oliver O'Donovan, *The Ways of Judgment* (Grand Rapids, MI: Eerdmans, 2008), p. 138.

[3] Ibid., pp. 248–249.

that people have material needs and wants that are in principle (at least in the latter case) unlimited but face constraints on the resources available to meet those needs and wants. Hence choices must be made about how best to deploy limited resources, including time, so as to satisfy the material needs and wants of people whose welfare the economic system is intended to promote.

How should these choices be made and by whom? Markets are institutional arrangements designed to facilitate negotiation between those seeking to acquire certain goods and services ("buyers") and those offering to supply them ("sellers"). The notion is that free negotiation between buyers and sellers over the terms of the exchange will solve the economic problem. That is, free negotiation will determine what gets produced, how it is produced, and for whom. The more intensely buyers demand a particular good or service, the more they are prepared to give up in order to get it (the higher the price they offer to sellers), and the more sellers are attracted to offer the good or service for sale. In the end, whatever is produced at the agreed market price will be sold to those buyers willing to pay at least the market price for each unit. The sellers in turn determine how to produce the amount of the good or service demanded by buyers, partly depending on the agreed market price and partly on the costs of production.

The beauty of market exchange is that it solves the economic problem without explicit direction from any external coordinating authority – "as if by an invisible hand," to quote Adam Smith's famous dictum. The assumption is that buyers and sellers are the best judges of their own interests and that free negotiation between them is the most reliable means of balancing their competing interests (generally regarding price) while maximizing their opportunities to satisfy their own needs and preferences. No other machinery is required to solve this problem; the interests of the parties in free negotiation resolve it spontaneously. This is the so-called genius of the market, beloved of economists.

When market exchange is competitive – that is to say, neither buyer nor seller can exercise market power over the other (generally because each has many alternatives to dealing with the other and knows this to be true) – the outcome will be an agreement to exchange a specified quantity of a good or service at a specified price, which agreement is voluntarily entered into by the two parties on a fully informed basis. Economists refer to this outcome as a *competitive market equilibrium*. Because the two parties to a competitive market exchange arrive at their agreement voluntarily and with full information, economists conclude that any attempt to alter the outcome (e.g., by changing the agreed amounts exchanged or the agreed price) would make one of the two parties worse off to the benefit of the other. This conclusion is generalized into the First Fundamental Theorem of welfare economics, which is that a competitive market equilibrium is a Pareto optimal allocation.

A Pareto optimal allocation is a set of quantities exchanged and prices at which they are exchanged that cannot be altered without making at least one of the parties to the exchange worse off. Judging whether a party is better off or worse off comes down to whether consumption possibilities are increased or diminished. This in turn reflects the assumption that economic welfare is essentially contingent on the consumption of goods and services and that more consumption is preferable to less.[4] Evidently, economic welfare is founded on a utilitarian calculus.

The genius of competitive market exchange in delivering Pareto optimal allocations is tempered by the fact that the outcome depends upon initial conditions, including the endowment of goods and services available to both parties before they begin the process of market exchange. Someone with little to sell cannot expect to obtain much of value in exchange, no matter how competitive the market. Yet the outcome of such an exchange will still be Pareto optimal, exposing the limitation of this concept as a measure of social welfare. Essentially, the Pareto criterion is incapable of making interpersonal comparisons of utility – that is to say, of deciding whether taxing Peter to pay Paul nevertheless leaves them both better off, because Paul values the gain in consumption more highly than Peter values the loss. Rearranging the starting conditions will deliver a different competitive market outcome that will also be Pareto optimal but unable to be ranked by the Pareto criterion higher or lower than an alternative competitive equilibrium derived from different starting conditions.

Economists attempt to escape this impasse by hypothesizing a social welfare function that explicitly weights the value to be placed on the consumption enjoyed by each party to an exchange so that aggregation (i.e., making interpersonal comparisons of utility) becomes possible. It then also becomes possible to envision circumstances in which intervention in market exchange to alter equilibrium outcomes might raise social welfare overall. Even so, the end result of such intervention is to alter the pattern of consumption, since social welfare, in the economist's conception, ultimately consists in the possibilities for consumption afforded to each individual.

[4] Thomas Carlyle contemptuously referred to this as the "pig principle," perhaps echoing St. Paul in Philippians 3:19 ("their god is their stomach"). But see footnote 2 for a broader conception of consumption possibilities.

## 2.3 THE LIMITATIONS OF MARKETS

How could free exchange between willing parties fail to serve the interests of those involved, let alone the public or common good? Economists describe such circumstances as "market failure," and they focus on conditions affecting the contracting (or "internal") parties themselves or else the impact of their interaction on unrelated (or "external") third parties. The conclusion that voluntary market exchange serves the interests of both contracting parties rests on the assumption that their bargaining power is broadly equal. If, however, bargaining power is unequally distributed, outcomes of the exchange will likely benefit one party more than the other, or even leave the weaker party worse off. One basic source of unequal bargaining power is "asymmetric information," that is, the circumstance in which one party has privileged (or "insider") information about the true nature of the product or service on offer or the bids being submitted by competing buyers or sellers. If both parties are not equally informed, or at least equally capable of informing themselves, the imbalance in their information can produce an imbalance in the terms of trade, favoring the party with the privileged information.

Bargaining power can also be unequally distributed if one party can block or interfere with the other party's right to choose a different buyer or seller. This is known as "exclusionary" behavior and is the essence of market power. A range of circumstances can confer market power on one side of a potential exchange and hence bias the gains from trade in favor of the party with market power. Structural conditions in markets, like economies of scale in production, can confer market power on sellers that achieve scale in advance of their competitors. This can enable an empowered seller to offer prices to potential buyers sufficiently below those offered by competing suppliers such that, eventually, only one seller remains in the market (the so-called monopoly).[5] Once this condition is achieved, the monopolist can raise its price above costs, safe in the knowledge that other potential suppliers will be unable to undercut the monopoly price without risking a "price war" that only the monopolist can win.

Other forms of exclusionary behavior include collusion among buyers or sellers not to offer competing bids and various forms of "vertical restraint" that allow wholesale suppliers to dictate the terms offered by retail suppliers to

[5] Prior to 1982, when divestiture was mandated, the Bell System of companies operated a monopoly of local telephone services in the United States and Canada. The system was broken up to force competition into a market that had become completely closed through monopoly ownership.

ultimate buyers. Again, the common feature is that buyers or sellers are blocked from dealing with other potential parties to an exchange or at different prices because these parties and/or competing offers are excluded from the market. Exclusion of potential competitors (either buyers or sellers) confers market power on incumbents.

Even absent information asymmetry or market power, free exchange may still undermine the interests of one or more of the contracting parties because of the nature of the good or service exchanged. Commonly cited examples include trade in drugs of dependence (both licit and illicit), gambling, and prostitution. The exchange itself may undermine a person's long-term material interest even if it meets a short-term material exigency. This is to say nothing of the potential impact on a person's character or moral virtue.[6]

Turning to circumstances in which the welfare of "external" as opposed to "internal" parties to an exchange is concerned, the issue here is that an exchange may well serve the material interests of the contracting parties and yet compromise those of parties uninvolved in the exchange. Economists refer to such outcomes of free market exchange as "negative externalities" (which can occasionally be positive, as in the rise in value of surrounding properties due to a homeowner's landscape gardening, but are more commonly negative). The parties to an exchange that creates negative externalities may or may not be aware of that fact, but they are generally assumed to ignore external costs and benefits when negotiating acceptable terms of trade. Hence an exchange that benefits two contracting parties may nonetheless compromise the common or public good on account of its negative impact on the material welfare of parties external to the exchange.

The above are examples of exchanges that should take place on different terms, or to a different extent, or perhaps not at all, in order to secure the public or common good. There are other instances where exchanges do not take place that should take place, or take place to a greater extent. Economists recognize a class of "public" goods (as contrasted with private goods), which, for various reasons, markets are less willing or even unwilling to exchange. The point here is that such goods raise social welfare; society is better off with them than without, or with more of them than the market will supply on its own terms. The market fails to supply enough public goods because of their nature: they are "non-rival" (i.e., one person's consumption does not diminish that available for

[6] Even if both parties are fully aware of the likely consequences of an exchange, myopic preferences can still lead people to discount the future consequences of current decisions, albeit irrationally. In such instances, free exchange can make one or both parties worse off in the long run, notwithstanding their complete awareness of that likelihood.

others to consume), "non-excludable" (i.e., it is not possible to prevent people from consuming a good or service whether or not they have paid for it), or both. The classic example of the pure public good is national defense, which is both non-rival and non-excludable. Social welfare is raised by the production of public goods, but some form of collective or coercive action is required to secure them. By itself, market exchange fails to produce enough public goods, since the normal requirement that exchange be requited is not fulfilled.

In principle, the social welfare function identifies circumstances in which the common good is served by intervening in market exchange to secure different outcomes. Free market exchange may fail to serve the common good because it fails to serve the interests of the parties to an exchange or of external parties or possibly both. The question then arises whether, and if so how, an external authority (generally a government) might intervene in an otherwise free market exchange so as to correct or eliminate the potential for harm to the parties involved, or to innocent bystanders, or to secure the production of public goods.

Government regulation of market activity takes many forms but ideally is shaped by the nature of the underlying market failure. Intervention, if it is to be beneficial, ought to address the underlying problem, or else the "cure" may be more harmful than the "disease." Regulation of market exchange is not without unintended consequences. Ideally, these must be anticipated and valued when the regulatory intervention is designed so as to maximize the chances of improving the common good relative to the unregulated free market alternative.

Typically, economists say that attempts to intervene in market exchange should pass a "public benefit" test. The test has two limbs: the first requires that intervention (by government regulation, for example) is the *only way* to secure or avoid a particular outcome (generally because free market exchange itself is the source of the problem); and the second requires that, even then, the *benefits secured by intervention should outweigh the costs* of intervening (since an imperfect market outcome may still be the lesser of two evils).

At the benign end of the spectrum, market failure grounded in asymmetric information may be remedied by a government agency acquiring and then publishing the missing information so that all parties to an exchange are equally informed.[7] This may be enough to rebalance the bargaining power of parties to an exchange so that one is no longer systematically advantaged in negotiation. Structural problems in markets that manifest as exclusionary behavior may be addressed by government efforts to penalize actions by buyers

7 For example, a public regulator (like the Securities and Exchange Commission in the United States) mandating disclosure of material changes in circumstances affecting publicly traded companies is generally regarded as sufficient to ensure the efficient operation of stock markets.

or sellers intended to exclude competitors. Competition law aims squarely at establishing such penalties and prosecuting breaches. Governments can also help lower entry barriers to markets, especially where the barriers are of a government's own making, including, for example, "red tape" licensing rules that unduly impede the efforts of new competitors to enter a market and make offers in competition with incumbents.

At the more extreme end of the spectrum is government intervention to set the terms of market exchange, including the parties permitted to contract and the terms on which they are permitted to contract – such as prices, quantities, and qualities. Governments may also decide that the only way to secure the common good is to curtail, or even ban outright, the exchange of particular goods or services. Such action may be motivated by an attempt to protect the interests of contracting parties in spite of themselves, or to protect the wider public interest from external costs imposed by the exchange.

While there is no doubt that market exchange can compromise the common good, it is not always clear that intervention by government improves the outcome, because the intervention might prove to be misdirected, ineffectual, or, in the worst case, counterproductive. The motivation of governments in seeking to manipulate market outcomes can also be questioned. Public choice theory emphasizes that governments, too, are economic actors with their own interests (and those of their constituencies) to serve. So what might appear to be public-spirited intervention may, in the most egregious instances, simply be a pretext for governments to favor particular interests for political gain, or even to raise revenue by covert taxation. In such cases, whatever gains there may be from constraining market exchange must be set against potential losses from displacing market outcomes with government-directed outcomes.

The economic costs of government intervention are not zero, even if the potential benefits of intervention are positive. The overriding concern that economists have in contemplating intervention in market exchange is to ensure that the *net social welfare benefit* of intervention is positive. Otherwise, market exchange, notwithstanding its costs to the common good in certain circumstances, may be the lesser of two evils.

## 2.4 CHRISTIAN ETHICAL NOTIONS OF THE COMMON GOOD

The chief Christian contribution to discussion of the common good is to deepen the concepts of both "common" and "good" beyond the utilitarian notions that prevail in modern political and economic discourse.[8]

[8] O'Donovan, *Ways of Judgment*, p. 138.

Among the Church Fathers, Augustine's contribution is outstanding by virtue of engaging with Cicero's discussion of the common good. Drawing on this definition, he argues that there can be no true commonweal apart from the service of God (*De Civitas Dei*, 19.21). A people are constituted by agreement about what is true and good; the ultimate truth and the ultimate good is God. Reworking Cicero's definition of what constitutes a people, Augustine asserts: "A people ... is a gathered multitude of rational beings united by agreeing to share the things they love ... [t]he better the things, the better the people; the worse the things, the worse their agreement to share them" (*De Civitas Dei*, 19.24).[9] Although this could lead Christians to either seek to dominate the earthly city or withdraw from it in anticipation of the heavenly city, Augustine instead shows that a knowledge of the ultimate good should lead Christians to value and pursue the penultimate, limited goods of the peace of the earthly city.[10] The fullness of the common good of communion with God cannot be achieved in the state, but it is partially foreshadowed in the church, in advance of the heavenly city (*De Civitas Dei*, 19.26).

Also among the Church Fathers' contributions to the idea of the common good, we find the sermons of John Chrysostom. On the basis of God's possession of all things – "The earth is the Lord's and the fullness thereof" (Psalm 24:1) – Chrysostom argues: "If our possessions belong to our common Lord, they belong to our fellow servants too."[11] All kinds of natural resources are common; but when someone tries to take exclusive possession, conflict arises. Wealth, therefore, understood as exclusive possession, cannot be called good; and the wealthy person can be called good only if he or she distributes that wealth.[12] Rather, true value is found when goods – which, for Chrysostom, include material as well as intellectual goods such as professional skills – are shared with others, with a view toward spiritual ends.[13] As Oliver

9 Translation from Oliver O'Donovan and Joan Lockwood O'Donovan, eds., *From Irenaeus to Grotius: A Sourcebook in Christian Political Thought* (Grand Rapids, MI: Eerdmans, 1999), p. 162.

10 See David Hollenbach, *The Common Good and Christian Ethics*, New Studies in Christian Ethics (Cambridge: Cambridge University Press, 2002), pp. 124–125.

11 "Twelfth Homily on 1 Timothy," in O'Donovan and O'Donovan, *From Irenaeus to Grotius*, p. 102.

12 Ibid., pp. 102–103.

13 See Jeremy Kidwell, "Radical or Realist? An Inquiry into the Social Ethics of John of Chrystostom as a Model for Resourcing the Tradition in Reflection on the Common Good," in *Theology and Economics: A Christian Vision of the Common Good*, ed. Jeremy Kidwell and Sean Doherty (New York: Palgrave Macmillan, 2015), pp. 127–142.

and Joan O'Donovan put it: "John [Chrysostom] has his own idea of equality as *unhindered access* to the benefits of common property."[14]

From the Middle Ages, Thomas Aquinas agrees that the ultimate good is communion with God and that "[t]he true good of persons is communion with other persons."[15] While this cannot be achieved in human society, the eschatological good of communion with God can provide a paradigm for human society in the present. In the twentieth century, Jacques Maritain drew on Aquinas to argue for a conception of the common good that "is more than an aggregation of individual goods and to which every individual as part of the social whole is subordinated."[16]

The late-medieval English theologian, John Wycliffe, further developed the notion of the common good that goes beyond the aggregated goods of individuals. Similarly to Chrysostom, Wycliffe's notion of the common good is grounded in the universal lordship of God over all things. This lordship was shared with Adam at creation and renewed to humanity in Christ so that "any and every righteous man is lord of the whole sense-perceptible world."[17] God communicates – that is, shares – the good of creation with his creatures, who also communicate it with one another. Because all share in Christ, who has lordship over all things, so anyone who is in Christ shares in all things. Thus, any good that one possesses in Christ – or, derivatively, as a member of Adam – is a good held in common. It belongs to all, even as it belongs to one.

Despite the substance of these patristic and medieval contributions, such writers rarely, if ever, venture a systematic definition of the common good. Nevertheless, as Hollenbach shows, at least one common element is clearly discernible – a holistic notion of the common good as opposed to an aggregative one.[18] It is the sharing of the good that makes it common, suggesting that the common good transcends mere material goods to the very community in which such goods are shared.

In the eighteenth century, the classical and Christian traditions gave rise to the Italian political economic notion of "civil economy." Bruni and Zamagni observe that "the central idea in civil economy – and therefore the basis for its practical implications – is that it sees human sociability and reciprocity as core

[14] O'Donovan and O'Donovan, *From Irenaeus to Grotius*, p. 91.
[15] Hollenbach, *The Common Good*, p. 130.
[16] Robert Song, *Christianity and Liberal Society*, Oxford Studies in Theological Ethics (Oxford: Clarendon Press, 1997), p. 134.
[17] "*Civil Lordship* 1.7.15d," in O'Donovan and O'Donovan, *From Irenaeus to Grotius*, p. 488.
[18] Hollenbach, *The Common Good*, pp. 7ff.

elements of normal economic life."[19] Market exchange is viewed as possible only because the parties to any exchange already share in a community. An economy is civil when exchanges within it conform to "the principle of reciprocity, and [do not] bend and destroy it."[20] This view of economy sees exchanges as embedded in existing social relationships, drawing on the "paradoxical" Christian notion that "happiness ... is constitutionally relational."[21] Value is conferred by the personal relationships that constitute the use and enjoyment of any good; that is, the common good is the only good of any substance.

Drawing on St. Paul's use of the term *koinonia* and the writings of John Wycliffe, Oliver O'Donovan argues that the possession of goods is necessary, but only as a moment in a wider context of social interaction: "The transmission of any good from one person to another creates a relation through which we enjoy the object in a new way together."[22] Private interest is satisfied in the communication of the goods of creation, but as a "median point" – dependent on the social value that gives rise to the moment of exchange and looking forward to that which it seeks to achieve.[23]

> Our relations with others may include commercial exchange-transactions; but exchange cannot be the whole truth of the relations and obligations formed around them. "This is a purely commercial transaction" can never be more than a specious explanation of social engagements that are either community-building or exploitative. No undertaking is "purely" commercial. Every engagement in which exchange takes place implies a social context of things held in common; our exchange-transaction either upholds the justice of that community, or it flouts it.[24]

The location of traditional (physical) markets in places where social interaction could occur in association with, as well as through, market exchange emphasized markets' social context, even if this was insufficient by itself to establish *koinonia*. The modern abstraction of market exchange from physical location – let alone social interaction – highlights the contrast with true communication of the goods and services exchanged. Referring specifically to the modern labor market and the communication of work (or lack thereof)

[19] Luigino Bruni and Stefano Zamagni, *Civil Economy: Efficiency, Equity, Public Happiness*, Frontiers of Business Ethics (Bern: Peter Lang, 2007), p. 17.
[20] Ibid., p. 41.
[21] Ibid., pp. 95–96.
[22] O'Donovan, *Ways of Judgment*, p. 244.
[23] Ibid., p. 249.
[24] Ibid., pp. 248–249.

in the modern workplace, O'Donovan bemoans the alienation of the modern worker, not just from his or her work (as per Karl Marx's diagnosis), but from the community of his or her fellow workers, leading to "restlessness and rootlessness [becoming] the ruling principles of the workplace rather than stability and growth."[25]

Yet it is possible to overstate the alienation inherent in market exchange. Especially in a modern context of global markets, exchange induces cooperation among people who are, and possibly remain, complete strangers. Where there is no relationship at all and perhaps not even the possibility of a relationship, market exchange facilitates cooperation in a co-creative endeavor. Although falling well short of *koinonia* in its purest form, some mutually advantageous relationship is better than none at all, and global markets, based as they are on modern communications, can create such a community of interest where none might otherwise have existed.

Of course, where "faceless" global markets undermine community by, for example, facilitating exploitation of human beings or despoliation of the natural environment, government intervention can be justified to secure the common good, including for noncitizens.

## 2.5 KOINONIA

Broadly speaking, Christian thought has counseled caution against giving either the market or the state too high a place in the project of human flourishing. Daniel Finn, surveying Christian approaches to economic ethics from the New Testament to the present day, writes:

> Because the Christian tradition has consistently seen the person as simultaneously individual and social, society is more fundamental than market and government, institutions that emerge from the interaction of persons in their daily lives.[26]

Brent Waters follows Oliver O'Donovan in placing *koinonia* or "communication" above both market exchange and state coercion as the source of human flourishing. O'Donovan's and Waters's choice of *koinonia* as the key biblical term for a Christian notion of collective human flourishing requires

[25] Oliver O'Donovan, *Entering into Rest* (Grand Rapids, MI: Eerdmans, 2017), p. 126.

[26] Daniel K. Finn, *Christian Economic Ethics: History and Implications* (Minneapolis, MN: Fortress, 2013), p. 370; see also Daniel K. Finn, *The Moral Ecology of Markets: Assessing Claims about Markets and Justice* (Cambridge: Cambridge University Press, 2006).

and repays careful scrutiny. Does *koinonia* capture the essence of a holistic conception of the common good?

At first blush, taking *koinonia* in this sense seems like an anachronistic overreach. In the New Testament, the term is regularly used for "fellowship" or close relationship with God, including the Father (1 John 1:3), Son (1 Corinthians 1:9), and Spirit (Philippians 2:1). In relation to human beings it can be used simply for harmonious relationships (as in Galatians 2:9: "the right hand of *fellowship*").

However, these usages by no means exhaust the word's wide semantic domain. *Koinonia* can also denote generosity, fellow-feeling, and altruism, and can even mean financial partnership and support. In the Apostle Paul's instructions concerning a collection for the poor in Jerusalem, the word is regularly translated as (financial) "contribution" or "sharing" (cf. Romans 15:26; 2 Corinthians 8:4; 9:13). The standard Greek lexica define *koinonia* quite broadly, as "close association involving mutual interests and sharing" or "an association involving close mutual relations and involvement."[27]

Even if the term is unable to bear the full weight of community-building and social interaction in the modern sense, concepts are bigger than words, and *koinonia* is a convenient label for the Bible's teaching about a range of related subjects. The Bible is replete with calls for believers to "do good to all people" (Galatians 6:10), understood quite broadly. In the New Testament, there are many "one another" admonitions that underscore the common good in the holistic sense, including "seek good for one another" (1 Thessalonians 5:15), "through love, serve one another" (Galatians 5:13), and "bear one another's burdens" (Galatians 6:2). Paul's insistence that thieves stop stealing, not in order to become independent but rather interdependent, is especially striking; he counsels them to "do something useful with their own hands, that they may have something to share with those in need" (Ephesians 4:28). *Koinonia* is as good a term as any to capture the biblical vision for corporate flourishing in community.

Waters argues that human beings flourish as they share or "communicate" the goods of creation. This involves a reciprocal giving and receiving – sharing in the sense of holding in common what is "ours" rather than "yours" or "mine" – and this reciprocity is captured neither in market exchange nor in state coercion.

[27] W. Bauer, F. W. Danker, W. F. Arndt, and F. W. Gingrich, *Greek-English Lexicon of the New Testament and Other Early Christian Literature*, 3rd ed. (Chicago: University of Chicago Press, 2002) and J. P. Louw and E. A. Nida, eds., *Greek-English Lexicon of the New Testament: Based on Semantic Domains*, 2nd ed. (New York: United Bible Societies, 1996), respectively.

> Neither markets nor states can engage directly in communicating goods, because the former is predicated on exchange and the latter on coercion. Moreover, the concept of communication reinforces the notion that humans do not flourish exclusively as consumers or citizens, but as individuals embedded within a society composed of associations or spheres of communication.[28]

On this view, even if markets are fully efficient in the economist's sense of delivering a Pareto optimal allocation, they will fail to deliver human flourishing, since the very foundation of market activity – namely, exchange – fails to "communicate" the goods exchanged and hence to create *koinonia*. By the same token, attempts by the state to overcome market inefficiency through regulatory intervention similarly fail to satisfy the requirements for human flourishing, since coercion, like exchange, falls short of the reciprocity inherent in "communication."

Note that this would be true even if state intervention completely neutralized market inefficiency, restoring a socially optimal allocation of resources in the economist's framework of thinking. To the Christian theologian – at least those who follow O'Donovan – "[m]arkets and political governance . . . are necessary in ordering human life, but neither is sufficient, and even both in tandem are insufficient, to promote human flourishing, because neither independently or together is a form of koinonia."[29]

If market regulation is insufficient to secure the common good by promoting human flourishing, why might it even be necessary? Here the role of government intervention differs from that in the economist's framework. In economics, state intervention to regulate markets aims to improve their efficiency, that is, the extent to which they promote social welfare. The Christian theologian, on the other hand, would sanction state intervention where this serves to promote *koinonia*, acknowledging that such intervention (involving as it does coercive action by the state) might itself compromise or even conflict with *koinonia*.[30]

The arena in which economists and theologians might both support government intervention in markets concerns the production of public goods.[31]

[28] Brent Waters, *Just Capitalism: A Christian Ethic of Economic Globalization* (Louisville, KY: Westminster John Knox Press, 2016), p. 148.

[29] Ibid., p. 150.

[30] Coercively raising taxes to fund the provision of public goods (discussed in the following paragraph) is an obvious example.

[31] Included within the category of public goods are so-called club goods and common goods. The arguments in this paragraph apply equally to these subcategories of public goods.

These are classically subject to market failure, as discussed earlier, and hence are produced in suboptimal quantities if they are produced at all. Yet public goods come closest to the notion of reciprocity or sharing that is inherent in "communication." People pay taxes according to their capacity and consume a public good according to their need or preference. It is consumed by "us" collectively rather than individually. The production of more public goods than the free market would provide promotes social welfare in the economist's calculus as well as *koinonia* in the Christian theologian's framework. Hence, regulating markets to secure the production of public goods helps to secure the common good in both views.

Broader yet, the theologian will look to the state to promote justice, a quality of human relationships that is implicit in *koinonia* but wider in its moral scope. Here the economist has precious little to say *qua* economist. Economics lacks any criterion for determining the justness of market outcomes. For the theologian, however, government comes into its own, under God, as an administrator of justice, a task described by O'Donovan as "judgment," or "an act of moral discrimination that pronounces upon a preceding act or existing state of affairs to establish a new public context."[32]

Economic relations among human beings are a constant opening for injustice. In the Old Testament, the nation Israel must keep God's "righteous decrees and laws" so that all the nations of the world will look enviously at the just and right ordering of their society and be attracted to God's wisdom (Deuteronomy 4:6–8). In particular, as God's representatives, judges must acquit the innocent, condemn the guilty, and expose false accusations and bribery (2 Chronicles 19:5–7). They are not to distort justice to favor the poor (Exodus 23:3) any more than to favor the rich. God also charges kings to act justly and instructs them to look after the weak and the defenseless. The psalmist prays, "Endow the king with your justice, O God ... May he judge your people in righteousness, your afflicted ones with justice" (Psalms 72:1–2).

Yet government interventions cannot of themselves secure justice within economic relationships, or more broadly. That comes only through humanity's participation in the salvation of Christ, which will be perfected only in the new creation. It is anticipated, however, in the life of the church, and of Christian believers, who learn to love one another as Christ has loved and loves them. The profound practices of generosity and fellowship (*koinonia*) that lie at the heart of the gospel, and to which human beings are called, can provide a model for governments to promote justice and flourishing in the

[32] O'Donovan, *Ways of Judgment*, p. 7.

world. Without such life in the midst of society, governments' attempts to defend the common good will be far more difficult.

While Christian moral theology thus provides frameworks for making moral judgments about markets and suggestions for areas where they might be regulated for the common good, it also recognizes that government cannot *create* the common good – rather, it can only *defend* it.[33] Christian moral theology therefore recognizes that the regulatory involvement of government is limited, both in scope and in effectiveness. There must be, in O'Donovan's phrase, "an *economy* of government ... authority may be exerted only where there is *prima facie* threat to the common good."[34]

This recognition does not give a theological rationale for "small" or "limited" government in the way those terms are usually used, but rather cautions against any vision of government as the vehicle for creating some kind of utopian society. On the other hand, this recognition cautions against any vision of self-regulating markets as vehicles for the same. Instead, government interventions should target threats to the common good – that is, specific classes of exchange or specific goods in exchange whose presence (or absence) hampers effective social communication between the parties to the exchange and within the communities of which they are part, including, for example, restraining the abuse of market power and mandating the provision of public goods.

Thinking of the market as one limited angle from which to view human community will, on the one hand, temper the economist's instinct against regulation, and also, on the other hand, temper the social reformer's instinct to override markets. In a Christian conception of the common good, government regulation of markets, where justified, should aim to ensure that market exchanges are properly *communications*. Regulation achieves this when it properly situates market transactions within the larger context of the community that confers real value on the goods and services exchanged through market mechanisms.

## 2.6 CONCLUSION

Economics and Christian theology offer distinct perspectives on the common good since they approach the notion from different vantage points. It is therefore hardly surprising that their respective views of the market as a contributor to or detractor from the common good should also differ. Similarly, their views of the capacity of governments to regulate markets to

33 Cf. O'Donovan, *Ways of Judgment*, pp. 138, 246–247.

34 Ibid., p. 66. Italics original.

meliorate their corrosive impact on the common good should also be expected to differ. The two disciplines reach different conclusions because they start out from different premises.

Economics is founded on utilitarian principles and so thinks of the common good in consequentialist terms. In principle, government regulation can moderate those aspects of market behavior that undermine the common good when measured using the economist's social welfare function. Government regulation typically brings its own shortcomings to bear, however, and whether or not the regulated market delivers higher social welfare (i.e., is more conducive to the common good) than does the unregulated or less regulated market is a matter for conjecture and, ultimately, empirical assessment.

Christian theology, on the other hand, adopting as it does a holistic rather than an aggregative conception of the common good, questions the very basis of market activity (i.e., exchange) as well as the very basis of government intervention (i.e., coercion). If neither exchange nor coercion properly communicates the goods of creation among God's people, then in neither case is *koinonia* upheld, and the market, whether regulated by coercive government intervention or not, will fail to promote the common good. This is clearly a higher threshold.

Is there a *via media*? The most obvious example is public goods, which economists concede the market will fail to supply in sufficient quantities to satisfy even their more limited notion of the common good, and, generally, notwithstanding the deficiencies of government coercion. In other words, even public goods supplied at government behest are better than no public goods at all. As for theologians, public goods are part of God's good creation and cannot be communicated among God's people if they do not even exist or at least do not exist in sufficient quantities.

In the end, economists will favor arrangements that deliver more of the things that people prefer (i.e., "goods and services") rather than less, allowing that this might involve some coercion by government. They worry less about the impact such arrangements might have on the broader communion that people enjoy (or not) during the process. Theologians, on the other hand, will worry a great deal about the impact of economic activity – whether coerced or not – on broader dimensions of human flourishing, especially human relationships, since how we love and serve one another ranks more highly in God's economy than what we eat or drink.

# 3

# Public Choice Theory and Interest Group Capture

CARROLL RIOS DE RODRÍGUEZ

The public choice research project made its appearance in the middle of the twentieth century, and is primarily the brainchild of American and British intellectuals.[1] The scholars associated with this research project focused on how individual actors participated in collective decision-making within the democratic, participative political systems of their time. Authors associated with the public choice research project point out that their work was inspired by, or derives from, the political economy practiced by Adam Smith, David Hume, Niccolò Machiavelli, and even Knut Wicksell and Joseph Schumpeter, whose work straddled the nineteenth and twentieth centuries. There was a time when the social sciences were less compartmentalized, and when the study of politics, economics, and even political philosophy was intertwined. As is common in the social sciences, few authors explore the intersection of the political sphere with Christianity, seen as a historical, cultural, and spiritual reality. Some may consider it unprofessional to use a faith-based lens to interpret a scientific discipline, while others may be influenced by their personal agnosticism or atheism.[2]

However, this chapter attempts to demonstrate that the claims made by public choice scholars regarding the political acts of individuals and groups correspond with the behavior of some historical figures featured in the Bible and with Christian thought more broadly. Even though individual citizens

1 International precursors and contributors to public choice theory include French mathematician Marie Jean Antoine Nicolas de Caritat, Marquis of Condorcet, Italian sociologist and economist Wilfredo Pareto, Scottish economist Duncan Black, and Swedish economist Knut Wicksell, among others.

2 Geoffrey Brennan, coauthor and friend of James Buchanan, states that Buchanan was "antagonistic to religion of all kinds." See Geoffrey Brennan and Michael Munger, "The Soul of James Buchanan?," *The Independent Review*, vol. 18, no. 3 (Winter 2014), pp. 331–342. Brennan is Anglican.

confront fewer opportunities to participate in sociopolitical decisions in systems where the decisions are taken by the top echelons of power, citizens can nonetheless lobby their authorities and seek from them certain protections or privileges. The Bible describes human behaviors that illustrate how interest groups interact with politicians in order to obtain benefits for their members. One interesting conclusion from this fact is that the theories regarding rent-seeking and regulatory capture, concretely, can also be applied to non-democratic political arrangements.[3]

Before delving into the work centered on interest groups, rent-seeking behaviors, and regulatory capture, it is important to describe four insights that undergird the entire public choice research program. These four insights deal with (1) how collective decisions are made, (2) how human action is conceived, (3) the importance of a realist approach to politics, and (4) the zero-sum nature of politics. Section 3.2 analyzes three complementary approaches to regulation: the regulatory capture theory developed by George Stigler, the interest group theory associated with the work of Mancur Olson, and the rent-seeking theory laid down by Gordon Tullock. Biblical passages are used to illustrate these approaches. The section ends with an exploration of Christians' attitudes toward, and participation in, rent-seeking activities. Section 3.3 reviews Christianity's teachings regarding democratic governance. Finally, Section 3.4 focuses on the constitution as a possible antidote to costly special interest regulation.

## 3.1 FOUR PUBLIC CHOICE BUILDING BLOCKS

### 3.1.1 Collective Decision-Making in Participatory Political Systems

Public choice theory is the subdiscipline of economics that explores how human beings participate in collective decision-making. As Christian anthropology postulates, humans are social beings.[4] Collective decisions are made in various arenas, such as the family, business boards, associations, and the political realm: a head of family may or may not consult with the children on where to dine on Sunday evening; a board of directors may or may not

[3] Other aspects of public choice theory, such as the study of voting rules and of alternate types of governance (for instance, parliamentarism or presidentialism), describe behaviors that generally occur in open and democratic contexts.

[4] See nos. 149–151 in the *Compendium of the Social Doctrine of the Catholic Church*, under the title "E. The Social Nature of Human Beings," www.vatican.va/roman_curia/pontifical_councils/justpeace/documents/rc_pc_justpeace_doc_20060526_compendio-dott-soc_en.html#THE%20SOCIAL%20NATURE%20OF%20HUMAN%20BEINGS

select the unanimity rule to approve voluminous expenses; in the political realm, individual citizens are only able to express their preferences when the rules enable them to partake in the decision-making; in extreme dictatorial settings, the tyrant dictates policy with limited consultation.

The context within which public choice emerged explains why the literature is applicable to, and seen through the optic of, open democratic systems in which voters, interest groups, politicians, and bureaucrats help shape the rules by which they govern themselves, as well as the specific decisions that are made within the institutional arrangements they give themselves. In 1963, twenty scholars gathered in Virginia, convened there by James M. Buchanan and Gordon Tullock, who had published *The Calculus of Consent* a year earlier. The group included philosophers, sociologists, psychologists, political scientists, and economists. William Riker, Mancur Olson, Vincent Ostrom, Anthony Downs, Duncan Black, John Rawls, Roland McKean, and Jerry Rothenberg were among those present. They first used the title "non-market decision-making" to refer to their research agenda; it was later renamed with the catchier, if not always clarifying, "public choice."[5]

For centuries, before and after the birth of Jesus Christ, ordinary citizens played a limited role in political choices. In its most radical form, the Athenian democracy, proposed by King Solon and then put in place by Cleisthenes, lasted about 186 years, from 508 BCE to 322 BCE. The Assembly was a group of citizens that took important decisions concerning the city, following an agenda set by the Council of Five Hundred. Slaves, women, children, and foreigners were excluded from this governing mechanism.[6] Lord Acton admired King Solon, "the wisest man to be found in Athens," because "[b]y making every citizen the guardian of his own interest Solon admitted the element of democracy into the State."[7] However, Acton's praise is not shared even by famous Athens residents, Plato and Aristotle, both of whom were critical of direct democracy.[8] According to Acton, Greece's democracy began to fail as majority rule became tyrannical and set aside legal

5 "Interview with James Buchanan," *The Region*, The Federal Reserve Bank of Minneapolis, September 1995, http://buscon.rae.es/draeI/SrvltGUIBusUsual?LEMA=teor%C3%Ada

6 See an article by Christopher W. Blackwell, prepared originally for a discussion sponsored by Harvard University's Center for Hellenic Studies, titled "Athenian Democracy: A Brief Overview," a Stoa Publication, February 28, 2003, www.stoa.org/demos/article_democracy_overview@page=all&greekEncoding=UnicodeC.html

7 John Emerich Edward Dalberg-Acton, "The History of Freedom in Antiquity," in *Ensayos sobre la libertad y el poder*, trans. Paloma de la Nuez (Spain: Union Editorial, 1998), p. 63.

8 Munroe Eagles and Larry Johnston, *Politics: An Introduction to Democratic Government* (New York: Broadview Press, 1985), p. 69.

and traditional limits. Eventually, after Alexander the Great rose to power, the Assembly ceased to be the main governing body in Athens.[9]

In Rome – which like Athens started out as a city-state – kings, aristocrats, and plebeians wrestled for power. The Senatus Populusque Romunus (SPQR or The Roman Senate and People) was, according to Greek poet and Rome resident Polybius, a hybrid combining facets of aristocratic, democratic, and monarchical government. Its checks and balances prevented the excesses of direct democracy. For example, consuls (monarchs) had to be elected by the people and the senate, in turn, provided funding.[10] Moreover, as Alexander Hamilton observed in *The Federalist* no. 34, two legislatures, one serving patrician interests and the other serving plebeian interests, "coexisted for ages, and the Roman republic attained to the utmost height of human greatness."[11] The system's mixed nature bears out Mary Beard's assessment to the effect that democracy was not a priority for Romans because the concept was "rooted politically and linguistically in the Greek world": "Romans fought for, and about, liberty, not democracy."[12]

As Rome grew and turned into an empire, male citizens faced fewer opportunities to influence policy. Acton observes that Julius Caesar "converted the Republic into a Monarchy."[13] Julius Caesar's successor, Octavian (also known as Augustus), ruled over the empire for forty years, from January 16, 27 BCE to August 19, AD. Beard suggests that the civil wars following Julius Caesar's assassination favored the emergence of an autocrat rather than the traditional sharing of powers.[14] Julius Caesar had been deified, and Augustus was called "Divi filius."[15] The term Augustus, itself, means "Revered One."[16] The investing of religious authority in the Roman emperor, and his pretention to be "Sone of the Divine," helped to enable his move to centralize de facto power. The Senate and other republican institutions were

9 See Blackwell, "Athenian Democracy."

10 Mary Beard, *SPQR: A History of Ancient Rome* (New York: W. W. Norton, 2015), pp. 188–189.

11 Alexander Hamilton (Publius), *The Federalist Papers: No. 34, On the Same Subject Continued, Concerning the General Power of Taxation, from the New York Packet*. Friday, January 4, 1788, https://avalon.law.yale.edu/18th_century/fed34.asp

12 Beard, *SPQR*, p. 189. For Romans, democracy was akin to "mob rule," adds Beard.

13 Dalberg-Acton, "History of Freedom in Antiquity," p. 70.

14 Beard, *SPQR*, p. 353.

15 Lord Acton finds in Roman politics a primitive form of republicanism that limits the kings' power and suggests the "collective supremacy of free men," but the emperor's centralized power. Lord Acton, "The History of Freedom in Christianity," Liberty Fund, Online Library, speech originally delivered on May 28, 1877, http://oll.libertyfund.org/titles/acton-the-history-of-freedom-and-other-essays

16 Beard, *SPQR*, p. 340.

simultaneously weakened.[17] This political context surrounded Jesus Christ's sojourn on this earth. During the years He lived among us, only the males who enjoyed the privileged legal status of Roman citizen could vote and hold office. Even in the city of Rome, a substantial number of inhabitants were not citizens: Scholars estimate that merely 4 million of the total 45 million inhabitants of the Roman Empire in 28 BC were citizens; around 600 were senators.[18] Civil liberty, participation, legitimacy, and voting were not concepts that featured in the mind of Pontius Pilate, the procurator of Judaea from 26 AD to 35 AD. In sum, a select group with strict entry barriers monopolized decision-making.

Political choices remained more or less closed off to the majority of the governed during the ensuing medieval feudal system, monarchical absolutism, and other variations of authoritarian rule throughout history, with the exceptions of the United Kingdom's constitutional monarchy after the Glorious Revolution (1688), with its Bill of Rights (1689) and parliamentary rule, and the republican regime put in place after the United States revolution and push for independence.[19] However, as pointed out earlier, regulatory capture and rent-seeking are phenomena that tend to be present whenever political power can be exploited for personal gain, both by the political leaders and interested individuals. Even absolutist governors can be petitioned and dispense favors. In other words, throughout history people have been able to use political power, and collective decision-making mechanisms, to carve out special interest benefits.

### 3.1.2 Fallible Decision-Makers

The research project known as public choice is rooted in the supposition that human beings made of flesh and blood populate the political, economic, and social arenas. "The individual is the unique unit of consciousness from which all evaluation begins," emphasize James M. Buchanan and Geoffrey Brennan.[20] A hypothetical person Andrew works in the Bureau of Land

[17] "Augustus, Gaius Julius Octavius," Roman Empire net, www.roman-empire.net/emperors/augustus.html

[18] "Roman Empire Population," UNRV History, Roman Empire, www.unrv.com/empire/roman-population.php

[19] See, for instance, Lord Acton's essay, "The English Revolution," in *Ensayos sobre la libertad y el poder*, trans. Paloma de la Nuez, pp. 181–193.

[20] James M. Buchanan and Geoffrey Brennan, *The Reason of Rules* (Indianapolis, IN: Liberty Fund, 2000). Originally published in 1985, http://oll.libertyfund.org/titles/brennan-the-collected-works-of-james-m-buchanan-vol-10-the-reason-of-rules

Management during the day, stops by the supermarket in the evening, and does house chores at night. Centuries ago, he may have been a scribe employed by the Roman emperor or the Israelite king. Then and now, Andrew's basic nature does not change as he shifts between political, economic, and social activities.

Thus, public choice warns against divorcing the *Homo economicus* from the *Homo politicus*: The social sciences should avoid "schizophrenic assumptions" regarding human action. The divide in anthropological models occurred when a more integral political economy was temporarily forgotten, as the field of economics was artificially cut off from other social sciences in the mid-twentieth century.[21] As Buchanan and Brennan state, "On the basis of elementary methodological principle it would seem that the *same* model of human behavior should be applied across different institutions or different sets of rules."[22]

Methodological individualism means that the unit of analysis for public choice is the individual, and not the group, nation, tribe, or other agglomeration. Concrete persons do the thinking, valuing, and the eventual selecting among alternative options. Inanimate aggregates, such as Jerusalem or the United Nations, do not breathe, think, or act. Individual people harbor disparate preferences. To this Christians add that, while God created each one of us in His image, and made us "capable of self-knowledge, of self-possession,"[23] as well as imperfect, or in theological terms, fallen creatures.

The exact nature of these creatures is more controversial. All would agree that individuals respond to incentives, but not all would champion the *Homo economicus* model as a realistic approximation of human action. Buchanan and Brennan affirm it is not a perfect model or an approximation of reality, but they defend the wealth-maximizer, rational, self-interested, and cost–benefit calculator as a useful fiction. The model does not always withstand empirical scrutiny, but it still holds greater predictive value than alternative models.

The *Homo economicus* model sometimes antagonizes Christians, as the caricature seems inevitably flat and egotistical. Humans do more than relate to others through economic transactions; familial, cultural, and religious relations are an integral part of human life.[24] Brian Fikkert and Michael

[21] Dimitris Milonakis and Ben Fine, *From Political Economy to Economics* (New York: Routledge, 2009), pp. 1–2, https://pauladaunt.com/books/From_Political_Economy_to_Freakonomics.pdf

[22] Buchanan and Brennan, *The Reason of Rules*, p. 56.

[23] *Catechism of the Catholic Church*, no. 357, www.vatican.va/archive/ccc_css/archive/catechism/p1s2c1p6.htm

[24] Moreover, these other types of relationships need not be contractual or transactional.

Rhodes, for instance, contrast *Homo economicus* with *Homo imago Dei*, "an inherently relational being created in the image of a relational God." *Homo imago Dei* is not an "autonomous, individualistic, purely self-interested, materialistic creature."[25] Fikkert and Rhodes deplore the transformation of some people from *Homo imago Dei* into *Homo economicus*, but they clearly suggest that *Homo imago Dei* can and should produce, consume, and trade in economic markets "in order to promote greater human flourishing."[26] In turn, Francis Woehrling puts forth an alternate model he calls *Homo economicus Christianus*: "[T]he Christian economic agent necessarily pursues individualistic objectives because he has to survive (and he knows this is a God-pleasing action) but at the same time he enjoys the company and the success of his co-contractants."[27] In sum, these two articles demonstrate that *Homo economicus*, as a model of human action, falls short of capturing the depth and richness of human nature as understood by Christians.

Bridges can be built to connect the Christian and the economic depiction of human beings. Human beings are not omniscient and cannot but operate based on our own perceptions of our particular circumstances,[28] taking into account the bits and pieces of information at our disposal. An individual has some advantage over all others in his "knowledge of the particular circumstances of time and place," writes Friedrich Hayek, "because he possesses unique information of which beneficial use might be made, but of which use can be made only if the decisions depending on it are left to him or are made with his active cooperation."[29]

Self-interest is not therefore synonymous with self-centeredness, egoism, or ugly avariciousness,[30] as people can and do care how their choices affect others. God-fearing and flawed individuals can *attempt* to live up to the expectations and commandments set down by the Lord, aided by the grace of God, following a difficult and bumpy path toward holiness. "While for model-building purposes 'self-interest' is frequently construed narrowly to

[25] Brian Fikkert and Michael Rhodes, "Homo Economicus versus Homo Imago Dei," *Journal of Markets and Morality*, vol. 20, no. 1 (Spring 2017), p. 102.

[26] Ibid., p. 118.

[27] Francis Woehrling, "'Christian' Economics," *Journal of Markets and Morality*, vol. 4, no. 2 (Fall 2001), p. 210.

[28] Here "subjective" alludes to personal perceptions, and is meant to neither deny objectivity nor promote relativism.

[29] Friedrich A. Hayek, "The Use of Knowledge in Society." This essay was first published in the *American Economic Review* in 1945, and is reprinted with permission by the Library of Economics and Liberty, www.econlib.org/library/Essays/hykKnw1.html

[30] Robert Sirico, *Defending the Free Market: The Moral Case for a Free Economy* (Washington, DC: Regnery Publishing, 2012), pp. 90–92.

mean wealth maximization, the rational actor model is in fact much more general," write William Shughart and Laura Razzolini.[31] "Public choice no more denies the existence of 'public spirit' than economics denies the existence of altruism."[32] In real life, the vast majority of people do not claim for themselves an "autonomy that precludes social obligation and responsibility."[33]

In everyday life and for most people, egotism, ruthlessness, materialism, or other antisocial sentiments are not the motivation behind their economic and political actions. Moreover, economic and political markets do not *require* that people act based on spurious goals. Morally bad choices made by select individuals should not serve to condemn the institutional arrangements themselves, in much the same way that we do not hold a highway responsible for the harmful consequences of a reckless driver's behavior.[34]

To a certain degree, economists exercise prudence when they abstain from judging the motivations of the agents they study: They cannot read people's minds and souls. They can evaluate the observable results of concrete actions.

### 3.1.3 Realism, Not Romanticism

Social science purports to discern particular truths about human action. Public choice economists first diagnose what individuals actually do, and only later do they transition into a more normative or prescriptive mindset.

Human interaction in the political sphere, as in the market, should not be romanticized, cautioned Buchanan. Scarce resources can be inefficiently assigned in both the economic and the political markets, depending on the incentives and institutions determining individual choices. "Regardless of any ideological bias, exposure to public choice analysis necessarily brings a more critical attitude toward politicized nostrums to alleged socioeconomic problems. Public choice almost literally forces the critic to be pragmatic in comparing alternative constitutional arrangements, disallowing any presumption

31 William F. Shughart II and Laura Razzolini, "Introduction: Public Choice at the Millennium," in *The Elgar Companion to Public Choice* (Cheltenham: Edward Elgar, 2001), p. xxii.

32 Ibid., p. xxvi.

33 Sirico, *Defending the Free Market*, p. 93.

34 There are numerous books and authors who are concerned with the morality of markets, including Leonard Read, Henry Hazlitt, Wilhelm Röpke, Michael Novak, Rafael Termes, Peter Berger, Paul Johnson, Robert Sirico, Samuel Gregg, and more. Some authors say economic markets are moral, others that they are amoral, and yet others that markets do not enter into contradiction with morality.

that bureaucratic corrections for market failures will accomplish the desired objectives."[35]

Realism dictates that public policies work best when designed for imperfect agents. This insight harkens back to James Madison's *The Federalist* no. 51:

> If men were angels, no government would be necessary. If angels were to govern men, neither external nor internal controls on government would be necessary. In framing a government which is to be administered by men over men, the great difficulty lies in this: you must first enable the government to control the governed; and in the next place oblige it to control itself. A dependence on the people is, no doubt, the primary control on the government; but experience has taught mankind the necessity of auxiliary precautions.[36]

Buchanan and Brennan are partial to David Hume's rendering of the same idea: "In constraining any system of government and fixing the several checks and controls of the constitution, *every man ought to be supposed a knave* and to have no other end, in all his actions, than private interest."[37] Thus, constitutional limits would restrain both angels and knaves who reach positions of power, and neither would be able to intentionally or unwittingly harm the governed.

### 3.1.4 A Zero-Sum Game

When individuals elect to transfer a particular decision from the private to the collective sphere, they move away from a positive-sum game and enter into a zero-sum game. Economists generally agree that voluntary transactions in a free market generate win–win results, because people only agree to exchange goods and services when they value what they receive more than what they give up. In truly free markets, where individuals trade without coercion, wealth is created and multiple preferences are simultaneously satisfied.

Collective decisions aggregate preferences so that some parties are more satisfied with the end result than others. There is a measure of coercion

35 James M. Buchanan, "Public Choice: Politics without Romance," *Policy*, the quarterly review of The Centre for Independent Studies, Spring 2003, www.montana.edu/hfretwell/documents/332/buchananpublicchoice.pdf

36 James Madison, *The Federalist* no. 51, "The Structure of Government Must Furnish the Proper Checks and Balances between the Different Departments," www.constitution.org/fed/federa51.htm

37 David Hume, "Of the Independency of Parliament," in *Essays, Moral, Political and Literary*, vol. 1 (London: Oxford University Press, 1963). As cited by Buchanan and Brennan, *The Reason of Rules*.

involved in collective decision-making. Even if the use of a majority rule is established consensually, for example, the outcome of a majority decision caters to the preferences of those in the majority coalition and imposes costs on the minority. Often, goods and services are redistributed from one group to another. In fact, unlike the economic market, government is not known as a wealth creator, but as a wealth redistributor.

An electoral process is likewise a zero-sum game. The members of the elected party decide on behalf of even those who did not vote for them. In other words, in a zero-sum scenario, the gain by some people is at the cost of others. The only rule in collective decision-making that does not impose external costs on some of the members of the group is unanimity rule, because by definition people will not knowingly inflict costs on themselves. Under unanimity rule, each voter has veto power and can therefore avoid unpalatable results.[38]

Why do we elect to play the zero-sum game at all? Public choice answers that most individuals value the social order brought about by political rules and their enforcement. In addition, the game is reiterated time and time again, so that individuals foresee winning every so often. And, of course, one must bear in mind Winston Churchill's reminder, pronounced in a 1947 speech at the House of Commons, that "democracy is the worst form of government, except for all those other forms that have been tried from time to time." Other political systems would provide even less opportunities for citizen participation in the decision-making process, and potentially involve even greater external costs for the governed.

## 3.2 CAPTURING THE REGULATOR

The theories of interest groups or collective action, rent-seeking, and regulatory capture are complementary approaches to one question: How are special interests advanced in a political market? The three economists associated with this line of research are George Stigler, Gordon Tullock, and Mancur Olson. Stigler is representative of the University of Chicago school public choice, while Tullock and Olson are usually considered part of the Virginia school of public choice. Olson published *The Logic of Collective Action* in 1965 and Tullock managed to publish "The welfare costs of tariffs, monopolies and theft" two years later, in 1967. Tullock had been working on the topic for years,

[38] James M. Buchanan and Gordon Tullock, "The Rule of Unanimity," in *The Calculus of Consent* (Ann Arbor: University of Michigan, 1965), p. 67, http://files.libertyfund.org/files/1063/Buchanan_0102-03_EBk_v6.0.pdf

and several leading journals, including the *American Economic Review*, rejected his paper before *The Western Economic Journal* finally accepted it.[39] The article by Stigler, "The theory of economic regulation," appeared in *The Bell Journal of Economics and Management Science* in 1971.

### 3.2.1 Industry and Regulators

George Stigler challenged the notion that regulators protect consumers from industrialists. Regulation, as Stigler understands it, involves the use of coercive political power to control, manage, or direct a particular activity, sometimes through legislation. The industry[40] and the regulators obscure their vested interests by publicly announcing that such policies protect the general interest or the consumer, but in reality they are "designed and operated primarily for the benefit" of the industry.[41] For example, regulations requiring washing machines to conserve energy elevate the cost of a washer, and only those manufacturers with the capacity to produce environmentally friendly products can sell their machines. Established producers protect themselves from potential competitors and obtain a higher profit margin. Another example would be the cumbersome procedures to obtain permits to install electricity power lines: Companies that can survive the expensive and time-consuming process corner the market.[42] "George Stigler changed the way economists analyze government regulation," writes fellow Chicagoan Sam Peltzman.[43]

The Stigler insight was foreshadowed in two seminal books: *The Calculus of Consent*, published by Gordon Tullock and James M. Buchanan in 1962,[44]

[39] Gordon L. Brady, "Rent Seeking: Valuing Tullock's Rejects," *Institute of Economic Affairs*, December 2002.

[40] Industry is understood as a company or group of companies that produce goods and services, as, for instance, the auto industry or the petroleum industry.

[41] George J. Stigler, "The Theory of Economic Regulation," *The Bell Journal of Economics and Management Science*, vol. 2, no. 1, pp. 3–21.

[42] William J. Novak, "A Revisionist History of Regulatory Capture," originally a chapter prepared for the Tobin Project, www.tobinproject.org/sites/tobinproject.org/files/assets/Novak%20Revisionist%20History%20of%20Regulatory%20Capture%20(1.13).pdf. See also Barry Posner, "Rent Seeking and Regulatory Capture," Penn State College of Earth and Mineral Science, The Pennsylvania State University, 2015, www.e-education.psu.edu/ebf200/node/160. The washing machine example is explained in Susan Dudley's video on regulatory capture, www.youtube.com/watch?v=U6CmyKt-65s.

[43] Sam Peltzman, "How George Stigler Changed the Analysis of Regulation," *Chicago Booth Review*, October 1, 1993, http://review.chicagobooth.edu/finance/archive/how-george-stigler-changed-analysis-regulation.

[44] James M. Buchanan and Gordon Tullock, *The Calculus of Consent: Logical Foundation of Constitutional Democracy* (Ann Arbor: University of Michigan Press, 1962).

and *The Logic of Collective Action*, by Mancur Olson.[45] Both of these sources point out that interest groups can effectively lobby politicians to obtain special interest legislation, depending on their relative access to power.[46] Industries, as Stigler described them, fit into the more general classification of the interest group. In fact, even a government bureau can capture the regulator.[47]

### 3.2.2 Industry Is One Type of Interest Group

Olson, Buchanan, and Tullock flesh out the concept of industry. It is not a monolithic black box.[48] The ones making rational choices are the individuals who populate the company. Common interest unites members of a group, but members are far from identical. Each member will have a unique preference that is not necessarily satisfied by the actual outcomes achieved, and his or her motivation to further the group goal will vary.

The size and cohesiveness of the group are also important. Politicians respond to large, well-organized groups that promise a great number of disciplined votes. Depending on what they have to offer, smaller groups can also advance their interests. In other words, political actors exchange scarce goods and services, and compete for potential favors with other pressure groups. Smaller groups can better control for free-riding behaviors that hamper the effectiveness of the collective.

Applying this perspective to the political intrigue leading up to Jesus's trial and crucifixion, we can see various interest groups played a part. Jesus was

45 Mancur Olson, Jr., *The Logic of Collective Action: Public Goods and the Theory of Groups* (Cambridge, MA: Harvard University Press, 1965).

46 Christopher Carrigan and Cary Coglianese, "Capturing Regulatory Reality: Stigler's The Theory of Economic Regulation," *Penn Law: Legal Scholarship Repository*, July 4, 2016, http://scholarship.law.upenn.edu/cgi/viewcontent.cgi?article=2651&context=faculty_scholarship

47 Many economists associated with the Chicago and Virginia Schools of Economics, and with public choice itself, tend to favor free markets. Their findings on regulation, therefore, could be construed as satisfying a predisposition. Yet Stigler's paper sets out to test the widely held view that regulation protects the consumer and hurts the regulated. His optimism regarding competitive political systems suggests he does not believe all industries capture all regulators. Just as Kenneth Arrow was personally disappointed to find that social welfare functions are impossible to calculate, it is probably the case that many public choice scholars were less critical of government interventions in markets *before* they researched the causes and effects of regulation. For example, James Buchanan intended to specialize on public finance until he gained awareness of how political decisions are actually made.

48 Ronald Coase once wrote that neoclassical economists tend to view the firm as a "black box," but he preferred to view it as a system of relationships. The same applies for industry in this example. R. H. Coase, "The Nature of the Firm," first published in 1937. www3.nccu.edu.tw/~jsfeng/CPEC11.pdf

seen as posing a threat to the political status quo and the balance of power. Various groups competed for distinct rulings. They exchanged political goods, mainly to keep the peace through convenient alliances, and purported to act in the interest of the populace.

The political factions include the Roman authorities, on the one hand, and the various Jewish groups or sects, including the Sadducees, Pharisees, Essenes, and Zealots, each of which varied in size and relative influence, as seen in Table 3.1. Discussion among these groups concerned religious topics, such as resurrection, and also political affairs. At the time, no separation was made regarding politics and religion.[49]

Caiaphas, a Sadducee and the chief priest and leader of the Sanhedrin from 18 AD to 36 AD,[50] maneuvered the discussion within that body, which operated as a legislative or supreme court and was composed of sixty-nine general members, a vice chief justice, and the high priest. According to the Bible, members were not unanimously in favor of accusing Jesus of the civil crime of sedition.[51] Some, like Nicodemus and Joseph of Arimathea, were secret disciples of Jesus.[52]

Jesus was neither political nor revolutionary, yet he criticized Sadducees and Pharisees alike. The Pharisees threated to excommunicate those who followed Jesus. He gained in popularity; many of the masses followed him. After he raised Lazarus from the dead, a remarkable miracle by any standard, many "believed in him." "So the chief priests and the Pharisees convened the Sanhedrin and said, 'What are we going to do? This man is performing many signs. If we leave him alone, all will believe in him, and the Romans will come and take away both our land and our nation'," writes John the Evangelist (John 11:47–48).

The Sanhedrin obtained a death penalty from the regulator, Pontius Pilate. They exerted pressure on Pilate by accusing the Messiah of sedition. Crucifixion was a frequently applied Roman punishment to subdue

[49] Felix Just, SJ, "Jewish Groups at the Time of Jesus," http://catholic-resources.org/Bible/Jewish_Groups.htm

[50] "Joseph Caiaphas," *New Advent Catholic Encyclopedia*, www.newadvent.org/cathen/03143b.htm

[51] Morris Gieselman, "Pharisees, Sadducees and the Sanhedrin," *Learning to Follow*, May 4, 2008, https://morrisgieselman.wordpress.com/2008/05/04/pharisees-sadducees-and-the-sanhedrin/

[52] *Catholic Catechism*, "The Profession of Faith," points 595–596, www.vatican.va/archive/ccc_css/archive/catechism/p122a4p2.htm

TABLE 3.1 *Major Jewish interest groups in the New Testament*

| Group | Main interest | General views | Characteristics and prominent members |
|---|---|---|---|
| Samaritans | Gained relatively more favor with Roman authorities than other Jewish groups | After a political division split Solomon's kingdom in two, other Jewish groups rejected the Samaritans. Samaritans considered the Pentateuch as inspired scripture and they offered sacrifices on Mount Gerizim. | Herod ruled from Samaria and his wife was Samarian.<br>The descendants of Joseph tribes accepted migrants into their community. |
| Zealots | Nationalists who opposed Roman rule | Zealots favored violent revolt against Roman occupants, rejected Roman taxation and believed theocracy should be law of land. | Judah was a leader, Simon, Barabbas and the two robbers crucified with Jesus were Zealots. |
| Publicans | Social-vocational sect | Others saw them as traitors because they made money by collecting taxes for the foreign occupants. | Men who served the Roman government as farmers or in public works, tax collectors. Matthew was a publican. |
| Scribes | Social-vocational sect | Scribes were mostly Pharisees, but some were Sadducees. | Provided reading and writing services, legal advice. |
| Levites | Social-vocational sect | Levites opposed Jesus Christ and sought to arrest and kill him. | Caiaphas and Annas were Levites. Many high and chief priests were from the tribe of Levi; Levites who were not engaged in priestly activities assisted in the operation of the Temple. Moses, Aaron, Ezekiel, and others were also Levites. |

(*continued*)

TABLE 3.1 (*continued*)

| Group | Main interest | General views | Characteristics and prominent members |
|---|---|---|---|
| Sadducees | Political interest group and religious sect with political influence, until after the Temple was destroyed in 70 AD | Sadducees defended the status quo and older doctrines because they wanted to maintain their privileged position. They refused to accept anything not written in the Torah, doubted the existence of spirit, and denied the possibility of physical resurrection. They oversaw formal national and international affairs of the state. They opposed the Pharisees. | Wealthy aristocrats and priests descendants from the lineage of Zadok, a high priest. Unpopular among commoners. |
| Pharisees | Largest religious sect and political interest group | Pharisees believed in the resurrection of the dead, that man has free agency and bears responsibility for his actions; they studied the Torah and oral law. They adapted and created laws to new situations, but sometimes did not live coherently. | Caiaphas, Nicodemus, and Paul the Apostle were Pharisees. (Religion and law are not separated in early Jewish communities.) |
| Qumran Community/ Essenes | Religious community of brothers | Essenes were more radical than Sadducees and Pharisees. As the Sadducees, they claimed to be high priests. They felt holy and pure, like the Pharisees. They rejected the resurrection of the | |

| Group | Main interest | General views | Characteristics and prominent members |
|---|---|---|---|
| | | body but believed in the immortality of the soul. They practiced their faith in the wild, not the temple. | |
| Nazarenes or early Christians | Religious group | Christian Jews who refused to give up their way of life. Mosaic law did not bind gentiles. Later absorbed into the Christian or Jewish groups. | First followers of Jesus Christ. |
| Herodians | Political supporters of the family of Herod Antipas | They conspired with the Pharisees to kill Jesus. | This was probably a small group. |

Sources: Victor L. Ludlow, Major Jewish Groups in the New Testament, The Church of Jesus Christ of Latter Day Saints, January 1975, www.lds.org/ensign/1975/01/major-jewish-groups-in-the-new-testament?lang=eng. See also "The New Testament Jewish Sects: Pharisees, Sadducees, Essenes, Zealots," www.bible.ca/d-jewish-sects-pharisees-sadducees-essenes-zealots.htm. Here they explain that sects were not extremists or isolated, as modern religious sects tend to be, but sometimes worked with one another and were an integral part of social life; Felix Just, SJ, PhD, "Jewish Groups at the Time of Jesus," http://catholic-resources.org/Bible/Jewish_Groups.htm. According to "Priests and Levites," Biblical Training, www.biblicaltraining.org/library/priests-and-levites, there is discussion as to the claim that the tribe of the descendants of Levi was charged with priestly duties. Non-Levites also performed priestly duties.

rebellions.[53] Ironically, the insurgent Barabbas was also accused of sedition.[54] Caiaphas mobilized the masses, which clamored outside of the palace of the prefect. This was at once a tangible sign of potential revolt, and apparent evidence of "majority" support for the crucifixion verdict. By pardoning Barabbas and crucifying Jesus, Pilate pleased a crowd and could construe a "general interest" justification for his actions. This conveniently obscured the fact that the high priests were protecting their privileged positions.

[53] Gunnar Samuelson, "Crucifixion in Antiquity," Laup and Gobel in Nehren, Germany, 2011, http://khazarzar.skeptik.net/books/crux002.pdf. For a more popular account, see also "How the Romans Used Crucifixion – Including Jesus' – As a Political Weapon," *Newsweek Special Edition*, April 4, 2015, www.newsweek.com/how-romans-used-crucifixion-including-jesus-political-weapon-318934

[54] "So the chief priests and the Pharisees convened the Sanhedrin and said, 'What are we going to do? This man is performing many signs. If we leave him alone, all will believe in him, and the Romans will come and take away both our land and our nation',"

### 3.2.3 Rent-Seeking

The rent-seeking theory developed by the Virginia school of public choice enriches the Chicago approach to regulation and Olson's interest group theory. Gordon Tullock defines rent-seeking behavior as "the use of resources for the purpose of obtaining rents for people where the rents themselves come from some activity that has some negative social value."[55] A few years after Tullock published his frequently cited paper,[56] Anne Krueger came up with the catchy phrase "rent seeking" in her 1974 piece, "The political economy of the rent seeking society."[57] Thus, Tullock and Krueger are widely recognized as the pioneers in the study of rent-seeking behavior. Rent-seeking includes legal activities such as lobbying, some forms of advertising, and illegal activities, such as corruption.

Economist Steven Horwitz writes that a better name for this phenomenon would be privilege-seeking: "The privilege is like another input that generates a return above opportunity cost. You might spend $100,000 lobbying to get a monopoly that generates $1,000,000 in profits. The extra profits are due to the government-granted privilege. The privilege generates a rent, or a return above cost."[58]

Looking at the New Testament, public choice would see the Sadducees and Pharisees as rent-seekers insofar as they invested time and resources into building a case against Jesus. They watched him closely and listened to his teachings in order to trap him into doing or saying something unlawful.[59] They asked him to perform miracles and accused him of breaking the Sabbath. Caiaphas's prolonged mandate was most likely proof that he cultivated the Roman occupants' sympathy, a standing that would help Caiaphas obtain a death sentence once the case was presented to Roman rulers.

Another example of rent-seeking can be found in Ezekiel. Recognized as a prophet by the Jewish, Christian, and Muslim traditions, Ezekiel predicted the fall of Jerusalem. He was sent into exile to Babylon eleven years before King

55 Gordon Tullock, Gordon Brady, and Arthur Seldon, *Government Failure* (Washington, DC: Cato Institute, 2002), p. 43.

56 Gordon Tullock, "The Welfare Costs of Tariffs, Monopolies, and Theft," *Western Economic Journal*, vol. 5, no. 3 (June 1967), p. 224.

57 Anne O. Krueger, "The Political Economy of the Rent Seeking Society," *The American Economic Review*, vol. 64, no. 3 (June 1974), pp. 291–303.

58 Steven Horwitz, "The Calling: Why Rent Seeking?," *The Future of Freedom Foundation Articles*, January 3, 2013, www.fff.org/explore-freedom/article/the-calling-why-rent-seeking/

59 Robert Bird, *Jesus, the Carpenter of Nazareth* (London: Kegan Paul, Trench, Trubner and Co. Ltd., 1890), www.google.com/search?tbm=bks&hl=en&q=pharisees+and+sadducees+spy+on+Jesus

Nebuchadnezzar II cracked the walls of the holy city, burned the Temple and took hold of the city in 586 BC, as described graphically in 2 Kings 25.[60] A large army encircled the city and limited food supplies for two years before its conquest. This was Nebuchadnezzar's response to the betrayal of King Zedekiah of Judah. Despite being installed as Judah's ruler by the Babylonian emperor himself, in 597 BC, Zedekiah switched sides and allied with Egypt's King Hophra because he wanted to stop paying tribute to Babylon. His actions mirrored those of his predecessor and nephew, Jeconiah or Jehoaichin, whose brief reign of little more than three months was also cut short by Nebuchadnezzar.[61]

Notwithstanding the role played by Babylonian outsiders in Jerusalem's fall, Ezekiel blames the city's inhabitants for the collapse: It was they who turned their back on God and sinned. The prophet mentions extortions, bribes, robbery, and other illegal acts:

- "In you are people who accept bribes to shed blood; you take interest and make a profit from the poor. You extort unjust gain from your neighbors" (Ezekiel 22:12).[62]
- "There is a conspiracy of her princes within her like a roaring lion tearing its prey; they devour people, take treasures and precious things and make many widows within her" (Ezekiel 22:25).
- "Her officials within her are like wolves tearing their prey; they shed blood and kill people to make unjust gain" (Ezekiel 22:27).

From Ezekiel we learn that the ruling class of Jerusalem awarded rents to some privileged inhabitants, and in so doing they inflicted harm on others, such as the poor. These were rents that the beneficiaries would not be able to attain if they did not have access to arbitrary political power. Ezekiel calls them "unjust gains." The mention of bribes reveals that the beneficiaries of the rent transfers first invested scarce resources (time and money) to persuade the rulers to extend them artificial favors. Thus, they incurred in the immeasurable but evident opportunity costs of diverting scarce resources away from more productive economic uses. The image painted by Ezekiel is graphic: The ruling class is depicted as a predatory wolf that blatantly abuses power, whereas the commoners are quite literally preyed upon and devoured.

60 See, for instance, Bible Gateway's citation of the Holman Christian Bible, www.biblegateway.com/passage/?search=2+Kings+25&version=HCSB

61 Shimon Bakon, "Zedekiah: Last King of Judah," *Jewish Bible Quarterly*, vol. 36, no. 2 (2008), pp. 93–99, http://jbq.jewishbible.org/assets/Uploads/362/362_zedekiah.pdf

62 *Bible Gateway*, New International Version (NIV) of the Bible, www.biblegateway.com/passage/?search=Ezekiel+22:12

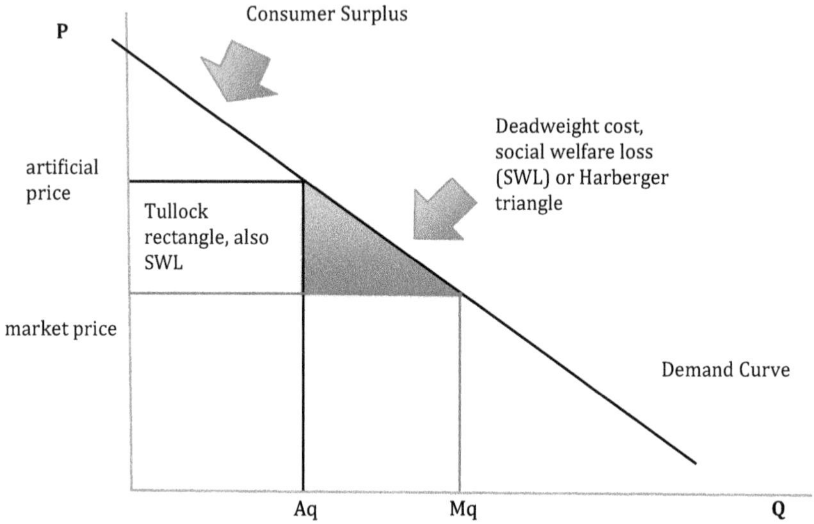


GRAPH 3.1 Tullock's rectangle

Tullock puts it succinctly: "The problem is, of course, that [a] small group may push for things where the benefit to them is smaller, indeed in many cases immensely smaller, than the injury inflicted on other people. Unfortunately, these rent seekers may get their way."[63] Tullock's principal insight is this: The social welfare costs associated with rent-seeking behaviors are not negligible, because lobbyists are willing to invest up to the total amount of the benefits transferred to them from the consumer surplus. This amount is added to the social welfare loss from a shrunken market, as seen on Graph 3.1.

Ezekiel is not the only prophet in the Bible who condemns the misuse of power by the regents and those who influence them, for personal enrichment or advancement. The repetition of the biblical admonitions is important, because it accentuates a conduct that is widespread. For example, prophet Isaiah (Isaiah 1:23) observes: "Your princes are rebels, accomplices of brigands. All of them greedy for presents and eager for bribes, they show no justice to the orphan, and the widow's cause never reaches them."[64] The Bible anticipates how self-interested human beings react to power in a zero-sum game setting.

[63] Gordon Tullock, "The Costs of Rent Seeking: A Metaphysical Problem," *Public Choice*, vol. 57, no. 1 (April 1988), p. 18.

[64] *Catholic Online Bible*, www.catholic.org/bible/book.php?id=29. A brigand is a member of a gang.

In turn, the prophet and judge Samuel has a revealing conversation with God regarding kings (1 Samuel 8:11–22). The people of Israel are clamoring for a king, but they don't know what they are asking for, God predicts. A king, any king, will force the people to serve him, and take away their property, their crops, their vintage, and also take them and their offspring as slaves. He will redistribute the confiscated goods "to his officials and attendants." One day will come when "you will cry out for relief from the king you have chosen, but the Lord will not answer you in that day."[65] Clearly, the king described here is an unrestricted despot who can dispose of the material goods and the people in his realm.[66] To him, the governed and their territories are personal property. Samuel goes on to describe how the people insist on having a king, because they want to be like "other nations," each with their respective ruler, "with a king to lead us and fight our battles."[67] One envisions a very reluctant God instructing Samuel to satisfy their headstrong plea.

A rent-seeking king or governmental authority is *extracting* rent. The industry or interest group does not always make the first move. Governments can and do effectively threaten citizens into paying bribes and making campaign donations. As God warns Samuel, the mere act of propping up political authorities creates incentives for rent extraction. Daron Acemoglu and James Robinson suggest that some states are shaped by extractive economic and political institutions to such a degree that the entire society becomes accustomed to appropriating wealth created by others and tolerant of predation and rent-seeking.[68]

In addition to interest group rent-seeking and government rent extraction, Tullock sees two other behaviors associated with this practice. Once an industry or group trumps the competition and is granted a privilege, it cannot rest on its laurels. It must *protect* its artificial rent, repeatedly investing scarce resources to prop up the barriers that award it monopoly power. The dynamic also sucks into the vortex more reluctant players, namely, those who are adversely affected by the advantages awarded to others. These actors must enter the political market to *defend* themselves against rent-seekers and offset

65 Ibid., www.biblegateway.com/passage/?search=1+Samuel+8

66 The right to own property is recognized by King Ahab (1 Kings 21:6–17), who through his wife's trickery ends up murdering Naboth, the rightful owner of a vineyard, in order to take possession of the land. Ahab's wife, Jezebel, mocks him for hesitating to use his political and military power to take what he wants.

67 *Catholic Online Bible*, www.catholic.org/bible/book.php?id=9&bible_chapter=8

68 Daron Acemoglu and James Robinson, *Why Nations Fail* (New York: Crown Business, 2012). See also the website: http://whynationsfail.com

the costs imposed on them. Like the rent-seekers, protectors, and extractors, they also divert scarce resources from the economic market.[69]

### 3.2.4 Do Christians Rent-Seek?

Appropriating other people's assets using government intervention and the threat of coercion is contrary to Christian teachings. Such actions are akin to theft or plunder and are thus forbidden by the eighth commandment. A severe Frederic Bastiat observed that once plunder is socially tolerated, men would "create for themselves a legal system that authorizes it and a moral code that glorifies it."[70] Making it legal does not make it right, even when appealing arguments apparently justify these activities. This problem was condemned as far back as 1563 in the Heidelberg Catechism: "God views as theft all wicked tricks and devices, whereby we seek to draw to ourselves our neighbor's goods, whether by force or with show of right."[71]

However, Christians participating in the political market may, conceivably, remain ignorant of the long-run costs their actions impose on others, and even on themselves. For instance, members of a symphony orchestra may lobby authorities for subsidies to sustain their musical ensemble, persuaded that the arts create positive externalities and that they serve the common good. Many Christians favor welfare programs that ostensibly help the indigent but that may in practice profit the opportunists.[72]

It is important to note that some economists, particularly George Stigler and Gary Becker, as well as some political scientists like Robert Dahl, minimize the costs of lobbying, rent-seeking, and special interest legislation. As long as political markets remain open for competing groups desiring a special interest advantage, this competition generates potentially the most efficient outcome. In Dahl's words, "societies are collections of competing, organized factions, each headed by an elite. These plural elites interact, compete, strike bargains

[69] Gordon Tullock, *The Society* (United States: Liberty Fund, 2005).

[70] Frederic Bastiat, *Economic Sophisms*, first published in 1845, USA: Liberty Fund, Library of Economics and Liberty, www.econlib.org/library/Bastiat/basSoph.html

[71] Cited in Dale Arand Moral, "Why Christians Care about Economics, Five Reasons," *Desiring God*, May 17, 2016, www.desiringgod.org/articles/why-christians-care-about-economics. The Christian Reformed Church Heidelberg Catechism can be found in www.reformed.org/documents/index.html?mainframe=http://www.reformed.org/documents/heidelberg.html

[72] An interest article is Aage B. Sørensen, "On Kings, Pietism and Rent-Seeking in Scandinavian Welfare States," *Acta Sociologica*, vol. 41, no. 4 (1998). The author says absolutist monarchs started the welfare programs to procure obedience from their subjects, but that the programs were perverted when generosity and obedience were supplanted by opportunistic rent-seeking.

and manage conflict within their own units."[73] According to this view, it is in the general interest that the most persistent or convincing pressure groups gain entitlements. Or, if the selection process fails to produce optimal outcomes, the transfers will somehow even themselves out in such a way that the whole is not worse off. These authors disagree with Tullock's affirmation that the pursuit of special interest benefits in a zero-sum political arena inevitably comports significant costs for society.

Some Christians who believe their actions are not in violation of their moral code do in fact seek rents. Although facts differ from country to country, many churches have obtained tax exemptions and other preferential treatments from their respective governments. Two justifications for this historical practice are that churches provide social services, as do nongovernmental organizations, and that their tax-exempt status avoids state meddling in religious affairs.[74]

Yet other churches have benefitted from a tax levied on parishioners. The Protestant and Catholic Churches of Germany are "closely involved in politics," explains David Conradt,[75] and depend on their local governments. Historically speaking, the local "princes granted a variety of special privileges to the churches (tax-free land, bishops' residences, salaries), many of which are still in effect." Conradt opines that the contemporary "church tax" is the most important privilege, as churches benefit directly from the 8–9 percent income tax[76] levied on workers who have not "contracted out" of their church affiliations. The Evangelical Church in Germany estimates that half of its total income comes from the church tax, again accentuating a financial dependency on government.[77]

In 1989, coauthors Ekelund, Hébert, and Tollison published a paper titled "An economic model of the Medieval Church: Usury as a form of rent

[73] Robert Dahl, *Pluralist Democracy in the United States: Conflict and Consent* (Chicago: Rand McNally, 1967), p. 24.

[74] See, for instance, "Should Churches Remain Tax Exempt? Background of the Issue," ProCon.org, https://churchesandtaxes.procon.org/view.resource.php?resourceID=006554; Pew Forum on Religion & Public Life, "Politics and the Pulpit 2008," pewforum.org, 2008, and "Why Are Churches and Religious Organizations Tax Exempt?," *Focus on the Family*, www.focusonthefamily.com/socialissues/religious-freedom/religious-freedom-after-the-obergefell-decision/why-are-churches-and-religious-organizations-tax-exempt

[75] David P. Conradt, *The German Polity* (USA: Rowman & Littlefield, 2013), p. 57, https://books.google.com.gt/books?id=HWE_DgAAQBAJ&dq=German+churches+dependent+on+tax+transfers

[76] Data obtained from http://blog.mygermanexpert.com/2013/06/10-Facts-about-German-Church-Tax.html

[77] "Church Taxes in Germany Generate Considerable Income and Mainline Decline," *Religion Watch*, Baylor Institute for Studies in Religion, vol. 31, no. 6, www.religionwatch.com/church-taxes-in-germany-generate-considerable-income-and-mainline-decline/

seeking."[78] They attempt to explain the economic behavior of the church through the framework of rent-seeking theory. The authors conclude that the medieval church was organized as a monopoly that faced incentives to rent-seek, and that religious authorities found it difficult to restrain those who wanted to take advantage of these incentives. "[T]he medieval doctrine of usury can be understood in terms of interest-group theory of government," they add. Whether their paper accurately portrays historical events or not, its mere existence suggests that religious institutions can be seen as interest groups in political markets, and that they can fall into rent-seeking behaviors.

Given that appropriating goods and services through force is mostly a sinful conduct, and that governments and legislation are the vehicles through which legalized transfers occur, have religious leaders advocated for controls to curtail these types of operations? Or have religious authors seemed more inclined to conceive politics romantically?

## 3.3 RELIGION AND DEMOCRACY

In the Old Testament passage cited earlier, God forewarns Samuel that rulers tend to extract rents and distribute favors to the interest groups of their liking. That is a realistic, not a romantic observation.

The passage also implies that government can be something that we give ourselves: the people beg God for a king.[79] At the same time, Christians have viewed government as an institution mandated and desired by God. For example, the *Catechism of the Catholic Church* states: "[E]very human community needs an authority to govern it." Human nature is seen as necessitating a state that brings unity and works for the common good. In Paul's letter to the Romans (13:1–2) we read: "Let every person be subject to the governing authorities. For there is no authority except from God, and those that exist have been instituted by God."[80] Thus, a benign disposition toward government stems from the conclusion that political authority is consonant with human nature and God's will.[81]

78 Robert B. Ekelund, Jr., Robert F. Hébert, and Robert D. Tollison, "An Economic Model of the Medieval Church. Usury as a Form of Rent Seeking," *Journal of Law, Economics and Organization*, vol. 5, no. 2 (Autumn 1989).

79 James M. Buchanan describes himself as a contractualist and a constructivist, meaning that he believes member of societies enter into figurative social contracts in order to arrange peaceful coexistence.

80 *Catechism of the Catholic Church*, nos. 1897–1899, www.vatican.va/archive/ccc_css/archive/catechism/p3s1c2a2.htm

81 According to the Late Scholastic scholar Francisco Suárez, "without political authority that which is in fact natural and indispensable, society, cannot be." See J. A. Fernández-

Acton believes that from Antiquity came the centuries-old belief that "in religion, morality, and politics there was only one legislator and one authority";[82] religion and state were melded together. This notion dominated until the ecclesiastical hierarchy and the feudal lords clashed over who could name prelates, and after a prolonged struggle over jurisdictions, the Church ceased to "buttress the thrones of the king whom it anointed," and the notion of civil liberty was born.[83] Regardless of the gradual separation of church and state authorities, there remains in Christianity a sense that all earthly political power *ought* to be accountable to God and enhance the community's well-being.

The government historically imagined by Catholicism was not a constitutional, liberal democracy, but rather the monarchical and authoritarian systems that dominated political landscapes until the turn of the nineteenth century. It wasn't until 1888, when Pope Leo XIII published the encyclical *Libertas* that we find a somewhat favorable reference to democracy. It is admissible to hold forth a form of government "moderated" by a democratic "element," as long as such methods do not contradict Catholic doctrine as to the origin of political power.[84] With time, social doctrine came to see participatory democracy in a more favorable light.[85] "Praise is due to those national procedures which allow the largest possible number of citizens to participate in public affairs with genuine freedom," states the pastoral constitution *Gaudium et Spes* (1965).[86]

Protestants may have embraced democracy more readily. In 1912, an American novelist named Winston Churchill[87] published an article titled

Santamaría, *Natural Law, Constitutionalism, Reason of State and Law* (New York: Peter Lang), 2005, https://books.google.com.gt/books/about/Natural_Law_Constitutionalism_Reason_of.html?id=Ennzm3L5dvcC&redir_esc=y

82 John Emerich Edward Dalbert-Acton (Lord Acton), "The History of Liberty in Antiquity," speech delivered on February 1877, Online Library of Liberty (Indianapolis, IN: Liberty Fund), http://oll.libertyfund.org/titles/acton-the-history-of-freedom-and-other-essays

83 Lord Acton, "The History of Liberty in Christianity," speech delivered on February 1877, Online Library of Liberty (Indianapolis, IN: Liberty Fund), http://oll.libertyfund.org/titles/acton-the-history-of-freedom-and-other-essays. Acton believes both Church leaders and feudal monarchs wanted to dominate the other, but in the end were unsuccessful. Introducing a degree of civil liberty was a solution that was not intended by the two parties in conflict.

84 Leo XIII, Encyclical *Libertas Praestantissimum*, 1888, no. 32, http://w2.vatican.va/content/leo-xiii/es/encyclicals/documents/hf_l-xiii_enc_20061888_libertas.html

85 See no. 191 of the *Compendium of Social Doctrine of the Church*, www.vatican.va/roman_curia/pontifical_councils/justpeace/documents/rc_pc_justpeace_doc_20060526_compendio-dott-soc_en.html

86 Pope Paul VI, *Pastoral Constitution on the Church in the Modern World, Gaudium et Spes*, 1965, www.vatican.va/archive/hist_councils/ii_vatican_council/documents/vat-ii_const_19651207_gaudium-et-spes_en.html

87 Not the same person as Great Britain's Prime Minister.

"Modern Government and Christianity," in which he claims that, by challenging hierarchy, the Reformation brought forth various churches or communities that "have been called by some modern writers democracies." Christ's ideal government, he adds, "is the least possible government."[88] In 1919, the *Harvard Theological Review* published "Christianity and Democracy," an address delivered by Arthur Cushman McGiffert. World War I, wrote McGiffert, forced Christians to take sides between autocracy and democracy. He affirms that a Christian democracy is "the only state of society worthy to be called the Kingdom of God on earth."[89]

The presumption that democracy is a system of government that improves on other alternatives is relatively recent. The advantages usually attributed to democratic methods include: finite terms in office, peaceful transitions, accountability to electors, citizen participation in decision-making, and legitimacy. In Friedrich Hayek's opinion, democracy is a process of discussion or a method of settling differences of opinion.[90] Negative externalities are theoretically lower when voter preferences are factored into the decision-making process, assuming the tyranny of the majority is averted.

According to the Center for Systemic Peace (CSP) and its Polity Project IV,[91] the number of governments with democratic characteristics grew from ten, in 1899, to approximately sixty in 1998.[92] The Democracy Index, generated by The Economist Intelligence Unit, counts 116 of the 167 sovereign nations evaluated in 2015 as being democratic, albeit only 20 are considered "full" democracies.[93] The remainder exhibits certain obstacles or mix authoritarian practices with features of democracy.[94]

As noted, the political regime does not have to be democratic for regulatory capture or rent-seeking to occur. When ordinary people are barred from

88 Winston Churchill, "Modern Government and Christianity," *The Atlantic*, January 1912 issue, www.theatlantic.com/magazine/archive/1912/01/modern-government-and-christianity/376203/

89 Arthur Cushman McGiffert, "Christianity and Democracy," *The Harvard Theological Review*, vol. 12, no. 1 (January 1919), pp. 36–50.

90 Friedrich A. Hayek, *The Constitution of Liberty*, as quoted in CIPE Development Blog, "What Is Democracy? Words of Wisdom from F. A. Hayek," www.cipe.org/blog/2006/07/20/what-is-democracy-words-of-wisdom-from-fa-hayek/#.WdD2S-lSyFJ

91 See Polity IV Proyect: Political Regime Characteristics and Transitions (1800–2013), www.systemicpeace.org/polity/polity4.htm. The new site of this organization is www.systemicpeace.org.

92 This data was taken from a graph attributed to Polity IV but found in the website *History of Democracy*, www.wikiwand.com/en/History_of_democracy

93 The Economist's Intelligence Unit report is titled "Democracy Index 2015, Democracy in an Age of Anxiety," www.yabiladi.com/img/content/EIU-Democracy-Index-2015.pdf

94 For instance, Norway occupies the first place among full democracies, whereas Israel and Singapore are considered imperfect democracies.

political participation, they can still organize themselves into groups, exert influence on their ruler, and provoke rebellions and revolutions. Even Niccolò Machiavelli, who counseled autocrats, knew rulers must consider the effects of their policies.[95] Terrifying tyrants *are* susceptible of being petitioned, and they regularly dispense favors. Two biblical figures that lobbied on behalf of the Jews were Queen Esther, who persuaded King Xerxes to stop the killing of the Jews in his Persian kingdom, and Joseph, who rose from slave to vizier after interpreting Pharaoh's dreams.[96]

Both democracies and autocracies can be unstable. Olson raised the issue of regime stability when he distinguished between "roving" and "stationary bandits." Stationary dictators "monopolize and rationalize theft in the form of taxes," writes Olson, but they also benefit from achieving peace and productivity in their territories. Incentives change when the ruler remains unknown or his tenure is short-lived: Such rulers behave more like roving bandits, because they tend to be more extractive and less concerned with the common good. "In a world of roving banditry there is little or no incentive for anyone to produce or accumulate anything," writes Olson.[97]

## 3.4 CONSTITUTIONS, AND GOD AS CONSTITUTION

A solution to the misuse of power presented in public choice literature is the establishment of constitutional restraints and of an effective judicial organism in charge of enforcing constitutional order. Outcomes are more aligned with the overall welfare of the group when members bind themselves to rules that must be obeyed by those who govern and those who are governed, and that presumably outlast a politician's term in office. Constitutional rules are metaphorically agreed upon before the political game commences. They are norms by which to make more specific rules. For example, laws that guarantee the right to private property are considered meta-rules, whereas municipal fees levied on property owners would be "rules within the rules." Constitutions can be written or unwritten, and they contain both formal and informal social norms.

Introducing the proper incentives into a constitutional design can discourage special interest legislation and rent-seeking. Seeking and granting

95 Nicolò Machiavelli, *The Prince*, written in 1505 and published in 1515, www.constitution.org/mac/prince.pdf, translated by W. K. Marriott.

96 See in the Bible, the Book of Esther and Genesis 41:1–56.

97 Mancur Olson, "Dictatorship, Democracy and Development," *American Political Science Review*, vol. 87, no. 3 (September 1993), www.svt.ntnu.no/iss/Indra.de.Soysa/POL3503H05/olson.pdf

privileges can become unattractive endeavors if the costs of pursuing these actions are sufficiently high. Restrictions on campaign contributions, limits to lobbying activities, and anticorruption legislation are attempts to reduce the net welfare costs of special interest transfers.

The paradox lies in the fact that it is neither in the interest of the regulator nor the regulated to put a stop to politics as usual, even though, in the long run, efficiency is in everyone's best interest. Holding their own power in check is not often attractive to legislators; even judges, purportedly neutral and relatively immune to the allure of special interest, have difficulty checking rent-seeking behavior.

A few exceptional kings in ancient times accepted constitutional limits. For instance, King Solon, described as "the most profound political genius in Antiquity"[98] by Acton, reputedly set down a Constitution that he expected "Athenians could be induced to accept," and then left Athens for ten years. He made the governed promise they would obey his rules in his absence. By removing himself from the scene, he effectively understood that societies need time to adjust to a change in norms. We have no way of knowing whether he also anticipated that his subjects would be tempted to lobby, complain and cajole in order to force Solon into modifying the rules to suit their personal benefit.[99] The general, abstract and impartial nature of his constitution was thus guaranteed by his "roving."

Judaism and Christianity created limits that serve much the same role as constitutions. These monotheistic religions made faithful kings and princes subservient to God and his commandments. Through Moses, God entered into a covenant with the people of Israel. The Ten Commandments are a critical part of this pact: Moses and those who followed him out of Egypt and into the Promised Land agreed to live in accordance with these laws.[100] The New Covenant, sealed by Jesus Christ's birth, death, and resurrection, "amplified" the Old Covenant and brought us the promise of eternal life. "The Son is his Father's definitive Word; so there will be no further Revelation after him," states the *Catholic Church's Catechism*. He is, in a sense, a living and permanent covenant.[101] Again, the conviction that all human beings will be judged for their actions and omissions by a merciful but just God, increases the payoff of treating the governed with respect. In *The Limits of Liberty*,

98 Lord Acton, "History of Freedom in Antiquity."

99 "Solon of Athens," www.thelatinlibrary.com/historians/notes/solon.html

100 Paul Suckling, "Biblical Covenants," *Life, Hope and Truth*, https://lifehopeandtruth.com/bible/covenants/biblical-covenants/

101 *Catechism of the Catholic Church*, no. 73, www.vatican.va/archive/ccc_css/archive/catechism/p1s1c2a1.htm

James M. Buchanan recognizes that the Mosaic tablets, the Book of Mormon, "natural laws inherent in man himself" and the Enlightenment social contracts are all possible historical explanations for the origins of constraints on political power.[102]

John Neville Figgis affirms that, for Lord Acton, "constitutional government was the sole eternal truth in politics, the rare but the only guardian of freedom." Acton explained that the constitutional principle evolved from the ideas of thinkers like Aristotle, Gaius, St. Thomas Aquinas, and the Late Scholastics like Francisco Suarez and Luis de Molina. Constitutionalism also has a Christian precursor in the Council of Constance's (1414–1418) final decree, the *Sacrosancta*. It declares the rights of the people, and binds the pope to the Council's finding, much as a constitution would.[103]

Zimmerman agrees: "Christian jurisprudence has played an enormously important role in the origin and development of modern constitutionalism. The view adopted by the American Founders is that people cannot know the natural moral order and their inalienable rights from their own reasoning unaided by God's revelation."[104] Both the United States *Declaration of Independence* and the *Constitution* are in debt with Western thinkers who believed that "higher" precepts can order social life and social liberty. God is explicitly mentioned as the source of civil rights, therefore relying on supernatural and human limits to political power.[105] For instance, in his first inaugural address, Thomas Jefferson, a deist, suggests that an acknowledged and adored God (Providence), together with the common practice of virtues such as temperance and honesty, play a role in sustaining a "wise and frugal Government, which shall restrain men from injuring one another, shall leave them otherwise free to regulate their own pursuits of industry and improvement, *and shall not take from the mouth of labor the bread it has earned*."[106]

[102] James M. Buchanan, *The Limits of Liberty, Between Anarchy and the Leviathan* (Indianapolis, IN: Liberty Fund, 2000), p. 17.

[103] The council was convened to end the Western Schism provoked by the three coexisting popes, and ended in the election of Martin V. See also Ivan Strenski, *Why Politics Can't be Freed From Religion* (Malden, MA: Wiley-Blackwell, 2010), https://books.google.com.gt/books/about/Why_Politics_Can_t_Be_Freed_From_Religio.html?id=FjVoalzP7gMC&redir_esc=y

[104] Augusto Zimmermann, "God, Locke and Montesquieu: Some Thoughts Concerning the Religious Foundations of Modern Constitutionalism," *The Western Australian Jurist*, vol. 1, 2010, www.murdoch.edu.au/School-of-Law/_document/WA-jurist-documents/WAJ_Vol1_2010_Augusto_Zimmermann—God-Locke-and-Montesquieu.pdf

[105] *The Declaration of Independence* can be found here: www.ushistory.org/declaration/document/. *The United States Constitution* can be found here: www.archives.gov/founding-docs/constitution-transcript

[106] Thomas Jefferson, *First Inaugural Address*, March 4, 1801, The Avalon Project at Yale Law School, http://avalon.law.yale.edu/19th_century/jefinau1.asp

Taking the idea further, God-fearing people may favorably submit to reasonable constitutional boundaries, and they may consequently be less likely to seek special interest regulation and demand the expansion of discretionary political powers.

Constitutional documents seem to lose force as Christian values and principles are forgotten or dismissed by secular and modern politics. Another reason for their migration away from abstract principles is that, as Bruno Leoni points out, these codes have become "more a sort of diktat that the winning majorities in the legislative assemblies impose upon the minorities."[107] It is in this context that James Buchanan attempts to build a foundation for a constitution that does not "presume the equality in some original position" and that is not "handed down" or revealed by a superior power, but rather that "might emerge from the non-idealistic, self-interested behavior of men."[108] This foundation is a contract among individuals under unanimity rule, minimizing external costs.

## 3.5 CONCLUSION

In the mid-1970s, Buchanan worried that "democracy may become its own Leviathan unless constitutional limits are imposed and enforced."[109] An unbridled, privilege dispensing, and redistributive government apparatus will continue to grow and expand, unless a constitutional revolution takes place. A decade later, Buchanan and Brennan recommend that this revolution be triggered by a "*civic religion*" – no less – that "will concentrate our attention on the rules that constrain governments rather than on innovations that justify ever-expanding political intrusions into the lives of citizens."[110] For this core idea to take hold in academia, and later in political circles, realism must prevail: Policy prescriptions and ideal constitutional texts are not presented to omniscient and benevolent despots, or angels, but to fallible men and women. "Both markets and governments fail, and there is no such benevolent wisdom."[111]

Mancur Olson injects some optimism into the discussion when he observes that, in comparison to other forms of government, democracies "have the great advantage of preventing significant extraction of social surplus by their

[107] Bruno Leoni, *Freedom and the Law* (Los Angeles: Nash Publishings, 1961), https://mises.org/files/freedom-and-law4pdf/download?token=YeFaaARq

[108] Buchanan, *The Limits of Liberty*, p. 69.

[109] Ibid., p. 205.

[110] Buchanan and Brennan, *The Reason of Rules*, p. 166.

[111] Buchanan, *The Limits of Liberty*, p. 220.

leaders." Democracy rests on the notion of individual rights, which in turn establishes boundaries for political operators.[112]

Public choice analysis of rent-seeking and regulatory capture does not essentially clash with Christian social thought. Christians may concur with public choice scholars that it is worth our while to compare the potential outcomes of institutional arrangements, so that realistic observations can be made regarding the best possible ways to organize open political markets. They would also agree that, given the fallen nature of human beings, interest groups tend to seek privilege and capture regulators. Checks and balances, including constitutional rules, are called for. Christian might add, hopefully, that the more pious the members of the polis are, the more likely we are to achieve a cooperative environment. In sum, even self-interested actors may choose morally upright – and socially beneficial – options in the political and economic arena, if they are God-fearing individuals.

[112] Olson, "Dictatorship, Democracy and Development."

# 4

# Christianity and Antitrust

## *A Nexus*

KENNETH G. ELZINGA AND DANIEL A. CRANE

### 4.1 INTRODUCTION

Ask anyone in the antitrust community the question, "Is there an intersection between contemporary antitrust enforcement and legal training?" and the answer would be, "Yes." Ask any of the same people, "Is there a connection between contemporary antitrust enforcement and the discipline of economics?" and the answer still would be, "Yes." But to the question, "Is there a relationship between Christianity and contemporary antitrust enforcement?" the response is likely an "I don't think so," or, just as likely, a blank stare.

The purpose of this chapter is to consider whether the Christian faith has a nexus with the institution of antitrust. It turns out it *doesn't* – and it *does*. For example, Christianity cannot explain why the Herfindahl–Hirschman Index is superior to the four-firm concentration ratio as a measure of industry concentration. Economics can. On the other hand, economics cannot explain why the per se rule against price-fixing is morally appropriate.[1] The Bible can.

In this chapter, we develop a triad of noteworthy connections between the institution of antitrust and the Christian faith.[2] First, we explore the historical connection between the institution of antitrust and Christianity. Understanding this link between Christianity and antitrust involves an exercise

The authors thank John Bigelow, Sarah Estelle, P. J. Hill, John Lunn, Edd Noell, Daniel Sokol, and Andrew Yuengert for comments and Charles Smith for excellent research assistance.

[1] Economics, as a science, can explain only the *consequences* for consumers and producers of a market's cartelization.

[2] While 3 is a special integer in the Christian faith, we don't contend there is anything inspired by this number of connections. Three is the number of the Trinity, the three persons of the Christian godhead (Matthew 28:19; John 14:26). It also is the number of strands in a cord that the Bible contends is not easily broken or severed (Ecclesiastes 4:22). The Bible also records that Jesus' resurrection took place on the third day (Luke 9:22; Luke 24:5–6; Luke 24:7; Luke 24:46).

in intellectual history. Many notable Christian thinkers, from the Catholic Aquinas to the Reformers Luther and Calvin, weighed in on such topics as markets, economic competition, and monopoly. But one person's influence, which we characterize as Christian, played a uniquely formative role in the development of modern antitrust policy – Adam Smith's. If antitrust had an economist patron saint, it would be Adam Smith. Smith's advocacy of the free market's capabilities revealed the importance of maintaining competition in markets. Because economics has made such inroads into antitrust, any link between Adam Smith and the Christian faith reveals a connection between antitrust and Christianity.

Second, we explore a Christian perspective on some of the major themes in antitrust, such as the meaning of rationality and efficiency, the morality of competition, and the importance of innovation. For example, when antitrust models human beings as either buyers or sellers, they are assumed to be *rational*. In the world of antitrust, the economic agents on the demand side and the supply side of the marketplace compare the price of a good or service (e.g., the value of opportunities foregone) with the benefits (in terms of utility derived from consumption). The decision calculus for buying or selling is based on weighing the costs and benefits inherent in such a choice. Poets, Romantics, Impulse Buyers, Hoarders, Don't-Give-a-Tinker's-Damn Type People, and the Deranged are never actors on the antitrust stage. Only rational actors need apply. In this second portion of our chapter, we explore what it means for antitrust to be based on rationality and we contend that there is a relationship between the rationality of man and the rationality of God, as both man and God are understood and portrayed in Christian theology.

Similarly, we explore how the purported goal of antitrust to promote economic efficiency may, in terms of Christian theology, be connected to *good stewardship*. The Bible, including several teachings of Jesus, contains many references to the concept of stewardship. Men and women, the only ones in creation who bear God's image, are to be good stewards over God's creation. A steward doesn't manage his or her own assets but rather is entrusted with the property or finances of someone else. While an owner can use their resources any way they want, a steward knows the day will come when his or her employer asks to examine the books. The Christian Scriptures draw this same parallel: humans act as stewards over all "God's good earth" – with a day of reckoning to come. The Bible also teaches the importance of equity, for we learn in the Scriptures that the Lord will judge with equity.[3] So it is important

3 Psalm 75:2.

to understand the connection between the institution of antitrust, efficiency, and equity.

The morality of competition as opposed to cooperation is another important theme at the intersection of antitrust and Christianity. Is it ethical for Christian business people to outcompete their commercial rivals? Or does loving one's neighbor as oneself require cooperating rather than increasing one's market share at a rival's expense? Can economic competition be justified on the grounds that, like athletic competition, it brings out the best in everyone?

Another theme intersecting antitrust and Christian doctrine is the role of innovation. While faulty narratives often portray Christianity as antagonistic to innovation, both Christian theology and Church history have been supportive of innovation. From God's mandate to Adam to "be fruitful and multiply and fill the earth and subdue it" in Genesis 1:28 throughout the biblical narrative, Christian doctrine squares with innovative methodologies to improve life and well-being. History chronicles the connection between the spread of Christianity and innovation. The institution of antitrust promotes competitive processes that have often enabled and incentivized innovation. Thus, as antitrust "subdues the earth" through providing a competitive framework with incentives to innovate, it is linked to Christianity's promotion of innovation.

In the third section of this chapter, drawing on the historical precedents and our analysis of antitrust's major themes, we examine a few legal domains of antitrust law. Our focus is on price-fixing. If antitrust were a meal, price-fixing would be the main course, and all the other business practices influenced by antitrust would be the soup, salad, or dessert courses. Every antitrust compliance program starts with warnings about price-fixing. Every antitrust practitioner knows that antitrust takes a dim view of price-fixing. We explore why the Christian faith underscores that view. We also offer some observations on mergers and monopolization.

## 4.2 A BRIEF INTELLECTUAL HISTORY OF CHRISTIANITY AND ECONOMIC COMPETITION

### 4.2.1 Medieval and Reformation Thought on Usury and Monopoly

Although it is customary to think of antitrust law as an artifact of American reaction to late nineteenth-century industrialization, there is a long tradition of intellectual thought and legal regard to the question of monopoly and competition. Influential church leaders have addressed such questions, directly or indirectly, for centuries.

Competition policy has roots in early Christianity, with edicts by Christian emperors prohibiting such market abuses as monopolies and cartels.[4] But it was not until the Middle Ages that Christian scholars began to work out general legal, ethical, and economic theories of economic competition. The medieval scholastics conceptualized such questions under the heading of "usury" and "just price theory."[5] Thomas Aquinas asserted that anyone pursuing an excessive profit to the detriment of the public is a dishonest trader.[6] Under canon law, monopoly profits were considered ill-gotten gains subject to claims for restitution.[7] Monopoly pricing was considered a deviation from just pricing, a transgression against principles of brotherly love and charity, and injurious to the community. Many writers in the Scholastic tradition, including Nicole Oresme (c. 1320–1382), San Antonio, Archbishop of Florence (1389–1459), and San Bernardino of Siena (1380–1444), wrote strongly against monopolies, either private or state-granted, and price-fixing cartels.[8] Although allowing that goods generally did not have an objective value and that interplay between supply and demand was necessary to determine the just price, medieval rules across Europe imposed extensive price controls in an effort to balance the interests of producers and consumers.[9]

By the time of the Reformation, an antimonopoly tradition had firmly taken root in the Christian mind.[10] Martin Luther, influenced by the Scholastic tradition in economic matters, lumped cartels and monopolies under the wider rubric of "usury" and the "lust for profits," by which he meant charging more than a fair price. Luther saw a rising moral problem in sixteenth-century Protestant Germany and identified cornering markets, or what the British common law called forestalling, regrating, or engrossing, as a particular problem:

> Again, there are some who buy up the entire supply of certain goods or wares in a country or a city, so that they may have those goods solely in their own power and can then fix and raise the price and sell them as dear as they like or

4 W. W. Thornton, *A Treatise on Combinations in Restraint of Trade*, § 20 (2d ed. 1928).

5 See generally Marcia L. Colish, *Medieval Foundations of the Western Intellectual Tradition 400–1400* (New Haven, CT: Yale University Press, 1997), pp. 330–334.

6 Raymond De Roover, "Monopoly Theory Prior to Adam Smith: A Revision," *Quarterly Journal of Economics*, vol. 65, no. 4 (1951), pp. 492–524.

7 Ibid.

8 Ibid., pp. 498–499.

9 Colish, *Medieval Foundations*.

10 For a non-Reformation analysis of the relationship between antitrust and Christianity, see Tihamer Toth, "Is There a Vatican School for Competition Policy?," *Loyola University Chicago Law Journal*, vol. 46, no. 3 (2015), pp. 583–616.

can. Now I have said above that the rule that a man may sell his goods as dear as he will or can is false and unchristian. It is far more abominable that one should buy up the whole commodity for that purpose. Even the imperial and temporal laws forbid this and call it "monopoly," i.e., purchase for self-interest, which is not to be tolerated in city or country, and princes and lords would stop it and punish it if they did their duty. Merchants who do this act just as though God's creatures and God's goods were made for them alone and given to them alone, and as though they could take them from other people and set on them whatever price they chose.[11]

Luther contrasted monopolistic market-cornering with the Genesis 47 account of Joseph buying up grain for storage during the seven fat years in anticipation of the coming seven lean years. This was not monopolistic, according to Luther, but rather a "common and honest purchase" because Joseph didn't prevent anyone else from buying and Joseph was motivated, through God's wisdom, by the public good rather than personal gain. Because antitrust economics does not distinguish whether monopoly profits are used for personal gain or personal philanthropy (the resource misallocation being the same), Luther's exegesis would not persuade most antitrust practitioners. Joseph's buying the grain in the seven fat years appears to the economist to be a voluntary market transaction. Likewise, when he sold the grain during the seven lean years, Joseph seems to the economist to have acted very much as a monopolist, forcing the Egyptians to give up everything they owned to Pharaoh.[12]

Luther also railed against predatory pricing:

When some see that they cannot establish their monopolies in any other way because other people have the same goods, they proceed to sell their goods so cheap that the others can make no profit, and thus they compel them either not to sell at all, or else to sell as cheap as they themselves are selling and so be ruined. Thus they get their monopoly after all. These people are not worthy to be called men or to live among other men, nay they are not worth exhorting or instructing; for their envy and greed is so open and shameless that even at the cost of their own losses they cause loss to others, so that they may have the whole place to themselves. The authorities would do right if they took from such people everything they had and drove them out of the country. It would scarcely have been necessary to tell of such doings, but I wanted to include them so that it might be seen what great knavery there is

[11] Martin Luther, "On Trading and Usury," in *Works of Martin Luther* (Philadelphia, PA: A. J. Holman Company, 1915), pp. 26–27.

[12] In addition to monopolies, Luther singled out price-fixing cartels as pernicious, and even described an issue of considerable interest to modern economics: mechanisms by which cartelists enforce their agreement internally and penalize "cheating." Ibid., p. 30.

in trade, and that it might be plain to everybody how things are going in the world, in order that everyone may know how to protect himself against such a dangerous class.[13]

Luther did not offer an opinion about how often business firms might operate at the "cost of their own losses" and under what conditions pricing below cost could become profitable. Contemporary antitrust scholarship has since examined this question in detail. While predatory pricing is actionable under the Sherman Act, antitrust now offers a cautionary perspective as to the likelihood of predatory pricing as a plausible monopolizing strategy.[14] The most recent pronouncements of the Supreme Court have followed in the grain of the academic scholarship on predatory pricing.[15]

Max Weber famously anointed John Calvin the father of modern capitalism due to the Protestant work ethic, but Calvin also was important to post-Reformation economics by breaking with Luther and the medieval tradition on usury. Calvin argued that Scripture did not condemn all lending for interest, but only unscrupulous lending to the poor, loans that benefited only the lender, and lending at excessive rates.[16] While Calvin did not deal as explicitly as Luther with monopolies and cartels, to the extent that the medieval Christian conception of monopoly was bound up in the conception

[13] Ibid., pp. 28–29.

[14] The taproot of this antitrust scholarship on this subject is John McGee, "Predatory Pricing: The Standard Oil (N.J.) Case," *Journal of Law & Economics*, vol. 1 (October 1958), pp. 137–169 and "Predatory Pricing Revisited," *Journal of Law & Economics*, vol. 23 (October 1980), pp. 289–230. For a summary of the issues, see Patrick Bolton, Joseph F. Brodley, and Michael Riordan, "Predatory Pricing: Strategic Theory and Legal Policy," *Georgetown Law Journal*, vol. 88, no. 1 (August 2000), pp. 2239–2330; and Kenneth G. Elzinga and David E. Mills, "Predatory Pricing and Strategic Theory," *Georgetown Law Journal*, vol. 89 (August 2001), pp. 2475–2494.

[15] *Matsushita Electric Industrial Co.* v. *Zenith Radio*, 475 U.S. 574 (1986). Here Justice Powell concluded, "There is a consensus among commentators that predatory pricing schemes are rarely tried, and even more rarely successful." *Matsushita* at p. 589. The Court's skepticism about the efficacy of predatory pricing continued in *Liggett Group, Inc.* v. *Brown & Williamson Tobacco Corp.*, 509 U.S. 209 (1993). This case is often referred to as *Brooke Group* because the Brooke Group acquired Liggett in the course of the litigation. In more recent cases, like *Pacific Bell Telephone Co.* v. *Linkline Communications, Inc.*, 555 U.S. 438 (2009) and *Weyerhaeuser Co.* v. *Ross-Simmons Hardwood Lumber Co.*, 549 U.S. 312 (2007), the Supreme Court has continued to hold to a skeptical view of predatory pricing cases. However, some lower courts have begun to cite a "post-Chicago" literature that views predatory pricing as a greater threat, even though these cases have still tended to reject predatory pricing liability on the facts before them. See *United States* v. *AMR Corp.*, 335 F.3d 1109 (10th Cir. 2003) (observing that, in light of Post-Chicago scholarship, the court would not approach predatory pricing claims "with the incredulity that once prevailed").

[16] Kathryn D. Blanchard, *The Protestant Ethic or the Spirit of Capitalism* (Eugene, OR: Cascade Books, 2010), pp. 36–40; John Calvin, *Letter of Advice on Usury* (1545).

of usury, Calvin freed Christian thought to deal with economic matters – and the role of capital and investment in particular – in a more open light. In so doing, he set the stage for the most important Christian writer of all time on economics – Adam Smith.

### 4.2.2 Adam Smith and His Immediate Influences

Conventional wisdom identifies Adam Smith as the father of modern economics.[17] Because antitrust is now joined at the hip with economics, it is worth revisiting the theological roots of Smith's economic contribution. While the intellectual and amicable connection between Smith and David Hume (no friend of the Christian faith) is well known,[18] and while most scholars consider Smith to have been a deist, Smith's intellectual debt to Presbyterian clergy is less commonly acknowledged.[19] Hence it is fitting to be reminded of what Smith wrote about this group:

> There is scarce perhaps to be found anywhere in Europe a more learned, decent, independent, and respectable set of men, than the greater part of the Presbyterian clergy of Holland, Geneva, Switzerland, and Scotland.[20]

These men were scholar-pastors who were deeply affected by the Protestant Reformation.[21] While Smith is commonly thought to have made an *economic case* for free markets and voluntary exchange, the Reformers who influenced Smith were making a *theological case* for free markets and voluntary exchange.

[17] Economists often remark, "It's all in Smith," meaning that the substantive issues and principles of economics have their taproot in *The Wealth of Nations*. A variation of this among economists is that "It's all in Marshall," referring to Alfred Marshall's magnum opus, *Principles of Economics*. Marshall's *Principles* was first published in 1890, the year antitrust was established as a national policy in the United States with the passage of the Sherman Act.

[18] David Hume, *The Life of David Hume, Esq: Written by Himself. To Which Is Added, a Letter from Adam Smith, LL.D. to William Strahan, Esq.* (Ann Arbor: University of Michigan Library, 2007), originally published in Dublin, 1777. The latest scholarship regarding Smith and Hume's friendship is Dennis C. Rasmussen, *The Infidel and the Professor* (Princeton, NJ: Princeton University Press, 2017).

[19] We are indebted to Samuel Gregg's scholarship in this regard. See Samuel Gregg, "Commercial Order and the Scottish Enlightenment: The Christian Context," in *Christian Theology and Market Economics*, eds. Ian R. Harper and Samuel Gregg (Cheltenham: Edward Elgar, 2008), pp. 43–59.

[20] Adam Smith, *An Inquiry into the Nature and Causes of the Wealth of Nations*, vol. 2, ed. Edwin Cannan (London: Methuen, 1904), p. 295.

[21] Countries such as France, Spain, and Italy, where the Reformation did not advance, are absent from Smith's list. Notably, Germany, the home of Martin Luther, also is absent.

Smith was a student of Francis Hutcheson, who was both a minister in the Church of Scotland and a professor at Glasgow. Hutcheson was influenced by Gershom Carmichael, a Presbyterian minister and a professor at St. Andrews and Glasgow. Carmichael was himself influenced by the natural law teachings of Hugo Grotius and Samuel von Pufendorf. If one were writing in the vernacular of the King James Version, Grotius and Pufendorf begat Carmichael, Carmichael begat Hutcheson, Hutcheson begat Smith, and Smith described the workings of what he called the "simple and obvious system of natural liberty."[22] In what follows, we describe the "begats." (Note: See Chapter 10 for an analysis of Smith, Pufendorf, and Hutcheson's views on price controls.)

Smith's work organized an economic way of thinking in an important – and now iconic – fashion. But some of his important principles had already been developed by "the Presbyterian clergy." For example, one of the most famous principles of economics, featured prominently in Smith, is that specialization and division of labor generate economic growth. Smith encountered this principle as a student of Hutcheson.[23] Hutcheson, the clergyman-professor, described "demand and supply" with as much clarity as Smith, his student:

> We shall find that the prices of goods depend on these two jointly, the demand on account of some use or other which many desire, and the difficulty of acquiring, or cultivating for human use.[24]

What is important for our analysis is not that Hutcheson, a professor of moral philosophy, was teaching economic principles before Smith was writing them down. Rather, for Hutcheson, economics as a discipline formed and generated these principles from a moral foundation. Market processes worked best not when people were driven by greed, but when they were motivated by biblical virtues of saving and diligent labor. Smith heard these (literally) "Proverbial" virtues taught by his teacher Hutcheson.[25] Smith's principle of self-interest was expressed famously with his words,

[22] Smith, *An Inquiry into the Nature*, p. 184.

[23] "Nay tis' well known that the produce of the labours of any given number, twenty, for instance, in providing the necessaries or conveniences of life, shall be much great by assigning to one, a certain sort of work of one kind, in which he will soon acquire skill and dexterity, and to another assigning work of a different kind, than if each one of the twenty were obliged to employ himself, by turns, in all the different sorts of labour requisite for his subsistence, without sufficient dexterity in any." Frances Hutcheson, *A System of Moral Philosophy, In Three Books* (Glasgow, 1755).

[24] Ibid., p. 54.

[25] Proverbs 6:6–8; Proverbs 21:5; Proverbs 21:20.

> It is not from the benevolence of the butcher, the brewer, or the baker that we expect our dinner, but from regard to their own interest. We address ourselves, not to their humanity but to their self-love, and never talk to them of our own necessities but of their advantages.[26]

Smith never uses the word greed as the motivator of buying and selling.

Smith's principle of self-interest finds its roots in his contention that, "In civilized society, [man] stands at all times in need of the cooperation and assistance of great multitudes, while his whole life is scarce sufficient to gain the friendship of a few persons."[27] It is this need for interaction between the buyer and seller of goods in which Love, the chief of Christian virtues, involves itself in the market economy.

Smith recognized the need for and presence of the virtue of Love in a market economy. Writing in *The Theory of Moral Sentiments*, he declared, "Humanity does not desire to be great, but to be beloved. It is not in being rich that truth and justice would rejoice, but in being trusted and believed, recompenses which those virtues must almost always acquire."[28] On this very idea of "being trusted and believed" most market interactions depend.[29]

Drawing from Hutcheson's ideas regarding the virtues of man, Smith recognized that the duties of man and God in extending benevolence differ practically. Smith observed that the notion that humans could manufacture "the general happiness of mankind" would require that people do something beyond their capabilities, but precisely in the abilities and desire of God.[30]

> The administration of the great system of the universe ... the care of the universal happiness of all rational and sensible beings, is the business of God, and not of man. To man is allotted a much humbler department, but one much more suitable to the weakness of his powers, and to the narrowness of his comprehension – the care of his own happiness, of that of his family, his friends, his country.[31]

26 Smith, *Inquiry into the Nature*, p. 16.

27 Ibid.

28 Adam Smith, *The Theory of Moral Sentiments*, ed. Dover Philosophical Classics (New York: Dover, 2006), p. 161.

29 There is, in fact, a branch of economic theory that explicitly pertains to "being trusted and believed." The literature regarding incentive compatibility in the context of asymmetric information explains how individuals reveal their truthful incentives in a market transaction only under certain rules that provide motivation to do so. Incentive compatible allocations that might yield Pareto efficient allocations are those for which the holders of private information will be willing to reveal it. See John O. Ledyard, "Incentive Compatibility," in *Allocation, Information, and Markets* (London: Palgrave Macmillan, 1989), pp. 141–151.

30 Ronald Coase, "Adam Smith's View of Man," *Journal of Law and Economics*, vol. 19 (1976), p. 17.

31 Smith, *Theory of Moral Sentiments*, p. 238.

Smith may even have drawn the title of his *magnum opus* from the title of his mentor's book. The full title of Smith's most famous work is: *An Inquiry into the Nature and Causes of the Wealth of Nations* (1776). The full title of Hutcheson's *magnum opus* is: *An Inquiry into the Origin of Our Ideas of Beauty and Virtue* (1725).

As mentioned earlier, Hutcheson was the most notable student of Carmichael in moral philosophy at the University of Glasgow. He then succeeded Carmichael on the faculty at Glasgow. Carmichael's convictions were derived from the works of Grotius and Pufendorf, who built upon the natural law tradition of Thomas Aquinas, and are responsible for Christianity's natural law tradition as applied to law and commerce. These predecessors of Adam Smith constructed two pillars that are predicates for antitrust to make sense. First, the law is to protect private property from theft and expropriation because there is a divine mandate for individuals to be able to exclude others from the use of their private property. Second, the law is to protect the market exchange of private property rights because there is a divine basis for individuals to engage in voluntary exchange of property.[32]

But, even with these two pillars in place, both Grotius and Pufendorf had concerns about the prospect of monopoly in a market-based economy. The views of Grotius on monopoly are expressed with examples of monopolizing (or "engrossing") agricultural products and the naval practices of the Spaniards:

[32] Pufendorf anticipated the State granting property rights to deter free riding on risky investments. He wrote:

> Besides, the Magistrate may give one Man, or one Company of Men the sole Power of Importing certain Commodities from certain Places, exclusive of all others. And there may be several good Reasons for the granting such a Privilege. For it requires vast Charges to settle a Trade with a very remote Nation, and perhaps after great Expenses it may not succeed at all; and therefore the Authors of such a Commerce ought in reason to have Security, that others may not intercept *gratis* what they have established at their great Risk and Charge; and besides such privileged Companies are better able to assist the Public with their Riches; upon any Emergencies, than private Persons: By this means too a greater Trade may be carried on, and with better Credit: Nor is this Method liable to so many Tricks and Shifts, since the Gain comes into the common Bank to be divided proportionally amongst them all. But as for these Privileges, a prudent Government will not grant 'em, but where the Commodities are imported from remote Places, and with great Hazard; and which do not so much concern the Necessities as the Superfluities of Life. Not even then must the Merchants be allowed to enhance the Price of those Things at their Pleasure; for it is against Reason to give a few an opportunity of scraping up exorbitant Riches out of the Fortunes of the rest, when the Public gets nothing by it. (Samuel von Pufendorf, *Of the Law of Nature and Nations: Eight Books*, 1729. Book V. Chapter V. Section VII).

> What, therefore, may seem so unjust as that the Spaniards should have the whole world tributary, so that they neither buy nor sell but at their pleasure? We hate and also punish engrossers of corn or other commodities in all cities. Nor doth any trade of life seem so wicked and hateful as this engrossing of corn. And that worthily too. For they do injury to nature which is plentiful and liberal to all in common. Nor is it to be thought that negotiation was found for a few men's uses, but to the end that what was wanting unto one should be recompensed through the plenty of another yet with a just advantage or profit propounded unto all who should undertake the danger and labor of transporting.[33]

Pufendorf expanded upon Grotius' work,[34] describing monopoly as contrary to natural law. He did not mince words:

> But a Monopoly, properly so called, as having the Force of Privilege, cannot be set on foot by private Men: For how can a private Man justify his hindering others from meddling with such a sort of Commodity, when he has no Command over, nor can lawfully use Force against them? And

[33] Hugo Grotius, *The Free Sea*, trans. Hakluyt. 1609. Reprint (Indianapolis, IN: Liberty Fund, 2004), p. 56.

[34] Despite being extremely similar in ideology, Pufendorf did not always see eye to eye with Grotius about monopoly. Grotius explains his justification of some natural monopoly structures, incorporating a biblical reference, in this excerpt:

> All Monopolies are not repugnant to the Law of Nature, for they may sometimes be permitted by the Sovereign upon a just Cause, and at a certain Rate; as may appear from the Example of *Joseph*, when he was Governor of *Aegypt*: So also under the *Romans*, the *Alexandrians* had the Monopoly, as *Strabo* tells us, of all Commodities brought from the *Indies* and *Aethiopia*. The like may be done by private Persons, provided they are contented with a reasonable Profit. But they, who, as the Oylmen in the *Velabrum*, do purposely combine to advance the Value of their Wares above the highest Degree of the current Price, and those also who use Force or Fraud to prevent the Importation of any greater Quantity, or else agree to buy up all, in Order to sell them again, at a Rate very exorbitant, considering the Season, commit an Injustice, and are obliged to make Amends and a Reparation for it. If indeed they do by any other Means hinder the bringing in of Goods, or ingross them to themselves, to vend them dearer, tho' at a Price not unreasonable for the Season, they act against the Rules of Charity as St. *Ambrose* proves by several Arguments, in his third Book of Offices, but properly speaking, they violate no Man's Right. (Hugo Grotius, *The Rights of War and Peace*, 1625. Reprint [Indianapolis, IN: Liberty Fund, 2005], vol. 2, chapter 12, section 16)

But Pufendorf disagrees with Grotius on the basis of Joseph's lack of use of market power:

> Grotius bring the Example of Joseph, when he was Viceroy of Egypt, in Justification of Monopolies; tho' that Example is not much to the Purpose: For neither did the King hinder others from buying up the Corn in the Years of Plenty, nor any from selling, who had too much: Neither had the Alexandrians in Strabo the Monopoly of Indian and Ethiopian Commodities from any Privilege, but from the Situations of the Place. (von Pufendorf, *Of the Law of Nature and Nations*)

> therefore the Monopolies of private Men are spurious and illegal, and do not depend upon Rights and Privileges, but are generally carried on by clandestine Frauds and Combinations: As if some few by a Trick should debar others from Trading to those Places from whence they have their Commodities, or should hinder those that have them from bringing them to Market: Or, if they should enter into a Combination to buy up all such sort of Commodities, and then stifle them, that so the Scarcity may enhance the Price. Against whom may be applied that of Apollonius Tyanaus in Philostr. in the Beginning. 'The Earth is the Mother of all, for she is just; but you being unjust have made her only a Mother to your selves.' The Knavery of such ought as much to be corrected, as those who enter into Compact to raise extravagantly the Prices of other things, by agreeing privately to sell nothing under such a Rate: Which piece of Roguery Labourers and Workmen are sometimes guilty of.[35]

In the quotation that follows, Pufendorf even anticipated Holmes' dissent in the *Northern Pacific* case.[36]

> In this place something maybe expected to be said concerning Monopolies, Whether any, or all of them be against the Law of Nature, or no? For 'tis an odious Name, and the Laws of many States brand it grievously. But here we must exempt several Things from the insidious Title of Monopolies, which indeed are not such. For sure 'tis prohibited by no Law, nor can it come under the Name of a Monopoly, if only one Man, in any Town, has got the way of making some sort of Manufacture, or if one Man only has got such a sort of Grain in his Ground, or if some certain Commodity be the Produce only of one particular Country. Since there is no such 'Produce of Alume in any other Country, which yet is of great Use, it is not to be wondered at, that the Lipareans have the Monopoly of it, and setting what Prices they please upon it, make vast Returns.' For Monopolies, as such, imply that others too would sell the same, did not one Man ingross the whole Trade to himself.[37]

35 Ibid.

36 "The law, I repeat, says nothing about competition, and only prevents its suppression by contracts or combinations in restraint of trade, and such contracts or combinations derive their character as restraining trade from other features that the suppression of competition alone. To see whether I am wrong, the illustrations put in the argument are of use. If I am, then a partnership between two stage coach drivers who have been competitors in driving across a state line, or two merchants once engaged in rival commerce among the States whether made after or before the act, if now continued, is a crime. For, again I repeat, if the restraint on the freedom of the members of a combination caused by their entering into a partnership is a restraint of trade, every such combination, as well the small as the great, is within the act." *Northern Securities Co.* v. *United States*, 193 U.S. 197, 410 (1904).

37 Pufendorf's paradigm of natural law anticipates the common law on restraint of trade with these words: "But if a Man, without contracting with the Others, should of his own Head aim

Gregg summarizes the Grotius-Pufendorf intersection this way:

> Grotius's Mare Liberum (1609) . . . made a powerful case for the liberty of all people of all nations to use the sea to trade freely (1609, 2004, pp. 49–51) and is commonly regarded as one of the first early-modern arguments against monopolies.
>
> Widely regarded as one of Grotius's most prominent intellectual disciples, a considerable portion of Pufendorf's theological and jurisprudential writings were concerned with applying Grotius's schema to a range of then-contemporary issues . . . [for example] when it came to the question of economic value and price, Pufendorf argued that the determining factors were a good's relative scarcity and its subjective utility.
>
> (Pufendorf, 1673, 2004, pp. 140–145)[38]

With Grotius and Pufendorf as the foundation, let's return to how Carmichael built upon it. He wrote this about competition:

> [The] further expenditure of labour and industry which the interest of human society requires in the way of competition in cultivating the things of the earth, is likely to achieve a greater stock of a certain kind of thing than our own personal use requires. In return for these we can acquire, by the use of agreements, other things that are useful to us. This further fruit of our labour should not be taken from us, provided we got it without fraudulent and unfair oppression of others, who should always be left the opportunity to get what their own use requires under fair conditions.[39]

Gregg summarizes the importance of Carmichael on competition this way:

> Carmichael highlights the importance of competition in stimulating the human creativity that delivers a surplus of privately-owned goods that people can then trade via voluntary transactions, while simultaneously insisting that others should have the opportunity to enter the circle of exchange. The implication is that it is unjust and not in the interests of the common good to unreasonably restrict market exchange. This amounts to a Christian natural-law argument for the moral necessity of free trade – an argument that would have resonated throughout much of the Scotland of Carmichael's time.[40]

at a Monopoly, by hindering some by Force, and others by clandestine Contrivances, from coming to the same Place, and by that means lay a Necessity upon all others to buy of him, it is plain that he offends against the Law of Humanity, and impudently breaks in upon the Liberty of the rest." von Pufendorf, *Of the Law of Nature and Nations*.

38 Gregg, "Commercial Order and the Scottish Enlightenment," p. 48.

39 Gershom Carmichael, *Natural Rights on the Threshold of the Scottish Enlightenment*, eds. James Monroe and Michael Silverthorne (Indianapolis, IN: Liberty Fund, 2002), p. 95.

40 Gregg, "Commercial Order and the Scottish Enlightenment," p. 50.

These words resonate "throughout much of the antitrust community of today" because Carmichael understood that competition was better than planning, that private property was a prerequisite of competition, that competition produced a "surplus" (or economic growth), that competition should not be to the benefit of some but not others, that competition should not be unreasonably restricted, and that there was a biblical basis for competition being given free reign. As Gregg summarized the linkage from Grotius and Pufendorf to Carmichael to Smith,

> Perhaps Gershom Carmichael's greatest contribution to the Scottish Enlightenment was to re-introduce the natural-law tradition, long dormant in Scotland since the Reformation, back into Scottish learning. While figures such as Hume reflected upon commercial society's emergence in ways that marked a break with Christian belief about human nature, most Scottish Enlightenment scholars – including, to a certain extent, Adam Smith, engaged in the same enterprise primarily within the context of the powerful theological and philosophical legacy bequeathed by the 17th century Protestant natural law tradition associated with figures such as Hugh Grotius (1583–1645) and Samuel von Pufendorf (1632–94).[41]

The encomium Smith gives to "Presbyterian clergy" is, at its taproot, recognition of a theory of law and commerce that was put forth by scholar-pastors who applied reason to Scripture. The result was a "natural law" that – like antitrust law – is friendly to market exchange, not hostile to it.[42]

Later scholars had no qualms about connecting Adam Smith's invisible hand to a providential order. Richard Whately wrote, "Man is, in the same act, doing one thing, by choice, for his own benefit, and another, undesignedly, under the care of Providence, for the service of the community."[43] In writing these words, Whately was influenced by Smith.[44] Thomas Chalmers rewrote the principle of the invisible hand this way:

> The greatest economic good is rendered to the community by each man being left to consult and to labour for his own particular good – or, in other words, a more prosperous result is obtained by the spontaneous play and busy

41 Ibid., p. 47.

42 Gregg contends that in Hutcheson's *System of Moral Philosophy*, the author further developed "economic ideas found in Grotius and Pufendorf, mediated through Carmichael, many of which anticipate theories subsequently developed in Smith's *The Wealth of Nations*" (1776, 1904).

43 Richard Whately, *Introductory Lectures on Political Economy* (London: B. Fellowes, 1832), p. 103.

44 Elizabeth Jane Whately, *Life and Correspondence of Richard Whately, DD.* (London: Longmans, Green, 1866).

> competition of many thousand wills, each bent on the prosecution of its own selfishness, than by the anxious superintendence of a government, vainly attempting to medicate the fancied imperfections of nature.[45]

In the ability of markets to translate the self-interest of economic agents into the good of others, Chalmers claimed this "bespeaks a higher Agent, by whose transcendental wisdom it is, that all is made to conspire so harmoniously, and to terminate beneficially."[46] If Providence has ordained that consumers appeal to the self-interest of sellers, who then compete in the marketplace for consumer patronage, any agent that eliminates competition, or suppresses it through regulation, squelches this "transcendental wisdom." This means that any institution that preserves and promotes market competition is an agent of Providence. Central planners search for proper levers of government regulation to allocate society's scarce resources. The default position of antitrust is to search for a market-based solution to allocate society's scarce resources. Grotius, Pufendorf, and their progeny presumably applaud antitrust from the heavenly sidelines.

Modern theorists often justify antitrust law in purely consequentialist terms. For example, Herbert Hovenkamp, a leading antitrust scholar and custodian of the highly influential *Areeda-Turner* treatise, asserts that antitrust law has "no moral content."[47] But the story of antitrust is not one of legal doctrine shorn of natural law.[48] The natural law that informed Adam Smith – the natural law two pillars are private property and voluntary exchange – remains fundamental to the institution of antitrust. Indeed, the institution of antitrust has no basis apart from a certain – if we may use the word – "reverence" for private property and voluntary exchange.

Joseph Schumpeter, in his classic *History of Economic Analysis*, claimed that economics, as a discipline, "gained definite if not separate existence" by

[45] Thomas Chalmers, *On the Power, Wisdom, and Goodness of God* (London: Bell and Daldy, 1869), p. 238.

[46] Ibid., p. 239.

[47] Herbert Hovenkamp, "Antitrust Violations in Securities Markets," *Journal of Corporation Law*, vol. 28 (2003), pp. 607, 609; see also Herbert Hovenkamp, *The Antitrust Enterprise: Principle and Execution* (2005), pp. 10, 54 (stating that antitrust is only concerned with the economic, not the moral, implications of conduct).

[48] Alvey offers two reasons why economics is, today, largely shorn of "moral concerns." "First, the natural sciences came to be seen as successful, and the attempt was made to emulate that success in economics by applying natural science methods, including mathematics, to economic phenomena. Second, the self-styled economic science came to adopt positivism, which ruled out moral issues from science itself." James E. Alvey, "A Short History of Economics as a Moral Science," *Journal of Markets and Morality*, vol. 2, no. 1 (Spring 1999), pp. 53–73.

way of Christianity's influence on law.[49] Jacob Viner, another historian of economic thought who paralleled Schumpeter in stature, wrote: "I am obliged to insist that Adam Smith's system of thought, including his economics, is not intelligible if one disregards the role he assigns in it to the teleological elements."[50]

## 4.3 ANTITRUST THEMES: RATIONALITY, EQUITY, EFFICIENCY, COMPETITION, INNOVATION

### 4.3.1 Antitrust and Rationality

The first thematic connection between antitrust and the Christian faith is theological: From whence cometh the basis for the institution of antitrust? The Christian faith offers a foundation for the same rationality upon which antitrust enforcement is founded.[51] In his book, *The Victory of Reason*, Rodney Stark explains:

> The Christian image of God is that of a rational being who believes in human progress, more fully revealing himself as humans gain the capacity to better understand. Moreover, because God is a rational being and the universe is his personal creation, it necessarily has a rational, lawful, stable structure, awaiting increased human comprehension.[52]

After creating "male and female" in his own image, "God blessed them and said to them, 'Be fruitful and increase in number; fill the earth and subdue it . . .'"[53] In what has come to be called the creation mandate, God directs men and women to be His stewards over the earth. This means that human beings – unlike all other living creatures – have been given a form of dominion over

[49] "It is within [the scholastics'] systems of moral theology and law that economics gained a definite if not separate existence, and it is they who come nearer than does any other group to having been the 'founders' of scientific economics." Joseph Schumpeter, *History of Economic Analysis* (New York: Oxford University Press, 1954), p. 97.

[50] Jacob Viner, *The Role of Providence in the Social Order* (Philadelphia, PA: American Philosophical Society, 1972), pp. 81–82.

[51] This is a very different topic than the familiar terrain, already explored, of the basis of antitrust in English common law or the legislative history of antitrust law. See William Letwin, "The English Common Law Concerning Monopolies," *University of Chicago Law Review*, vol. 21, no. 3 (1954), p. 355; and Donald Dewey, *Monopoly in Economics and Law* (Chicago, IL: Rand McNally and Company, 1959), especially chapters IX and X; and Hans Thorelli, *The Federal Antitrust Policy* (Baltimore, MD: Johns Hopkins Press, 1955).

[52] Rodney Stark, *The Victory of Reason: How Christianity Led to Freedom, Capitalism, and Western Success* (New York: Random House, 2007), pp. 11–12.

[53] Genesis 1:27–28.

God's creation, not out of merit, but rather because God was pleased to create them in His image. Man is able to exercise good stewardship over the earth because God, as Stark describes it, created the earth as a "rational, lawful, stable structure, awaiting increased human comprehension." As the field of antitrust has grown in its "human comprehension," antitrust is better positioned to "subdue the earth" to the extent it applies a "rational, lawful, stable structure" to the task of stewardship that the Bible claims God ceded to mankind.[54] The rationality postulate undergirds most of economic analysis.

A presupposition of antitrust is that the rational economic actor model applies to both buyer and seller. Where antitrust economics stands in tension with the Christian faith is where Christianity also sees men and women as sinners, in need of redemption offered in the Gospel through Jesus Christ. Whereas antitrust seeks to optimize the choice set that consumers face, Christianity questions some of the choices that buyers and sellers make. Consumer preferences, to be met by competing sellers at congenial prices, are not a necessary or sufficient condition for human flourishing.

Describing economic agents through the lens of Christian theology, Brennan and Waterman explain:

> Their desires do not reflect their true interest. Their actual behavior has no presumptive normative authority. Man is sinful. Agents know what they ought to do, but they do something else ... As St Paul puts it: "That which I would not, that I do. And that which I would, I do not."[55]

Thus, while antitrust seeks the optimization of consumer choices,[56] Christianity questions the morality of those choices. Paul's writings in Romans 7:15, referenced above, describe the insufficiency of consumer choice alone for human flourishing. However, as we've argued in this section, the fundamental rationality necessitated by antitrust's rational actor model

[54] Pufendorf described the creation mandate this way: "For, not being born for himself alone, but being therefore furnished with so many excellent Endowments, that he may set forth his Creator's Praise, and be rendered a fit Member of Human Society; it follows hence, that it is his Duty, to cultivate and improve those Gifts of his Creator which he finds in himself, that they may answer the End of their Donor; and to contribute all that lies in his Power to the Benefit of Human Society." Samuel von Pufendorf, *The Whole Duty of Man According to the Law of Nature*, 1673. Reprint (Indianapolis, IN: Liberty Fund, 2003).

[55] Geoffrey Brennan and Anthony M. C. Waterman, "Christian Theology and Economics: Convergence and Clashes," in *Christian Theology and Market Economics*, eds. Ian R. Harper and Samuel Gregg (Northampton, MA: Edward Elgar, 2008), p. 91.

[56] Economics as a science lacks the language to create "moral norms," but rather the moral concerns of individuals within the context of Pareto efficiency, which analyzes individuals' preferences as data apart from value judgments. While economic theory provides no basis for value judgments, Christianity stands ready to fill the gap.

coincides with the biblical mandate to "subdue the earth" along with the biblical description of God as a rational, ordered being.

### 4.3.2 Equity and Efficiency[57]

The pursuit of equity and efficiency provide us with an additional intersection between Christianity and the institution of antitrust. Throughout the biblical narrative, the revealed nature of God is one of equity and justice.[58] In the Sermon on the Mount, Jesus even blesses the materially poor.[59] Additionally, the Bible upholds the wise allocation of resources in an efficient manner.[60] The goal of antitrust squares with the biblical values of both equity and efficiency.

In his Godkin lecture, Arther Okun claimed: "We can't have our cake of market efficiency and share it equally."[61] The conventional wisdom is that there is a trade-off between the pursuit of efficiency and the pursuit of income equality.[62] True, the operating assumption of most economic analyses is to hold the distribution of income constant (or assume it as given) and, from that, to analyze efficiency problems. But no one seriously entertains the notion that some distributions of income, because of their structure of incentives and rewards, will not yield a larger basket of output than others.

In light of this trade-off, it is notable that antitrust enforcement generally serves to help those at the low end of the income distribution range without decreasing economic efficiency. Antitrust achieves this double benefit when it promotes efficiency in resource allocation by preventing the cartelization or monopolization of markets patronized by low-income consumers. The economic logic is straightforward: Prices will be made lower in a competitive market so that for any given income, a larger basket of goods and services can be purchased. Antitrust policy, therefore, need not concern itself with increasing the purchasing power of the poor because it does this when it thwarts cartels and monopolies in its pursuit of economic efficiency.

57 This section draws upon Kenneth Elzinga, "Goals of Antitrust: Other than Competition and Efficiency, What Else Counts?," *University of Pennsylvania Law Review*, vol. 125, no. 6 (1977), pp. 1191–1213.

58 Psalm 99:4; Proverbs 1:3.

59 Luke 6:20.

60 Proverbs 31:27; Psalm 90:12; Proverbs 21:5; Psalm 39:4–5.

61 Arthur Okun, *Equality and Efficiency, the Big Tradeoff* (Washington, DC: The Brookings Institution, 1975).

62 C. Brehm and T. Saving, "The Demand for General Assistance Payments," *American Economic Review*, vol. 54, no. 1 (1964), pp. 1002–1018.

Antitrust actions may not always improve both income distribution and efficiency. For example, the breakup of a cartel of artist-merchants who handcraft porcelain will be efficient but will bestow its distributional benefits only upon the economically privileged who shop in this market, thus arguably increasing inequality. But such situations are not the norm – in most circumstances antitrust gives the efficiency–equality trade-off the characteristic of having one's cake and eating it too. While a direct assault on inequality through income redistribution might lead to a reduction in efficiency, a direct assault on inefficiency through antitrust will not necessarily result in any reduction in equality.

In sum, the pursuit of efficiency goals through antitrust enforcement is consistent with the objective of equitable distribution of income.[63] This is not to say that antitrust policy alone is a sufficient redistributive tool. Most analyses of the poverty problem in the United States attach only minimal importance to inadequate antitrust enforcement as a causative agent. The problem of poverty is attributed more often to the low level of education and job skills of the poor, insufficient aggregate demand, the distorted incentives of current welfare policies, drug addiction and alcoholism, racial discrimination, and a cognitive bias in favor of short-term over long-term satisfaction.[64] Thus, the pursuit of egalitarian income distribution through antitrust enforcement is likely to have limited results.[65] Nonetheless, the congenial quality about antitrust is that the equity objectives that bear on its enforcement do not seriously conflict, and at times even harmonize, with the pursuit of economic efficiency.

[63] Private recovery of treble damages, 15 U.S.C. 15 (1970), also has an apparent connection with this equity goal of antitrust. Not only is it supposed to promote equity by compensating the injured from the fruits of an antitrust violation, but it also reduces income inequality if we make the assumption that those who commit violations generally have higher incomes than those they injure.

[64] See Robert J. Lampman, "Approaches to the Reduction of Poverty," *American Economic Review*, vol. 55, no. 1 (1965), pp. 521, 524–525. See generally Edward Banfield, *The Unheavenly City* (Boston, MA: Little Brown and Co., 1970).

[65] In fact, antitrust pursuit of equity goals is foreclosed in some areas. For example, those "restraints of trade" effected by labor unions and minimum wage laws directly contribute to income maldistribution, but, with only a few exceptions, antitrust is unable to strike at labor market restraints. In *Apex Hosiery Co.* v. *Leader*, 310 U.S. 469 (1940), the Sherman Act was held not to apply to "restraints on the sale of the employee's services to the employer." Ibid., 503. See also *United States* v. *Hutcheson*, 312 U.S. 219 (1941). The broad union exemption under Apex Hosiery was narrowed in *Connell Constr. Co., Inc.* v. *Plumbers & Steamfitters* 100, 421 U.S. 616 (1975). Antitrust also has made important inroads on restraints upon competition by professional associations. For example, *Goldfarb* v. *Virginia State Bar*, 421 U.S. 773 (1975).

### 4.3.3 The Morality of Competition

Antitrust policy is predicated on the assumption that business firms will create public benefits when they compete hard against one another by improving products and offering lower prices, or what Scherer and Ross describe as "conscious[ly] striving against other business firms for patronage ... for potentially incompatible positions."[66] Christian thinkers continue to debate competition as a matter of Christian ethics and morality.[67] One can debate, for example, how Jesus' admonition to turn the other cheek[68] and Paul's admonition to train ourselves like competitive athletes and run the competitive race before us[69] inform Christian ethics in the marketplace.

There are several ways to reconcile these ostensible (and, we believe, only ostensible) conflicts in Scripture. Competition as an industrial value need not imply a society organized on selfish and ruthless disregard of others, or what C. S. Lewis gives as the state of hell: "A state in which everyone is perpetually concerned about his own dignity and advancement ... where everyone lives the deadly serious passions of envy, self-importance, and resentment."[70] To the contrary, competition can be salutary for society and for the individual competitor.

First, antitrust policy is focused on a systemic rather than personal level, and as such, it is designed to advance social welfare. On average, what producers lose through competition is more than made up for by consumers' gains.[71] Thus, an antitrust policy mandating competition rather than cooperation is not designed to enrich some at the expense of others, but rather to confer public benefits. The public benefits of market interactions may be seen as the sum of the mutual benefits gained by individuals in Smith's "obvious and simple system of natural liberty." Bruni and Sugden (2013) argue that mutual benefit is not only a fortunate by-product of the pursuit of self-interest, but actually the *telos* of the market: that buyers and sellers in a competitive

66 F. M. Scherer and David Ross, *Industrial Market Structure and Economic Performance* (Dallas, TX: Houghton Mifflin, 1990).

67 Clive Breed has assembled recent literature in "Jesus and Competition," *Faith & Economics*, vol. 45, no. 1 (Spring 2005), pp. 41–57.

68 Matthew 5:39.

69 Hebrews 12:1–2; I Corinthians 9:27.

70 C. S. Lewis, *The Screwtape Letters* (London: Geoffrey Bles, 1942), p. vii.

71 Robert Bork, *The Antitrust Paradox* (New York: Basic Books, 1978), p. 110.

marketplace actually *intend* for mutually beneficial transactions.[72] Thus, in preserving competition among producers, antitrust enables the marketplace to flourish in the mutually beneficial manner that an economy of central planning or rent-seeking does not produce. As Paul Rubin has argued, market competition is a form of unplanned cooperation to secure systemic economic benefits.[73]

Even at a personal level, competition within ethical and legal boundaries can be considered salutary for all involved. Shane Clifton argues from the Pentecostal tradition that "[c]ompetition is not a way for the powerful to crush the powerless, but for each person to reach their potential."[74] In the same way that an athlete running her hardest may hope to spur on her rivals to better performances, the Christian in business who competes hard for business need not wish her rival to perish, but may indeed hope that her competition spurs other firms to improvement. As Judge Learned Hand recognized in the *Alcoa* case, "Many people believe that possession of unchallenged economic power deadens initiative, discourages thrift and depresses energy; that immunity from competition is a narcotic, and rivalry is a stimulant, to industrial progress; that the spur of constant stress is necessary to counteract an inevitable disposition to let well enough alone."[75]

Finally, although antitrust law requires competition, it also establishes limits on competition (i.e., prohibiting predatory or anticompetitive tactics), as do separate strands of law, particularly contracts, torts, intellectual property, and the law of unfair competition. Thus, the competition that antitrust law mandates is not cutthroat or unlimited, but bounded by legal principles grounded in ethics and morality.

### 4.3.4 Innovation

Among contemporary economists, there is widespread agreement that market systems promote innovation. There is considerably less agreement on whether antitrust enforcement promotes for innovation, or whether it instead gets in

[72] Luigino Bruni and Robert Sugden, "Reclaiming Virtue Ethics for Economics," *Journal of Economic Perspectives*, vol. 27, no. 4 (2013), pp. 141–164.

[73] Paul H. Rubin, "Emporiophobia (Fear of Markets): Cooperation or Competition?," *Southern Economic Journal*, vol. 80, no. 4 (2013), pp. 875–889.

[74] Shane Clifton, "Pentecostal Approaches to Economics," in *The Oxford Handbook of Christianity and Economics*, ed. Rachel M. McCleary (Oxford: Oxford University Press, 2014), p. 275.

[75] *United States* v. *Aluminum Co. of America*, 148 F.2d 416 (1945).

the way. This debate is often styled as the Schumpeter–Arrow divide, following the work of the Austrian economist Joseph Schumpeter and the American Nobel Laureate Kenneth Arrow,[76] and has taken a prominent place in recent antitrust enforcement actions in high-tech industries, such as those concerning Microsoft, Google, and Intel. We do not propose to resolve the Schumpeter–Arrow divide here but rather offer more general comments on the value of economic innovation from a biblical perspective.

As mentioned earlier, faulty narratives often have portrayed Christianity as historically antagonistic to innovation. But both Christian theology as well as Church history are positively disposed to innovation.[77] A thorough historical analysis demonstrates the connection between Christian movements and innovation. Rodney Stark has argued that Christianity, by focusing on theological abstraction and rationality and recognizing property rights, became a catalyst for technological and scientific innovation throughout Western Europe.[78] Joel Mokyr has disputed what he views as Stark's "argument based on some inherent superiority of Western or Christian culture" in advancing innovation, but does credit the Puritan embrace of science as a driving force behind the British Industrial Revolution.[79]

In the antitrust pursuit to "depart from laissez faire in the ultimate interests of laissez faire,"[80] the antitrust institution seeks to promote competitive processes that enable and incentivize innovation. This goal of promoting industrial innovation and progress finds ample support within a long-standing Christian tradition. Although Christian theology has relatively little to offer informing precisely *how* antitrust should spur innovation – whether by intervening aggressively to correct market failures or staying its hand out of solicitude for experimentation and robust competition – the Christian tradition strongly supports innovation as a goal.

76 Herbert Hovenkamp, "Competition and Innovation," in *The Making of Competition Policy: Legal and Economic Sources*, eds. Daniel Crane and Herbert Hovenkamp (Oxford: Oxford University Press, 2013).

77 Anne Bradley catalogues the relationship between Christianity and Innovation in her article "Innovation, Change, and Economic Growth: A Christian Economist's Perspective," *Institute for Faith, Work and Economics*, March 11, 2013, https://tifwe.org/innovation-change-economic-growth-a-christian-economists-perspective/. She writes that the Bible documents and upholds innovation in the forms of Construction (Genesis 6:14; 1 Kings 5–6), Metallurgy (Proverbs 25:4; Zechariah 13:9; Isaiah 48:10), Clothing (Genesis 37), and Shipping (James 3:4; John 21:11).

78 Stark, *The Victory of Reason*.

79 Joel Mokyr, A *Culture of Growth: The Origins of the Modern Economy* (Princeton, NJ: Princeton University Press, 2017), pp. 229, 314.

80 Joel B. Dirlam and Alfred E. Kahn, *Fair Competition* (Ithaca, NY: Cornell University Press, 1954), p. 17.

## 4.4 APPLICATION TO SELECTED DOMAINS OF ANTITRUST LAW

### 4.4.1 The Bible and Cartels[81]

The quotation from Adam Smith that most antitrust lawyers know (particularly members of the plaintiffs' bar) is: "People of the same trade seldom meet together, even for merriment and diversion, but the conversation ends in a conspiracy against the public, or in some contrivance to raise prices."[82] Because price-fixing and other forms of cartel conduct occupy center stage in US antitrust enforcement, if there is any connection between the Christian faith and antitrust, it should show up here. And it does.

Suppose that a group of firms becomes weary of competing against each other so they divide up the market geographically, each firm agreeing not to poach on customers outside its designated territory. Or a group of sellers become unhappy with prevailing prices so they agree to a floor price below which sales will not be made. Or consider a market where prices are determined by competitive bidding, but sellers meet in advance in order to rig bid prices. Economists recognize each of these collective strategies as a variation of cartel behavior. Antitrust lawyers recognize each as being illegal per se under federal antitrust laws. The Bible, in turn, recognizes such concerted conduct as immoral.

The ninth commandment prohibits bearing false witness.[83] This amounts to a condemnation of the deceptive nature of cartels as a matter of Christian morality. When a company holds itself out to its customers as an independent center of initiative in the marketplace, yet buyers are uninformed that the market has been parceled out, or that a floor price has been set, or that the bidding is phony, the firms in the cartel have borne false witness. Indeed, many cartel agreements involve the submission of bogus bids or other forms of dissimulation to prevent buyers from detecting the fact that quoted prices have been fabricated through collusion. Antitrust laws that deter cartels deter the bearing of false witness.

The ninth commandment, in its brevity, makes no distinction between white lies and major falsehoods. In like fashion, Section One of the Sherman Act draws no distinction as to whether the cartel raises prices and restricts

[81] This section draws upon Kenneth G. Elzinga, "Controversy: Are Antitrust Laws Immoral? A Response to Jeffrey Tucker," *Journal of Markets and Morality*, vol. 1, no. 1 (1998), pp. 83–89.

[82] Adam Smith, *An Inquiry into Nature and Causes of the Wealth of Nations*, ed. Edwin Cannan (Indianapolis, IN: Library of Economics and Liberty, 1904), p. 137.

[83] Deuteronomy 5:20.

output by large amounts or small. Participants in a cartel bear false witness whether the cartel is weak or strong.

Any decision by prospective members to form a cartel involves the calculation of prospective costs and benefits. Absent antitrust deterrence, the major economic hindrances to cartelization would be the free rider problem, cheating by members of the cartel, and fending off prospective new entrants. Absent antitrust deterrence against cartels, one of the major moral deterrences to cartelization would be any unwillingness on the part of sellers to portray themselves as independent economic agents – when they are not. *Ceteris paribus*, economics teaches that without antitrust deterrence, there will be more cartels. Antitrust is a concession to the inability of the ninth commandment to thwart cartels fully.

When the Justice Department announces a criminal enforcement action against companies or individuals involved in cartel agreements, it often issues a press release equating the price-fixing agreement to a form of theft from consumers. While we have no quarrel with that characterization, we would suggest that the Christian tradition emphasizes an additional evil of the cartel agreement – its inability to operate without a high degree of dishonesty and deception.[84]

### 4.4.2 The Bible and Mergers

If cartels are the meat and potatoes of antitrust enforcement, mergers and acquisitions are the soup and salad courses. Does the Christian faith offer a perspective on anticompetitive mergers and acquisitions as it does cartel conduct? Indirectly, yes.

A merger to monopoly may restrict output and raise prices (just as a cartel will do). Whether one considers these effects immoral depends upon whether one considers sellers extracting wealth from consumers by output restriction – rather than by superior skill, foresight, and industry – to be immoral.

The Scriptures are favorably disposed to the pursuit of profits when it entails good stewardship over society's scarce resources, honesty in one's dealings, and honoring God by giving Him the first fruits of the return.[85] Economic theory teaches that monopolistic output restriction is inefficient. Inefficiency

[84] Jonathan Crowe and Barbara Jedlickova describe the wrongness of cartels as pertaining to both the negative economic consequences of cartels to the competitive marketplace as well as the immorality of deception, which reflects the analysis in our chapter of cartels violating both economic and moral rules. Jonathan Crowe and Barbara Jedlickova, "What's Wrong with Cartels," *Federal Law Review*, vol. 44 (2016), pp. 401–418.

[85] Proverbs 3:9–10.

in a world of scarcity may itself be immoral from the standpoint of the biblical principle of stewardship.[86]

A business community that outwardly prides itself on the virtues of free enterprise, but engages in extensive horizontal integration that eliminates competing sources of supply, can hardly expect to persuade customers of the merits or the morality of free enterprise. For consumers, free enterprise connotes not only freedom of contract between buyers and sellers but also the freedom for buyers to shop among alternative sources of supply. At the taproot, that is what the antimerger law seeks to accomplish.

In a fallen world, many questions are hard to answer. Even antitrust experts often disagree on the merits of a particular merger. In the case of horizontal mergers, the combining firms may secure market power that will harm consumers or exploit economic efficiencies that will benefit consumers. The market may discipline a combination of business firms that, hindsight reveals, made no economic sense. It is sometimes tricky to sort mergers into competitive and anticompetitive categories. Should we, for that reason, give all corporate marriages a pass so long as all the firms come to the altar willingly? It is an act of faith (in markets, not the Scriptures) to believe we can dispose of antitrust in the merger arena just because antitrust authorities may sometimes stop benign or efficient mergers or neglect to unravel anticompetitive mergers.

### 4.4.3 The Bible and Economic Dominance

The third major heading of contemporary antitrust law is monopolization, or what the Europeans call "abuse of dominance." Monopolization remains a poorly defined antitrust offense, with significant ongoing policy contestation around such questions as whether dominant firms should be subject to special obligations to avoid perpetuating their dominance and where the line should be drawn between aggressive but permissible competitive behavior and unlawfully predatory behavior. Antitrust practitioners agree that the proverbial act of blowing up the competitor's factory should be considered monopolization, but consensus beyond that is scarce.

The Scriptures contain no secret code on how to write contemporary monopolization law, but they do provide ethical principles regarding the accumulation of earthly riches. On the one hand, the Scriptures are replete with warnings to the wealthy and powerful. For example, I Timothy 6:9–10 warns that the love of money is the root of all sorts of evil. And, in Luke 6:24,

[86] See also Proverbs 31:18; Luke 19:13.

Jesus pronounces a woe to the rich, who have already received their consolation. But Jesus' parables also underscore the virtue of prudent investment, including reaping just rewards for risk-taking. In the Parable of the Bags of Gold,[87] Jesus hypothesizes an employer who entrusts bags of gold – five, two, or one – to three servants while he's away on a journey. Upon his return, he learns that the servants with five or two bags made prudent investments during his absence, each doubling the master's principal, but that the third servant, entrusted with a single gold bag, hid it in the ground and therefore earned no return on investment. This servant attempts to justify himself on the basis that, knowing his master was a hard man, he ensured the safety of the money entrusted. His master rebuffs this excuse, pointing out that even a very safe investment with bankers would have garnered some interest, and has the "wicked and lazy" servant punished.

Although Jesus meant this parable to have a primarily spiritual connotation regarding the Kingdom of God, its economic moral buttresses a strand of monopolization jurisprudence holding that firms should not be penalized for reaping the benefits of their risky investments and that less efficient firms should not have standing to complain when their more efficient rivals grow market share: "For whoever has will be given more, and they will have an abundance. Whoever does not have, even what they have will be taken from them."[88]

## 4.5 CONCLUSION

Geoffrey Brennan and Anthony Waterman make this statement about economics:

> Economists have long paid lip service to the idea of economics as a pure science that cannot authorize them to offer "a single syllable of advice." [quoting Nassau Senior] But in practice, they have rarely been able to resist making policy recommendations of all sorts – recommendations that necessarily commit them to underlying normative foundations. As one influential moral philosopher has put it, thinking of economics as it is actually practiced, "economics is a branch of ethics . . . (quoting Broome)."[89]

Our analysis of the intersection of antitrust and Christianity runs parallel to that of Brennan and Waterman. While antitrust is about law and economics, antitrust is also about ethics. And the ethics of antitrust can be viewed

87 Matthew 25:14–29.
88 Matthew 25:29.
89 Brennan and Waterman, "Christian Theology and Economics," p. 86.

profitably (no pun intended) through the lens of the Christian faith. Indeed, the institution of antitrust connects with the Christian faith in several ways. The historical foundation of antitrust finds its roots in the Christian thinkers of the Scholastic tradition, the Reformation movement, and the Scottish Enlightenment. Adam Smith, the patron saint of economics, was himself influenced by the Presbyterian clergymen of the Scottish Enlightenment. Smith's "simple and obvious system of natural liberty" has been codified with the most famous metaphor in all of the social sciences: *the invisible hand*. It is this "simple and obvious system of natural liberty" – Smith's invisible hand – which modern antitrust endeavors to protect and promote.[90]

The themes of antitrust, such as rationality, equity, efficiency, competition, and innovation, are all congruent with biblical foundations and Christian principles. This chapter also explores a triad of contemporary applications of Christian thinking and antitrust litigation: cartelization, mergers, and economic dominance. Overall, we illustrate the deep interconnectedness – historically, thematically, and contemporarily – of the Christian faith with antitrust as a discipline.

[90] Adam Smith's less well-known *The Theory of Moral Sentiments* can be read as a bridge between the Christian ethics of Hutcheson and the secular ethics of Hume. The many attempts to exegete what the discipline of economics means by the pursuit of self-interest is derivative of Smith's endeavor to mediate between Hume's dismissal of a supernaturally grounded basis for ethics and Hutcheson's insistence on a revelation revealed basis for morality.

# 5

# Christianity and Corporate Purpose

STEPHEN M. BAINBRIDGE

The 2020 Democratic Presidential nomination contest was unique in recent American history in that multiple candidates explicitly embraced social democracy and, in Bernie Sanders' case, even outright socialism. Given the political importance of social democracy in many other Western economies, it seems curious that it has not played a significant role in American politics up to now. Various explanations have been offered for that failure,[1] but one especially provocative explanation for it is the success of the American public corporation.

John Micklethwait and Adrian Wooldridge quote German sociologist Werner Sombart's observation that "on the reefs of roast beef and apple pie socialist utopias of every sort are sent to their doom."[2] In turn, they argue, those reefs existed because of the general rise in prosperity – despite frequent panics and slumps – associated with the emergence of large industrial corporations. These "new companies plainly improved the living standards of millions of ordinary people, putting the luxuries of the rich within the reach of the man in the street."[3] In addition, as Michael Novak likewise observed, rising prosperity made possible by the tremendous new wealth created by industrial corporations was a major factor in destroying arbitrary class distinctions, enhancing personal and social mobility.[4] Many of the wealthiest

William D. Warren, Distinguished Professor of Law, UCLA School of Law. Thanks to David A. Skeel for very helpful comments.

1 See, e.g., Seymour Martin Lipset and Gary Marks, *It Didn't Happen Here: Why Socialism Failed in the United States* (New York: W.W. Norton, 2001).

2 John Micklethwait and Adrian Wooldridge, *The Company: A Short History of a Revolutionary Idea* (London: Phoenix, 2005), p. 77.

3 Ibid.

4 Michael Novak, *Toward a Theology of the Corporation* (Washington: The AEI Press, 1990), p. 42.

businessmen of the latter half of the nineteenth century began their careers as laborers rather than as scions of coupon-clipping plutocrats. It was difficult for the class struggle to take hold when virtually every laborer hoped to also become a millionaire someday.

The rise of modern corporations did more than just expand the economic pie. The legal system that facilitated their rise necessarily allowed individuals freedom to pursue the accumulation of wealth. Economic liberty, in turn, proved a necessary concomitant of personal liberty – the two have almost always marched hand-in-hand. In turn, the modern public corporation has turned out to be a powerful engine for focusing the efforts of individuals to maintain the requisite sphere of economic liberty. Those whose livelihood depends on corporate enterprise cannot be neutral about political systems. Only democratic capitalist societies permit voluntary formation of private corporations and allot them a sphere of economic liberty within which to function, which gives those who value such enterprises a powerful incentive to resist both statism and socialism. As Novak observed, private property and freedom of contract were indispensable if private business corporations were to come into existence.[5] In turn, the corporation gave liberty economic substance over and against the state.

Other commentators, however, paint a far less rosy picture. Critics claim that "individuals with antisocial tendencies are overrepresented in the ranks of corporate leaders," as "a sub-category of so-called 'successful psychopaths' may be more adept at climbing the corporate ladder than most others."[6] Indeed, the corporation itself has been described as a "dangerous psychopath" relentlessly pursuing the economic self-interest of its managers and shareholders regardless of the consequences to others.[7] At the very least, corporations have proven effective engines for generating externalities.[8] In the wake of the significant disruptions caused by the financial crisis of 2008 and the resultant Great Recession, these criticisms have taken on renewed weight, as illustrated by the pervasive skepticism of large corporations exhibited in the 2020 Democratic primaries.

5 Ibid., p. 45.

6 Renee M. Jones, "The Irrational Actor in the CEO Suite: Implications for Corporate Governance," *Delaware Journal of Corporate Law*, vol. 41 (2017), pp. 713, 721.

7 Joel Bakan, *The Corporation: The Pathological Pursuit of Profit and Power* (New York: Free Press, 2005).

8 *Territory of U.S. Virgin Islands* v. *Goldman, Sachs & Co.*, 937 A.2d 760, 795 (Del. Ch. 2007), aff'd, 956 A.2d 32 (Del. 2008) ("equity holders often take profits that are inflated by externalities foisted by their corporations").

This debate plays out in various aspects of corporate governance but especially with respect to the purpose of the corporation. One school of thought argues, as Milton Friedman famously opined, that the social responsibility of business is to increase its profit.[9] The other school of thought contends that corporations can and should "strengthen the society which gives them existence."[10]

Because "Catholicism is an 'incarnational faith' that sees God in everything, and the Gospel is a living message, intended to be infused into the reality of the world in which we live,"[11] it is important for those of us who are Catholic "to ask the question whether there is a Catholic vision of the corporation."[12] That question is pertinent to non-Catholics as well, because "all who are concerned with the moral and religious quality of human systems should find [the Catholic social] tradition both instructive in itself and parallel to developments in their own intellectual histories."[13]

As the United States' largest religious faith, where Catholicism comes down on the corporation and its proper purpose, also has political and economic significance. If the Church were solely concerned with changing the hearts and minds of ruthless businessmen, it would have little relevance to the study of corporate law and governance outside of business ethics classes at Catholic schools. In fact, however, the US Conference of Catholic Bishops' well-known 1986 pastoral letter on economic justice explicitly stated the Bishops'

9 Milton Friedman, "The Social Responsibility of Business Is to Increase Its Profits," *N.Y. Times*, September 13, 1970, sec. SM, p. 12.

10 *A. P. Smith Mfg. Co.* v. *Barlow*, 98 A.2d 581, 590 (N.J. 1953).

11 Susan J. Stabile, "A Catholic Vision of the Corporation," *Seattle Journal for Social Justice*, vol. 4 (2005), p. 181.

12 Ibid.

13 Michael Novak, *Catholic Social Thought & Liberal Institutions: Freedom with Justice*, 2nd ed. (New Brunswick, NJ: Transaction Publishers, 1989), p. xxiii. Having said that, however, it should be noted that some skeptical commentators have argued that moral treatises – including those based on Catholic Social Thought – are unhelpful in dealing with practical problems of business ethics. Scott Fitzgibbon, "'True Human Community': Catholic Social Thought, Aristotelian Ethics, and the Moral Order of the Business Company," *St. Louis University Law Journal*, vol. 45 (2001), pp. 1247, 1252. My own view is that although "broad amorphous statements of moral norms typical of Catholic social teaching (and much commentary thereon) are a blunt instrument poorly suited to the sort of fine detail work demanded of lawyers, judges, and legislators," they can be useful in thinking about big picture questions such as that of the corporations' proper purpose. Stephen M. Bainbridge, "The Bishops and the Corporate Stakeholder Debate," *Villanova Journal of Law and Investment Management*, vol. 4, no. 1 (2002), pp. 3, 6. Put another way, broad statements of moral norms may not help us decide whether the capacity within which one learns of a corporate opportunity should be relevant to whether one may take that opportunity without breaching one's fiduciary duty, but they can help us decide whether or not self-dealing ought to be permissible.

intent "to add our voice to the public debate."[14] Likewise, the key "papal documents have consistently recognized that there is a role for law in regulating the economy,"[15] while positing the pertinence of Catholic social thought to debates over how the law should do so. Catholic social teaching and the law of corporate purpose thus inevitably join together in a normative dialectic.

## 5.1 THE DISTINCTION BETWEEN USURY AND PROFIT IN SCRIPTURE AND TRADITION

Scripture has relatively little to say of direct relevance to modern incorporated business. To the contrary, the scriptures were written in and reflect the concerns of a predominantly agrarian economy, although trade was becoming more important in Christ's time than it had been in early Israel.[16] Likewise, Tradition has little to say about modern corporations. Until the groundbreaking work done by Saint Pope John Paul II in his papal encyclicals on the economy, Catholic social thought – the part of the Church's tradition most directly pertinent to questions of corporate social responsibility – comprised mainly nostalgic yearning for a long dead agrarian economy.[17]

Having said that, however, both Scripture and Tradition offer important broad normative principles that inform certain questions of corporate governance. Perhaps the most famous of their economic dictates is the proscription of usury. The Old Testament contains a number of strong condemnations of usury, such as:

- Do not exact interest in advance or accrued interest, but out of fear of God let your kindred live with you.[18]
- You shall not demand interest from your kindred on a loan of money or of food or of anything else which is loaned.[19]
- I myself, my kindred, and my attendants have lent the people money and grain without charge. Let us put an end to this usury![20]

[14] National Conference of Catholic Bishops, *Economic Justice for All: Pastoral Letter on Catholic Social Teaching and the U.S. Economy* (Washington, DC: National Conference of Catholic Bishops, 1986), p. 27.

[15] Stabile, "Catholic Vision," p. 194.

[16] Edd S. Noell, "A 'Marketless World'? An Examination of Wealth and Exchange in the Gospels and First-Century Palestine," *Journal of Markets & Morality*, vol. 10 (2007), pp. 85, 92–98.

[17] Novak, *Liberal Institutions*, p. 24.

[18] Leviticus 25:36 (NAB).

[19] Deuteronomy 23:19 (NAB).

[20] Nehemiah 5:10 (NAB).

- There are those in you who take bribes to shed blood. You exact interest and usury; you extort profit from your neighbor by violence. But me you have forgotten – oracle of the Lord GOD.[21]

Although the New Testament contains no such comparable prohibitions, the Church Fathers early on incorporated the Judaic ban on usury into Christian doctrine.[22]

The definition of usury in Jewish law at the time of Christ was complex and highly manipulable.[23] At its core, however, was moneylending – i.e., the extension of a loan to be repaid with interest.[24] This remained the core definition of usury in Catholicism at least until the nineteenth century. Although some commentators deny that Church teaching on usury has evolved towards a more permissive attitude to usury is somewhat controversial, it seems clear that modern Catholic social thought defines usury simply as "the acquiring of gain and profit in the situation where one did not undertake any effort or incur any expense or risk."[25] Because most lenders take on some risk, the modern prohibition thus is largely limited to excessive rates.

Critically for our purposes, however, the ban on usury was not driven by antagonism toward profit. Scripture contains a number of favorable references to profitmaking. In Matthew 13:45, for example, Christ compared "the kingdom of heaven" to "a merchant searching for fine pearls," which would be an odd analogy if trade were inherently sinful. In the Apocrypha, Wisdom 14:1–2 recognized that "one preparing for a voyage" is motivated by "the urge for profits."

The Parable of the Talents is especially pertinent to our discussion.[26] The goal of Jesus' parables was to stimulate thought, encourage people to think for themselves, and thus to puzzle out religious mysteries. In order to facilitate that process, parables were told as if they were true tales – even if sometimes highly improbable ones – that the listeners could accept as factual bases from which to extrapolate theological lessons. Put another way, Jesus' parables were effective as

[21] Ezekiel 22:2 (NAB). For a more comprehensive list of Old Testament prohibitions of usury, see William Woodyard and Chad G. Marzen, "Is Greed Good? A Catholic Perspective on Modern Usury," *BYU Journal of Public Law*, vol. 27 (2012), pp. 185, 192–193.

[22] John D. Skees, "The Resurrection of Historic Usury Principles for Consumption Loans in a Federal Banking System," *Catholic University Law Review*, vol. 55 (2006), pp. 1131, 1142–1144.

[23] J. Duncan M. Derrett, *Law in the New Testament* (Eugene, OR: Wipf & Stock, 2005), pp. 65–66.

[24] As Derrett observes, the law, "according to the rabbis of the Pharisees, provided by direct enactment that loans at interest by Jews to Jews were unlawful." Ibid., p. 56.

[25] Woodyard and Marzen, "Is Greed Good?," p. 200.

[26] Matthew 25:14–30.

teaching tools precisely because his listeners "could readily identify with the roles people filled, work that they did, relations that were broken and restored, losses they sustained and happiness they experienced."[27] The Parable of the Talents thus likely was premised on a legal backstory about the fiduciary duties of servants that would have been well understood by those who heard the Parable, which permits us to draw inferences about the contents of that background law. The master clearly believed that his servants had an obligation to affirmatively advance his best interests. In particular, the master evidently believed his servants had a duty not only to preserve his funds but also to affirmatively deploy them in trade so as to increase their value.[28] Accordingly, the Parable can be understood as implicitly endorsing the expectation that a business should show a profit. It contrasts the satisfaction of the capitalist when his agents invested his funds profitably to God's satisfaction when his faithful get "on with the very serious business of doing God's bidding."[29]

To be sure, some early Christian theologians condemned profitmaking. To Chrysostom, for example, it was illicit to sell a good "entire and unchanged" at a profit.[30] Even under this restrictive view, moreover, it was licit to sell for a profit something that one had improved.[31] In contrast, Aquinas suggested that trading for profit was, at worst, neutral and could be commendable when the gains are spent on charity or some other virtuous end.[32] In some situations, the Church has even used the profit motive to induce desired behavior. For example, "the papacy held out the prospects for economic gain as a motivation for Crusaders from the very first crusade."[33] Today, the Catechism endorses profitmaking, explaining that profits "make possible the investments that ensure the future of a business and they guarantee employment."[34]

Why do Scripture and Tradition treat profits from moneylending as problematic while endorsing profitmaking in general? The Biblical condemnation

[27] Simon J. Kistemaker, "Jesus as Story Teller: Literary Perspectives on the Parables," *Masters Seminary Journal*, vol. 16 (2006), pp. 49, 52.

[28] Stephen M. Bainbridge, "Parable of the Talents," in *Research Handbook on Fiduciary Law*, eds. D. Gordon Smith and Andrew S. Gold (Cheltenham: Edward Elgar, 2018), p. 97.

[29] Derrett, *Law in the New Testament*, p. 279.

[30] Thomas Aquinas, "Of Justice and Cheating," in *On Moral Business: Classical and Contemporary Resources for Ethics in Economic Life*, eds. Max L. Stackhouse, Dennis P. McCann, Shirley J. Roels, and Preston N. Williams (Grand Rapids, MI: William B, Eerdmans Publishing, 1995), p. 167.

[31] Ibid., p. 168.

[32] Ibid.

[33] Robert B. Ekelund et al., *Sacred Trust: The Medieval Church as an Economic Firm* (New York: Oxford University Press, 1996), p. 132.

[34] United States Catholic Conference, *Catechism of the Catholic Church*, 2nd ed. (Washington, DC: United States Catholic Conference, 1997), p. 2432.

of usury reflects God's special concern for the poor, being grounded in "the deep and consistent message of the Bible demanding kind and just treatment of poor and vulnerable members of society."[35] The Church Fathers thus condemned usury in large part because they believed it led to oppression of the poor. In particular, indebtedness could lead to slavery,[36] as illustrated by the Parable of the Unfaithful Servant, in which a king decided to settle accounts with his servants. One of the servants was unable to repay a large debt, so the king "ordered him to be sold, along with his wife, his children, and all his property, in payment of the debt."[37]

In contrast, a profitable business can lift up the poor. A transaction familiar to the Jews of Christ's time was the capital services partnership, in which a wealthy capitalist invested funds with a merchant or other entrepreneur who lacked funds and eventually shared the profits between them. It was regarded at the time as "good to offer such a partnership to a poor man."[38] The Church likewise has long accepted the legitimacy of partnerships in which one partner put up capital and the other provides labor. The prohibition of usury thus was not intended to prohibit gaining profits that could be fairly characterized as reimbursement for one's efforts and risk-taking.[39] Accordingly, as the Compendium of the Social Doctrine of the Church explains, while "recourse to usury is to be morally condemned ... the quest for equitable profit is acceptable in economic and financial activity."[40]

## 5.2 PROFITMAKING VERSUS PROFIT MAXIMIZATION

The Church's endorsement of profit is not unconstrained. Indeed, as Pope Benedict XVI taught, "[t]reating human activity – including economic activity – as a purely technical matter leads to 'confusion between ends and means,

35 Christopher L. Peterson, "'Warning: Predatory Lender' – A Proposal for Candid Predatory Small Loan Ordinances," *Washington & Lee Law Review*, vol. 69 (2012), pp. 893, 978.

36 John Thomas Noonan, *A Church That Can and Cannot Change: The Development of Catholic Moral Teaching* (Notre Dame, IN: University of Notre Dame Press, 2005), p. 130. The prohibition of usury also rested on a philosophical argument drawn from Aristotle about whether money could bear offspring and another by Aquinas that use and value cannot be distinguished, both of which are beyond the scope of this essay. Murray N. Rothbard, *An Austrian Perspective on the History of Economic Thought*, vol. 1 (Auburn, AL: Ludwig von Mises Institute, 2006). See generally John Thomas Noonan, *The Scholastic Analysis of Usury* (Cambridge, MA: Harvard University Press, 1957).

37 Matthew 18:25 (NAB).

38 Derrett, *Law in the New Testament*, p. 20.

39 Ekelund et al., *Sacred Trust*, p. 116.

40 *Compendium of the Social Doctrine of the Church* (Washington, DC: United States Conference of Catholic Bishops, 2005), p. 341.

such that the sole criterion for action in business is thought to be the maximization of profit.'"[41]

> The Church acknowledges the legitimate role of profit as an indication that a business is functioning well. When a firm makes a profit, this means that productive factors have been properly employed and corresponding human needs have been duly satisfied. But profitability is not the only indicator of a firm's condition. It is possible for the financial accounts to be in order, and yet for the people – who make up the firm's most valuable asset – to be humiliated and their dignity offended. Besides being morally inadmissible, this will eventually have negative repercussions on the firm's economic efficiency. In fact, the purpose of a business firm is not simply to make a profit, but is to be found in its very existence as a community of persons who in various ways are endeavouring [sic] to satisfy their basic needs, and who form a particular group at the service of the whole of society. Profit is a regulator of the life of a business, but it is not the only one; other human and moral factors must also be considered which, in the long term, are at least equally important for the life of a business.[42]

Church teaching thus draws a sharp distinction between the pursuit of profit as a business goal and treating profit maximization as the purpose of a business.

Why does the Church draw this distinction? On the one hand, there is a concern for the manager whose relentless pursuit of profit leads him into sin. In the Scriptures, Jesus repeatedly warns of the temptations faced by those whose work is focused on building wealth. The Medieval Church had considerable experience with the potential risks associated with amassing great wealth, having seen how Cistercian monasteries became increasingly corrupt as their economic profits grew.[43] On the other hand, Scripture is also concerned with the social consequences of a rich man's cupidity. Avarice leads the rich man to breach the Biblical command to love one's neighbor. In the context of a modern industrial economy, that command manifests itself as a concern that pursuit of profit will lead the owner to overwork or otherwise oppress the firm's workers and other stakeholders.

We see this concern expressed even more profoundly in the Church Fathers and, especially, post-Rerum Novarum Catholic social thought. Most

[41] Pope Benedict XVI, *Caritas in Veritate*, June 29, 2009, http://w2.vatican.va/content/benedict-xvi/en/encyclicals/documents/hf_ben-xvi_enc_20090629_caritas-in-veritate.html,71.

[42] Pope John Paul II, *Centesimus Annus*, May 1, 1991, p. 35, http://w2.vatican.va/content/john-paul-ii/en/encyclicals/documents/hf_jp-ii_enc_01051991_centesimus-annus.html.

[43] Ekelund et al., *Sacred Trust*, p. 45.

of the early Church Fathers were still embedded in a primarily agrarian economy, in which land was the source of all wealth. They understood the Scriptures to teach that land was originally a gift from God to all but observed that land in Roman society was increasingly concentrated in the hands of fewer and fewer wealthy magnates. In response, they developed the concept of a social mortgage. While many of the Fathers (albeit not all) recognized, as does the modern Church, a right to private property, they qualified that right by insisting that one's use of the land had to be socially responsible.[44] It was a modest step from that underlying principle to the notion that the profits of economic activity generally likewise must be devoted to the common good.

The Church thus teaches that the pursuit of profit maximization without regard to the common good "reflects a misunderstanding of the very concept of the economy."[45] Properly understood, profitmaking "is useful if it serves as a means towards an end that provides a sense both of how to produce it and how to make good use of it. Once profit becomes the exclusive goal, if it is produced by improper means and without the common good as its ultimate end, it risks destroying wealth and creating poverty."[46] In modern society, "the all-consuming desire for profit" and "the thirst for power" thus are closely related sins that are opposed to the will of God and the common good.[47]

## 5.3 TRANSLATING CHURCH TEACHING ON PROFIT INTO CORPORATE GOVERNANCE TERMS

In his encyclical *Laudato Si'*, Pope Francis built on the teaching laid out in the preceding part to ask whether it is "realistic to hope that those who are obsessed with maximizing profits will stop to reflect on the environmental damage which they will leave behind for future generations?"[48] His answer was that the pursuit of profit maximization made such hope unrealistic. Those who are concerned solely with profit maximization ignore "the rhythms of

44 Albino Barrera, *Economic Compulsion and Christian Ethics* (Cambridge: Cambridge University Press, 2007), p. 95. Hence, for example, the Medieval Church condemned price-fixing and monopolies, believing that the profits therefrom came at the expense of exploited consumers. Ekelund et al., *Sacred Trust*, p. 123.

45 Pope Francis, *Laudato Si'*, May 24, 2015, p. 195, http://w2.vatican.va/content/francesco/en/encyclicals/documents/papa-francesco_20150524_enciclica-laudato-si.html.

46 Pope Benedict XI, *Caritas in Veritate*, p. 21.

47 Pope John Paul II, *Sollicitudo Rei Socialis*, December 30, 1987, p. 37, http://w2.vatican.va/content/john-paul-ii/en/encyclicals/documents/hf_jp-ii_enc_30121987_sollicitudo-rei-socialis.html.

48 Pope Francis, *Laudato Si'*, p. 190.

nature, its phases of decay and regeneration, or the complexity of ecosystems which may be gravely upset by human intervention."[49]

> As long as production is increased, little concern is given to whether it is at the cost of future resources or the health of the environment; as long as the clearing of a forest increases production, no one calculates the losses entailed in the desertification of the land, the harm done to biodiversity or the increased pollution. In a word, businesses profit by calculating and paying only a fraction of the costs involved.[50]

In economic terms, of course, Pope Francis is describing the problem of externalities. Like all businesses, corporations inevitably externalize some costs onto others. By virtue of their potential size and complexity, however, corporations are an especially powerful generator of externalized costs. Almost as soon as the modern large corporation emerged in the latter half of the nineteenth century, abuses and scandals became rampant.[51] Even absent outright abuses, corporations will still externalize costs. Although large corporations are run not by their shareholder-owners, but rather by the board of directors and, especially, by the managers to whom the board delegates operational authority, management will generally make decisions that advance shareholders' interests.[52] As a result, even though many corporate actions have deleterious effects on some stakeholders, the interests of those stakeholders are rarely taken into account.[53]

While there is not much dispute over the question of whether corporations should be induced to internalize the costs it would otherwise impose on society, there is great dispute over how best to accomplish that goal. As might be expected from our review of Church teaching, the Church has come down squarely on the side of those who advocate corporate social responsibility.

The most explicit endorsement of corporate social responsibility came in the US Catholic Bishops' 1997 pastoral letter on economic justice, in which the Bishops asserted that a board of directors' decisions affect a much broader class of constituency groups than merely their shareholders. Employees, managers, customers, creditors, suppliers, and communities all contribute to

49 Ibid.

50 Ibid., p. 195.

51 The nineteenth-century scandals are described in detail in David Skeel, *Icarus in the Boardroom: The Fundamental Flaws in Corporate America and Where They Came From* (New York: Oxford University Press, 2005).

52 Manuel G. Velasquez, "Ethics, Religion, and the Modern Business Corporation," in *The Catholic Challenge to the American Economy: Reflections on the U.S. Bishops Pastoral Letter on Catholic Social Teaching and the U.S. Economy, with the Final Text of the Pastoral Letter*, ed. Thomas M. Gannon (New York: Macmillan, 1987), pp. 55, 73.

53 Ibid., pp. 73–74.

the enterprise, all have a stake in its success, and all are affected by its actions. Hence, the corporate decision-making process must also reflect their interests. To be sure, the Bishops acknowledged the directors' and officers' legal obligation to maximize shareholder wealth. They argued, however, that "morally this legal responsibility may be exercised only within the bounds of justice to employees, customers, suppliers, and the local community."[54] In other words, corporate decision-makers have a moral obligation to balance a decision's impact on stakeholders against its economic impact on shareholders.

In order to operationalize those broad statements of principle, the Bishops proposed several institutional changes to corporate governance designed to promote stakeholder participation in firm decision-making. For example, they urged greater use of worker ownership and worker determinism.[55] They also urged labor unions to explore new relationships with management.[56]

The Bishops' Letter was extremely controversial.[57] But while its specific policy proposals probably do not have Magisterial status, the basic principle of corporate social responsibility has been incorporated into the Magisterium. The *Compendium of the Social Doctrine of the Church*, for example, states that:

- "It is essential that within a business the legitimate pursuit of profit should be in harmony with the irrenounceable protection of the dignity of the people who work at different levels in the same company."[58]
- "Due to the increasing complexity of business activities, decisions made by companies produce a number of very significant interrelated effects, both in the economic and social spheres. For this reason the exercise of responsibility by business owners and management requires – in addition to specific updating that is the object of continuous efforts – constant reflection on the moral motivations that should guide the personal choices of those to whom these tasks fall."[59]
- "Business owners and management must not limit themselves to taking into account only the economic objectives of the company, the criteria for economic efficiency and the proper care of 'capital' as the sum of the means of production."[60]

54 National Conference of Catholic Bishops, *Economic Justice for All*, p. 305.
55 Ibid., p. 300.
56 Ibid., p. 304.
57 Stephen M. Bainbridge, "Corporate Decisionmaking and the Moral Rights of Employees: Participatory Management and Natural Law," *Villanova Law Review*, vol. 43 (1999), p. 741.
58 *Compendium of the Social Doctrine*, p. 340.
59 Ibid., p. 344.
60 Ibid.

The Catechism likewise teaches that business owners and managers "are responsible to society for the economic and ecological effects of their operations. They have an obligation to consider the good of persons and not only the increase of profits."[61]

## 5.4 THE LAW OF CORPORATE PURPOSE

At least in Delaware – the premier state in American corporate law – the law and Catholic social thought appear to stand in sharp opposition. Unlike the latter, Delaware law of corporate purpose is well settled in favor of shareholder wealth maximization.[62] Directors have a fiduciary duty to sustainably maximize shareholder wealth over such time horizon as the board deems fit.[63] Numerous Delaware cases have so held.[64] True, many commentators have sought to explain away or otherwise distinguish these decisions, but as former Delaware Chief Justice Leo Strine explained in detail, "[T]hese

[61] *Catechism*, p. 2432.

[62] See, e.g., Alan J. Meese, "The Team Production Theory of Corporate Law: A Critical Assessment," *William & Mary Law Review*, vol. 43 (2003), pp. 1629, 1702 ("Delaware, at least, has apparently decided that the principal-agent model, and with it the shareholder primacy norm, is superior to alternative models of corporate governance."); David G. Yosifon, "The Law of Corporate Purpose," *Berkeley Business Law Journal*, vol. 10 (2013), pp. 181, 184 ("Delaware demands shareholder primacy in corporate governance."). I have elsewhere insisted that "the terms shareholder primacy and shareholder wealth maximization" should not be used interchangeably, because the former encompasses both the latter and a claim that shareholders do (or should) control the corporation. Stephen M. Bainbridge, "Director v. Shareholder Primacy in the Convergence Debate," *Transnational Lawyer*, vol. 16 (2002), pp. 45, 47. I therefore agree with David Yosifon's argument that "[w]e should stop using 'shareholder primacy' to refer to both purpose and means. It inhibits clear expression and exchange of ideas." David G. Yosifon, *Corporate Friction: How Corporate Law Impedes American Progress and What to Do about It* (Cambridge: Cambridge University Press, 2018), p. 1.

[63] See Leo E. Strine, "Our Continuing Struggle with the Idea That For-Profit Corporations Seek Profit," *Wake Forest Law Review*, vol. 47 (2012), pp. 135, 155 (observing that "corporate law requires directors, as a matter of their duty of loyalty, to pursue a good faith strategy to maximize profits for the stockholders").

[64] See, e.g., *In re Trados Inc. S'holder Litig.*, 73 A.3d 17, 20 (Del. Ch. 2013) ("Directors of a Delaware corporation owe fiduciary duties to the corporation and its stockholders which require that they strive prudently and in good faith to maximize the value of the corporation for the benefit of its residual claimants."); *eBay Domestic Holdings, Inc.* v. *Newmark*, 16 A.3d 1, 34 (Del. Ch. 2010) (stating that "the fiduciary duties and standards that accompany [the corporate] form … include acting to promote the value of the corporation for the benefit of its stockholders"); *TW Servs., Inc.* v. *SWT Acq. Corp.*, 1989 WL 20290, at *7 (Del. Ch. March 2, 1989) (stating that it is "non-controversial" that, "broadly, directors may be said to owe a duty to shareholders as a class to manage the corporation within the law, with due care and in a way intended to maximize the long run interests of shareholders").

commentators essentially argue that Delaware judges do not understand the very law they are applying."[65]

## 5.5 RECONCILING THE LAW OF GOD AND OF MAN

Delaware corporate law and Catholic social teaching seem to express incompatible visions of corporate purpose. The Church allows the pursuit of profit – arguably somewhat begrudgingly – but teaches that seeking to maximize profit leads to illicit externalities. The law seemingly commands that a corporation's directors and managers maximize shareholder profits without regard to those externalities.

In fact, however, the conflict is more apparent than real. First, business decisions rarely involve a choice between profit and environmental catastrophe. To the contrary, most business decisions are win-win situations in which the size of the economic pie gets bigger for everyone. Second, corporate law requires directors and officers to conduct the business within the bounds of law,[66] which imposes substantial constraints on a corporation's ability to externalize costs onto society.[67] Finally, corporate law does not require directors and managers to maximize short-term profit at the expense of the long term. To the contrary, in most situations, the law allows corporate decision-makers to focus on long-term, sustainable growth of profits.[68]

In such situations, the business judgment rule provides directors with substantial discretion to balance competing considerations.[69] Suppose a board

[65] Leo E. Strine, "The Dangers of Denial: The Need for a Clear-Eyed Understanding of the Power and Accountability Structure Established by the Delaware General Corporation Law," *Wake Forest Law Review*, vol. 50 (2015), pp. 761, 766–767. See also Yosifon, "Corporate Purpose," p. 184 (arguing that "the black letter law of corporate governance is shareholder primacy" and identifying "the missteps that ... other scholars have made in interpreting that doctrine").

[66] *Guttman* v. *Huang*, 823 A.2d 492, 506 (Del. Ch. 2003). ("[O]ne cannot act loyally as a corporate director by causing the corporation to violate the positive laws it is obliged to obey.")

[67] Some commentators argue that the Supreme Court's decision in *Citizens United* v. *FEC*, 558 U.S. 310 (2010), allows corporations to evade those constraints by making "political expenditures to elect candidates supportive of lax regulation." Leo E. Strine and Nicholas Walter, "Conservative Collision Course?: The Tension between Conservative Corporate Law Theory and Citizens United," *Cornell Law Review*, vol. 100 (2015), pp. 335, 343). I have elsewhere explained why that argument is flawed. See Stephen M. Bainbridge, "Corporate Social Responsibility in the Night-Watchman State," *Columbia Law Review Sidebar*, vol. 115 (2015), p. 39.

[68] Strine, *Dangers of Denial*, pp. 772–773.

[69] *Lewis* v. *Anderson*, 615 F.2d 778, 781 (9th Cir. 1979) ("The business judgment rule applies to all discretionary decisions by the board "), cert. denied, 449 U.S. 869 (1980); *Gaillard* v. *Natomas Co.*, 256 Cal. Rptr. 702, 710 (Cal. App. 1st Dist. 1989). ("The common law 'business judgment

of directors is advised that short-term profit could be maximized by closing an antiquated plant in a US Rust Belt state. Updating the plant will reduce short-term profits but will benefit various stakeholders and also produce substantial gains for shareholders in the future. If the board chooses to update the plant and that decision is challenged by a shareholder, the business judgment rule will give the board legal cover.[70]

The business judgment rule, however, has no application where the board of directors is disabled by conflicted interests.[71] In such cases, concern for director accountability trumps protection of their discretionary authority. In corporate takeovers, for example, a well-known conflict of interest taints target company director decision-making. Not surprisingly, therefore, the law denies directors the discretion to consider the interests of non-shareholder constituencies in the takeover setting. Under the Delaware supreme court's decision in *Revlon, Inc.* v. *MacAndrews & Forbes Holdings, Inc.*,[72] a target's board of directors may not protect stakeholder interests at the expense of shareholder interests.[73] Rather, any management action benefiting stakeholders must produce ancillary shareholder benefits. In addition, once an auction of corporate control begins, stakeholders become entirely irrelevant. In such an auction, short-term shareholder wealth maximization is the board's only appropriate concern. Indeed, in this context, considering any factors other than shareholder wealth violates the board's fiduciary duties.[74]

There is thus a small set of business decisions in which corporate law requires directors to take actions that Catholic social teaching condemns. Yet, one can argue that corporate law is consistent with the broader principles of that teaching.

rule' refers to a judicial policy of deference to the business judgment of corporate directors in the exercise of their broad discretion in making corporate decisions.")

70 As Professor Branson observes, "the types of decisions ordinarily given business judgment rule protection include directors decisions to make an acquisition or build a new plant." Douglas M. Branson, "The Rule That Isn't a Rule – The Business Judgment Rule," *Valapariso University Law Review*, vol. 36 (2002), pp. 631, 649. Similarly, Professor Simmons explains that "routine operational decisions, such as the decision to build a foreign production plant or what products to produce, are protected under state law through the business judgment rule." Omari Scott Simmons, "The Corporate Immune System: Governance from the Inside Out," *University of Illinois Law Review*, vol. 2013 (2013), pp. 1131, 1159.

71 *Bayer* v. *Beran*, 49 N.Y.S.2d 2, 6 (Sup. Ct. 1944) (explaining: "The 'business judgment rule' … yields to the rule of undivided loyalty. This great rule of law is designed 'to avoid the possibility of fraud and to avoid the temptation of self-interest.'").

72 506 A.2d 173 (Del. 1986).

73 Ibid., p. 182.

74 Ibid., p. 185.

It is one thing for a sole proprietor to decide that agapic love should be his or her guiding star in making business decisions. When they choose a less profitable course of conduct for altruistic reasons, they are in effect spending their own money. In contrast, when a corporate director or manager does so, he or she is spending someone else's money and therein lies a critical difference.

Why does Catholic social teaching fail to draw that distinction? Part of the problem is that Catholic social teaching lacks a fully realized theology of the corporation. It speaks of business without making fine distinctions between the various types of legal entities secular civil law allows a business to be organized. In particular, Catholic social teaching largely ignores the separation of ownership and control characteristic of American corporations as well as the agency costs that arise from that separation.

As a result, the Church basically says that it is morally proper for managers to spend other people's money – i.e., the shareholder's residual claim on corporate assets and earnings – to advance management's chosen objectives. The implicit assumption is that management will make the ethically correct choice. In effect, Catholic social thought appears to assume that men are angels.

In contrast, the law declines to assume that directors and managers are angels. The law thus recognizes the legal regime "must be based on a certain realism about human beings and, therefore, on a theory of sin and a praxis for dealing with it."[75] Here, the sin in question is that of self-interest. While corporate social responsibility empowers honest directors to act in the best interests of all the corporation's constituents, it also empowers dishonest directors to pursue their own self-interest. There is a very real risk that directors and managers given discretion to consider interests other than shareholder wealth maximization will use stakeholder interests as a cloak for actions taken to advance their own selfish interests.[76]

[75] Novak, *Toward a Theology*, p. 22.

[76] One problem for any system of business ethics is how to make choices among competing interests in zero-sum situations, in which any decision will leave some stakeholders worse off. How does one prioritize the interests of the many different stakeholders in a large corporation? It might be objected that Catholic social thought gives managers too little guidance as to how to do so, because – like all stakeholder theories – it does not provide "the kind of systemic, prescriptive, prioritizing guidance that is so crisply present in shareholder wealth-maximization theory." Lee A. Tavis, "Modern Contract Theory and the Purpose of the Firm," in *Rethinking the Purpose of Business: Interdisciplinary Essays from the Catholic Social Tradition*, eds. S. A. Cortright and Michael J. Naughton (Notre Dame, IN: University of Notre Dame Press, 2002), pp. 215, 221. In fact, however, Catholic social thought offers two straightforward principles for prioritizing among stakeholders, namely, the preferential option for the poor and the special

The failure of Catholic social teaching to address this point is surprising. Christianity is not a utopian faith – rather it is quite realistic about human beings. In particular, the central doctrine of the Fall of Man tells a coherent story about the nature and origins of human preferences in an unredeemed world. To be sure, Christians are called to a higher standard of behavior than that of fallen man. In making social policy, we must remember that all have sinned. Consider the Parable of the Talents. The faithless steward put his own self-interest ahead of that of his master, which is precisely what faithless directors might do.

Accordingly, it is consistent with the Christian worldview to insist that a realistic social order must be designed around principles that fall short of Christian ideals. In particular, the rules must not be defined in ways that effectively require every citizen to be a practicing Christian. Christian visions of Justice therefore cannot determine the rules of economic order. Instead, legal rules and predictions about human behavior must assume the fallen state of Man.[77]

## 5.6 CONCLUSION

Insofar as prudential judgments about the economy are concerned, Saint Pope John Paul II emphasized that the "church has no models to present."[78]

position of workers within the firm. By itself, of course, this point does not disprove the validity of shareholder primacy as a normative guide for corporate decision-making; it simply eliminates one argument against Catholic social thought's wider perspective.

[77] The third servant in the Parable of the Talents illustrates this point quite nicely. Recall that the servant returned the talent with which he had been entrusted, telling his Master that "out of fear I went off and buried your talent in the ground" (Matthew 25:25). The Master took the talent away from the unfaithful servant, giving it to the servant with ten talents, and ordering that the "'useless servant [be cast] into the darkness outside, where there will be wailing and grinding of teeth'" (Matthew 25:30). Recognizing that human nature meant some of his servants might prove faithless, as did the third servant, that Master had given the servants discretion as to how the end of enhancing the Master's wealth was to be accomplished, but no discretion to change that duty. The unfaithful servant who did nothing to fulfill the mandate given him effectively ignored and thus de facto changed the assigned end. By exceeding the scope of his discretion, the servant disrespected his obligation and by extension his Master, which in turn may help explain the severity of the sanction imposed on the unfaithful servant. There is an interesting analogy here to *Dodge* v. *Ford Motor Co.*, 170 N.W. 668 (Mich. 1919), which held that "[t]he discretion of directors is to be exercised in the choice of means to attain that end [i.e., shareholder profit], and does not extend to a change in the end itself, to the reduction of profits, or to the nondistribution of profits among stockholders in order to devote them to other purposes." Ibid., p. 684. In effect, the court gave corporate directors the same command as did the Master in the Parable.

[78] Pope John Paul II, *Centesimus Annus*, p. 13.

The Church thus especially encourages lay initiative "when the matter involves discovering or inventing the means for permeating social, political, and economic realities with the demands of Christian doctrine and life."[79] As applied to the specific problem of corporate purpose, we have seen that the specifics of Church teaching are difficult to reconcile with those realities. In this instance, the law of man is more consistent with the Church's understanding of human nature than is Catholic social teaching on corporate purpose.

[79] *Catechism*, p. 899.

# 6

# Is Entrepreneurship Christian?

## *Theology, Market Structure, and the Ethics of Market Behavior*

ANDREW GODLEY

### 6.1 SETTING THE AGENDA

In recent years, entrepreneurship has become identified by policymakers across the spectrum as something unambiguously good to promote. Entrepreneurs promote innovation, innovation spurs wealth creation, and richer people have more fulfilling lives, runs the logic. In the context of what has been described as the " contained depression" of the ongoing financial crisis[1] – where macroeconomic policy levers appear to have been successful in placing a floor under economic collapse but are impotent in stimulating anything but slow economic growth – so entrepreneurship and innovation are further identified as potential solutions to the immediate and present danger of secular stagnation.

In the face of near universal support for entrepreneurship and innovation among policymakers, legitimized by strong consensus among academic economists, we might expect similar support from other leading commentators. But one section of society appears notably skeptical of the alleged benefits of entrepreneurship and market-related innovation: the church.

The outcome of the well-publicized Occupy London, St Paul's Cathedral protest camp in late 2011 to early 2012 suggested that many in the Church of England supported the anticapitalist movement's ideals. Former Archbishop of Canterbury Rowan Williams has decried modern market freedoms as "corrosive of morality," and policy debates "trapped in discussions about efficiency and the maximization of choice."[2] Pope

[1] Martin Wolf, "We Still Have That Sinking Feeling," *Financial Times*, July 10, 2012. www.ft.com/content/c57bod1e-ca81-11e1-89be-00144feabdco.

[2] Rowan Williams, "From Faust to Frankenstein," *Prospect*, April 23, 2012. www.prospectmagazine.co.uk/2012/04/from-faust-to-frankenstein/.

Francis in 2014 claimed free markets were a "new tyranny"![3] Such skepticism is not simply the immediate response to the financial crisis. A few years earlier, the World Alliance of Reformed Churches' Accra Declaration of 2004 equated economic freedom and entrepreneurial activity with neoliberal ideology, and formally called for this to be rejected as idolatry. This seemingly extreme perspective was received with sympathy from many church voices.[4] To academic economists almost all these criticisms are the products of naïveté at best, or a gross misjudgment of the human condition at worst.

This divergence in opinion between economists and policymakers, on the one hand, and large sections of the church, on the other hand, is worse than unhelpful. The most intractable of world problems and their solutions, ranging from the immediate (the consequences of reducing debt in the absence of growth) to longer term (feeding a growing global population and combating environmental degradation) are largely economic in nature. The moral authority of the worldwide orthodox Christian church carries tremendous force in shaping world opinion. Consider how unanimity within the church contributed to the articulation and astonishing progress toward the attainment of the United Nations' Millennium Development Goals, for instance. If the question in the title of this chapter was addressed seriously and constructively by the leading Christian denominations, the outcome would likely be hugely influential in addressing the response to the ongoing economic and environmental crises, either by constraining current policy consensus, or by offering an additional mandate with powerful moral underpinnings.

A different outcome would be felt among the world's growing community of academic Christian economists. As the Christian population of the world has grown so quickly over the past two decades or so, there has also been a spillover into the world's university campuses and faculties. The extraordinary growth of Christianity in much of Asia, Latin America, and sub-Saharan Africa has coincided with a rapid growth in university participation there. As far as we can tell, university faculties – including academic economists – around most

[3] *Telegraph*, "The Pope's Attack on Capitalism," June 17, 2014. www.telegraph.co.uk/finance/economics/10906849/The-Popes-attack-on-capitalism-shows-he-knows-nothing-about-how-the-world-really-works.html

[4] World Alliance of Reformed Churches, "Covenanting for Justice in the Economy and the Earth," Accra, Ghana, 2004; Peter Armstrong, *Critique of Entrepreneurship: People and Policy* (New York: Palgrave, 2005); Stan du Plessis, "How Can You Be a Christian and an Economist? The Meaning of the Accra Declaration for Today," Stellenbosch Economic Working Papers 02/10, University of Stellenbosch, 2010.

of the world are increasingly Christianized, drawn as they are from increasingly Christianized populations.[5]

Intellectually, however, economics is the social science that has become the most removed from its moral and ethical foundations as it has become ever more technical. The efficient markets hypothesis allows the models to work but at the cost of making a series of assumptions about the underlying ethics of market behavior, which are rarely properly articulated. An additional benefit of the church's constructive engagement with modern economics would be the intellectual support given to Christian economists in universities around the world wanting to reconnect the discipline with its moral underpinnings.

This chapter, therefore, aims to be a catalyst in stimulating informed and constructive debate on the relationship between Christianity and enterprise. The chapter proceeds following the normal convention of, first, defining terms. There is much necessary abbreviation here, given that entire libraries have been written on what economics and entrepreneurship are; and much of the history of Western civilization is a (frequently troubled) meditation on the meaning of Christianity! This is followed by a section outlining this Christian economist's attempt to develop a theology of entrepreneurship. Inevitably this involves me stepping outside my area of expertise, and so is offered tentatively but in the spirit of promoting dialogue. The chapter then goes on to discuss two governing ethical principles and highlights how criticisms of capitalism emerging from the church are often informed by the ethical principle of social justice. Economics, by contrast, as a system of thought privileges the ethical principle of autonomy. Moreover, because of key theoretical assumptions, consideration of the role of justice within economics is overwhelmingly passive. Herein lies a key to the current dialogue of the deaf between the church-based critics and economists and policymakers. Each side privileges a different ethical principle in addressing common problems. The chapter then goes on to show how a critique of entrepreneurship and entrepreneurial behavior informed by the principle of autonomy nevertheless highlights economic behavior unacceptable to both the Christian and the economic worldviews. Focusing on the ethical principle of autonomy then provides some insight into how Christian-informed ethics might help to inform economic thinking about – and policymaking for – a modern and complex world

5 There are sadly only fragmentary data. The best come from surveys of North American philosophy academics, where a quarter are now professing Christians, a remarkable increase from only 1 percent over thirty years ago (cited in Timothy Keller, *The Reason for God: Belief in an Age of Scepticism* [New York: Hodder, 2008], p. x).

economy. This is not to diminish concerns about market behavior informed by the principle of justice, but simply to assert that, because economics as a system of thought has largely assumed these problems away, it would seem sensible to begin a constructive dialogue on the basis of shared assumptions.

## 6.2 DEFINITIONS: ENTREPRENEURSHIP AND CHRISTIANITY

### 6.2.1 Entrepreneurship

The most widespread definition of entrepreneurship in the academic literature is that "entrepreneurship involves the nexus of two phenomena: the presence of lucrative opportunities and the presence of enterprising individuals."[6]

There are several important implications here. First is the presumption of the existence of modern economic institutions (the "lucrative opportunities"). This contains three axioms.

1. Individuals are self-aware, rational, and optimizers. They are able to specialize in activities to which they are most suited and then trade whatever product is surplus to their own requirements. Extending the principle of Smithian specialization across populations (Ricardian comparative advantage) means that everyone gains from cooperative trade.
2. Technological innovation increases productivity and so increases the output that can be traded through cooperative behavior. This also leads to net welfare gains.
3. In order for individuals to cooperate there must be institutions that facilitate cooperation. Overwhelmingly, this is through trading in markets (although firms and bureaucracies also allocate resources internally through their hierarchies). For markets to function efficiently and fairly, the property rights of market participants, buyers and sellers, must be secure, and sufficient information about any given transaction and its near alternatives must be available.

Then there is the presumption that entrepreneurs are different (they are "enterprising individuals"). They exercise their imaginations in fundamentally creative ways and are willing to commit resources to imaginary futures in the absence of certainty. This ability to exploit an opportunity is described in the

6 Scott Shane and S. Venkataraman, "The Promise of Entrepreneurship as a Field of Research," *Academy of Management Review*, vol. 26, no. 1 (2000), p. 218.

economics literature as exercising "judgment."[7] In the popular mind, entrepreneurship is mostly identified with technological change. But innovations in how goods are traded and in organizational structures also provide significant opportunities for entrepreneurial behavior.

Entrepreneurial opportunities are only real if there is the possibility of generating sufficient revenue to cover the full cost of production. Concerns about entrepreneurship in the church often appear to revolve around the notion of profits, especially the notion of "excessive profits" (which notion is typically not well defined). But from the perspective of economic theory, profits are simply the reward for innovation and investment. If markets function efficiently, then profits also provide signals to competitors, who then are likely to enter such markets and bid away the entrepreneur's profit. Thus, from the perspective of economics, profit is morally neutral. If markets and competitive forces function properly, there is no scope for "excessive" profits to be anything other than temporary returns to first movers. It follows then that any ethical evaluation of entrepreneurial behavior must have the structure and properties of the market at its heart. If a level of profit is somehow morally unacceptable, it is an outcome of a particular market structure that has allowed such an outcome to emerge. A clearer understanding of the nature of entrepreneurship, therefore, ensures that any attempt to answer the question whether it is "Christian" or not must focus on the properties and structures of markets.

### 6.2.2 Christianity

Defining Christianity also runs the risk of partiality and superficiality. The Apostles' Creed is perhaps the most succinct summary of key beliefs among all orthodox denominations. For present purposes this leads to four important observations:

1. First, the Creator God is both just and loving, and the collection of individuals in humanity represents the focus of God's love.
2. Second, sin is the result of mankind's disobedience and has the consequence of separating the disobedient humanity from a just and loving Creator God. Separation from God is eternal damnation.

[7] Mark C. Casson, *The Entrepreneur: An Economic Theory Robertson* (Oxford: Martin Robertson, 1982); Sharon Alvarez, Andrew Godley, and Mike Wright, "Mark Casson, *The Entrepreneur* at Thirty: Continued Relevance?" *Strategic Entrepreneurship Journal*, vol. 8, no. 2 (June 2014), pp. 185–194.

3. Third, Jesus of Nazareth was both fully God and fully human, and by allowing himself to be executed on the cross became the atoning sacrifice for mankind, paid to overcome the penalty of disobedience. Atonement provides for the possibility of forgiveness. Damnation, or separation, is overcome. Complete intimacy with God, the concept of Heaven, is really going to happen at some point in the future. Christianity is therefore a religion that states that redemption is only possible when done by God, not by good works or pilgrimage or anything else under man's agency. Without Christ there is literally no basis for Christianity.
4. Fourth, at Pentecost, after Jesus' resurrection and ascension to Heaven, the Holy Spirit came and filled Jesus' followers, the first Christians. The indwelling of the Holy Spirit then leads to the spiritual regeneration of the believer in the present. The tension between sin and grace in our fallen world means the regeneration of the believer by the Holy Spirit is never complete in this world. For that we must await the second coming of Christ.

The church, the community of believers, is therefore not simply a collection of individuals who subscribe intellectually to a set of doctrines but rather a community of individuals who through faith in Jesus Christ have been redeemed and through the Holy Spirit are being regenerated. It is this regeneration that gives the church its character. Regeneration imparts to the believers God's love for the entire body of humanity, God's desire to be reunited with every individual on earth, and a desire to see every individual attain their true fulfillment as a created being. The more complete that regeneration is in the present, the greater the church's focus on its mission as the vehicle of God's love for the world. A loving approach to interacting with others precludes tolerance of economic subjugation or poverty. So, the church is missionary, and missionary activity must have some economic aspect to it.

But how does Christianity relate to entrepreneurship? Superficially the answer seems straightforward. Where entrepreneurship leads to poverty reduction, enhances individual dignity, and benefits the wider society, it clearly fits within God's economy. It is worth noting in passing how entrepreneurial activity around the world has so dramatically reduced global poverty since 2000, with private sector wealth creation having an impact on the United Nations' Millennium Goals by an order of magnitude greater than aid.[8] But it

[8] Angus Deaton, "Price Indexes, Inequality, and the Measurement of World Poverty," *American Economic Review*, vol. 100, no. 1 (2010), pp. 5–34.

is equally the case that entrepreneurship and innovation in the financial sector were largely responsible for the financial crisis and its ensuing economic and social devastation. So simply equating free markets and the innovation they encourage with progressive outcomes consistent with the church's concern for the world is clearly absurd. Outside a few libertarians, no academic economist would subscribe to this overly simplistic view of entrepreneurship and markets. The first step to begin the process of encouraging constructive dialogue is to develop a theologically informed understanding of markets and entrepreneurship.[9]

## 6.3 A THEOLOGY OF ENTREPRENEURSHIP

If miscommunication is at the heart of the lack of dialogue between church and economists, then we need to articulate a theology of entrepreneurship and markets that is consistent with economic thought to function as a common intellectual meeting ground. The recorded teachings of Jesus in the Gospels represent the high-water mark of Christian theology and Christian ethical teaching. What can we elucidate about entrepreneurship from these teachings? Jesus did make frequent references to (broadly defined) entrepreneurs and entrepreneurial behavior, sometimes with approval (the Good Samaritan, the wise builder, selling all to buy the precious pearl) and sometimes not (dishonest scales, the parable of Lazarus, the overturning of the tables in the Temple, "den of thieves"). Jesus was evidently aware of the contemporary version of the institution of private property and the principle of profitable market exchange, but no plain reading of the Gospels can offer unambiguous support for any unbridled capitalist system of exchange. But the Gospel record fails to offer up any obvious condemnation of autocracy and summary execution, yet Jesus was fully aware of such practices. Any straightforward, plain reading of the Gospels fails to provide any particularly obvious evidence of Jesus' attitude toward entrepreneurship (or summary executions or dictatorships). Focusing solely on the Gospels is, in other words, unlikely to be the most fruitful route to developing an economically literate theology of entrepreneurship. Of course, it is only possible to understand the Gospels when they are interpreted within the context of the entire Bible, from Creation to the second coming and the new heaven on earth. It might be more sensible,

[9] John H. Dunning, "The Moral Imperatives of Global Capitalism: An Overview," in *Making Globalization Good: The Moral Challenges of Global Capitalism*, ed. John H. Dunning (Oxford: Oxford University Press, 2003), pp. 11–40.

therefore, to begin our theology of entrepreneurship by focusing on the Creation narrative.

This narrative states that God is the source of all goodness, and so the outcomes of all his actions are good (Genesis 1:9; Exodus 33:19, 34:6–8). Mankind was created in God's image (Genesis 1:27), so created mankind is fundamentally good (and actually "very good"; Genesis 1:31). Work is a key activity for mankind in Creation (Genesis 2:15), so both work itself and the product of work must also be "very good." Work in Creation is more than the production of basic individual needs – Eden is not some agrarian fantasy. Work in Eden is creative, intellectual, and even results in conspicuous consumption (Genesis 2:19–20, 2:12).

The Creation narrative also underlines the significance of relationships among humans, between humans and God; and among humans, God, and the environment. God created Eve as a helpmate, heralding intimacy, mutual commitment, and support between Adam and Eve (Genesis 2:20–25: "flesh of my flesh"). God enjoyed walking in Eden "in the cool of the day" (Genesis 3:8–10), when he would talk with Adam and Eve (Genesis 3:9). The Creation narrative therefore gives a clear picture of a deeply fulfilling intimacy and friendship between men and women ("be united with") and among men and women and God. Relationships involve mutual exchange. In the Garden of Eden, the context for these relationships is described as work.

Furthermore, while the Creation narrative has the stylized individuals of Adam and Eve representing men and women, it is clear from the prophetic vision of the "new heaven and a new earth" in Revelation (Revelation 21) that God's intention is for Eden-like conditions to be extended to all redeemed nations (Revelation 21:24–26). God created all of mankind to enjoy fruitful relationships with one another and with God – and work is central to these. Given the elevated status of work in Eden, so work and its product must form some part of the redeemed nations' "splendour" and "glory and honor" that is brought into the New Jerusalem (Revelation 21:24–26).

The nations are different, and they were given different names in Genesis (Genesis 10) to reflect different characteristics.[10] So the product of their redeemed work also differentiates one nation from the other. Mutual exchange of the product of redeemed work allows all nations, and all residents of heaven, to benefit from the gains of trade. In the Garden of Eden, the

[10] "Nations" in the Old Testament is a synonym for the gentiles; their differences from one another are secondary to their pejorative state relative to the Jews. But the nations in Revelation 21 are redeemed, and so national differences are redeemed.

exchange of the product of work was restricted to the mutual cooperation between one man and one woman.[11] But in the depiction of the New Jerusalem, the benefits of mutual exchange would be felt across many peoples from many different nations.

The initial preconditions for market exchange can therefore be discerned in the biblical representations of the two ideal states of grace: Eden and heaven. Residents are productive, and their individual product differs. There is a supply of various goods and services. Furthermore, these goods and services are desirable. They are the product of redeemed work; they are associated with the nations' splendor, glory, and honor. There is a demand. Finally, the number of individuals in heaven is so great that mutual exchange cannot be based simply on rich-content discourse, as might be the case between the united man and woman in Eden. There will need to be some sort of institutional arrangement to support mutual exchange. This institutional arrangement is what economists call a market.

Theologians take note: There will be markets in heaven. Moreover, if there are any moves away from market equilibrium (surely not unlikely in the context of eternity), then there will be entrepreneurs in heaven too.

### 6.3.1 Markets under Creation and Fall

If it is remotely possible that markets might exist in heaven, then it is worth exploring what such markets might look like. To economists markets deal with the problem of scarcity by rationing goods and services to those willing to pay the highest price. Scarcity and its twin, price, are fundamental to the operation of a market as understood by economists.[12] But it is scarcity itself that is rare in heaven! In heaven there is an infinite supply of goods and services, so no need to ration them (Revelation 21:4–6, 22:2–3). Residents in heaven will "reign for ever and ever" (Revelation 22:5), so even time scarcity is reduced effectively

[11] Although Genesis 2:12 implies that Eden may have traded with the land of Havilah for its gold, onyx, and aromatic resin.

[12] Or, that fixed amounts of capital and labor at any particular moment (a definition of scarcity) are only able to produce more output by bidding other capital and labor inputs from other sources of employment, thus bidding up the price of the cost of inputs – and hence the cost of supply – leading to an upward sloping supply curve. Because consumers have fixed amounts of resources to devote to consumption, correspondingly, they will prefer to consume less of a product the more expensive it becomes. This leads to relatively stable markets at equilibrium prices. Of course, there are many types of markets where such conditions of supply and demand don't function (several discussed subsequently) and, so, where price rationing does not always produce optimal outcomes.

to nought.[13] So while there will be both a demand for and a supply of goods and services, and there will be some sort of process to match supply and demand, the institutional nature of the exchange process will be different from that seen in markets familiar to us in the fallen world. Because the supply of redeemed human work-product is infinite, and because residents are immortal, there is no scarcity in heaven. There is, therefore, no scope for the price mechanism to operate.

One caveat (and this is really a digression for economists) is related to what economists call transaction costs. They are the costs associated with the actual transaction, or market exchange, itself. These involve the costs of searching for information, negotiating an agreement, and completing the contractual transfer of the rights of ownership from the seller to the buyer. For many products and services these transaction costs are so low as to be insignificant in the actual exchange. But in more complex transactions (such as buying and selling real estate or businesses), the transaction costs can become quite large. Transaction cost economics is the branch of the discipline that explores what happens to economic activity when transaction costs become high.

Will transaction costs in heaven be high or low? In heaven there is no scarcity, so economic resources will typically have very low exclusivity; there will always be an abundance of near-substitutes. Property rights will not be very valuable.[14] So the costs of negotiation will be low. The residents of heaven are honest, so the costs of contracting will also be relatively low. There is no scarcity of time, so search costs are low. Transaction costs will therefore surely be low in heaven and therefore unlikely to inhibit market exchange. Aficionados of transaction cost economics will be alert to the implication that the allocation of goods and services in heaven will therefore likely be through some sort of market rather than through some sort of bureaucracy or hierarchy.

Without scarcity there will be no basis for prices to exist in heaven. There will be demand for the product of redeemed work, so there will be markets with some exchange function. Entrepreneurs will intermediate between changing demand and supply. But in the absence of prices, how will these transactions take place? Entrepreneurs will have to exercise enormous creativity to be able to fulfill their intermediating function in heavenly markets without access to price signals. One possibility that is consistent with both

[13] Theoretically, heaven's residents may encounter some time scarcity in having to choose between consuming one good or service rather than another at any given time. But in the context of eternity, the potential for non-simultaneous consumption to lead to rationing is likely to be low.

[14] Any consideration of what the nature of property rights might be in heaven (private versus common or state, etc.) goes well beyond the confines of this chapter.

the imagery of Eden and heaven, as well as with Jesus' teaching in the Gospels, is that exchange in heaven will come through some form of blessing mechanism (Genesis 1:28). God blessed mankind, leading to mankind enjoying a state of fulfilling abundance ("Be fruitful and increase in number"; Genesis 1:28). Humans, made in the image of God, are to bless each other, reinforcing the tendency toward divine-ordained abundance (e.g., Matthew 19:29; Luke 14:15–24; John 14:2–3). The Abrahamic covenant revolves around the benefits arising from the mutual blessing of the nations and Abraham's descendants (Gen 12:2–3). Heavenly entrepreneurs will then be responsible for taking the product of redeemed work from among the nations and allocating it to other residents of heaven to meet their desires. In the absence of any price mechanism, this process will be analogous to giving the product to selected consumers. There will be no price to pay, because the price mechanism cannot operate in the absence of scarcity. But the process cannot be indiscriminate giving. Clearly, the concept of a gift is insufficiently powerful to communicate the welfare gains associated with these heavenly transactions. Because each product of redeemed work carries the properties of divinity with it (the "splendor," "glory and honor" of the redeemed nations in Revelation), so each recipient is blessed. Entrepreneurs in heaven are the intermediaries of heavenly blessings.

But what does this mean in practice? Many of the biblical descriptions of heaven are confusing. The proposition that there might be an alternative to the price mechanism –the blessing mechanism – that enables entrepreneurs to function in markets and to allocate products in heaven is theoretically and theologically consistent. But it is difficult to conceive how it might operate in practice. Consider that one of the uses of prices is their role to signal to potential entrepreneurs where the demand is growing. If heavenly markets don't have prices because there is no scarcity, how will heavenly entrepreneurs know where to allocate product? There is currently no satisfactory answer to this. The unsatisfactory answer is that heavenly entrepreneurs may utilize the charismatic gift of discernment (1 Corinthians 12:7–11). While it is an unsatisfactory answer, it is at least a partial answer. Some further insight can be gained from the discussion in the next section by moving from considering how markets might operate under the states of grace in Eden and heaven, to considering how they might function in the fallen world before and after the atonement.

### 6.3.2 Markets in the Fall

The curse of Adam focuses on work, changing what was the context for Adam and Eve's intimate and wholly satisfying relationship with God in Eden into "painful toil." The Fall introduces scarcity, the product of fallen work is "thorns and thistles" rather than the fruit of Eden (Genesis 3:17–19). As scarcity enters, so demand exceeds supply, and the price mechanism operates. Furthermore, this is compounded by sin, leading to selfishness, greed, and exploitative behavior in market transactions, employers exploiting workers, and one party in any transaction seeking to exploit the other. In such markets the powerful exploit the weak, earning God's condemnation (Isaiah 23). In such markets the weak withdraw from transactions, exacerbating their vulnerable economic situations.

The economy of the ancient Jews was based on subsistence agriculture, with quasi-markets operating to trade surpluses, supported by the minimal protection given to property rights under the autocratic feudalism of the times. The death and resurrection of Jesus Christ then enabled the partial spiritual regeneration of the church. Because regeneration is always partial until the second coming of Christ, the economic characteristics of a regenerated state of grace will always compete with the economic characteristics of the Fall. Work even among the redeemed will always involve toil. The product of work will always be insufficient to overcome scarcity, so markets will continue to be rationing institutions that use prices. But regeneration does allow glimpses of heavenly markets to enter the church's realm. Redeemed market exchange and redeemed entrepreneurship in a fallen world might be understood to operate dualistically, responding both to the blessing mechanism and the price mechanism.

A helpful analogy here is healing. In recent years, the consensus theological position in the orthodox denominations has shifted under the increasing empirical evidence of miraculous healings. If God heals in today's fallen world, so the Holy Spirit is able to bring elusive fragments of the promise of the heaven to come (Revelation 22:2b: "the leaves of the trees are for the healing of the nations") into the fallen world. The curse of Adam is fully broken at the second coming (Revelation 22:3 and Isaiah 65:17–25), and so there will be no illness and no crying in heaven. Yet glimpses of this prospect of the complete restoration of health are presently breaking into the church through occasional miraculous healings. These remain rare, however, even in those churches that see the most healing. So for the church today the prospect of miraculous healing appears to be real (James 5:14), but rare, so Christians are always encouraged to seek medical help for their ailments (1 Timothy 5:23). This is an unsatisfactory dualism, but it remains best pastoral practice.

This analogy is helpful when wanting to understand a fuller theology of entrepreneurship. For while entrepreneurship in a state of grace is an aspect of God's blessing and leads to the blessing of others, under the conditions of the

Fall, entrepreneurship can lead to harmful outcomes. Redeemed entrepreneurs may therefore operate in markets using the blessing mechanism to allocate resources, but (just as miraculous healings are rare in the fallen world and Christians are advised to consult doctors) so entrepreneurs will also have to operate dualistically using the pricing mechanism under conditions of scarcity. Perhaps it was to this unsatisfactory dualism that Jesus was referring when he instructed he followers to be as "shrewd as snakes and as innocent as doves" (Matthew 10:16)? It is unsatisfactory because there is no way to understand what might be the boundary conditions for entrepreneurs moving from operating according to the price mechanism to the blessing mechanism.

There is anecdotal evidence to support the idea of Christian entrepreneurs using a blessing mechanism at least occasionally in their market transactions. A strong theme in the economic history literature focuses on the relationship between Christianity, entrepreneurship, and inclusive economic gain. There appears to be a reasonable relationship between Christian revival (or accelerated regeneration) and economic growth, including the recent notable example of China.[15]

But the conclusion of this initial discussion of the theology of entrepreneurship remains unsatisfactory. Perhaps that is not surprising. If the theological underpinnings of market activity and entrepreneurship were straightforward, there would be less scope for the obvious gaps in worldviews between church leaders and economists to have emerged in the first place. Nevertheless, the focus of this section has been to assert that a theology of entrepreneurship can emerge, but only when we begin by drawing out principles of market exchange from the Creation narrative and the prophetic pictures of the new heaven. Developing further this theology of entrepreneurship and market activity would undoubtedly promote constructive debate between the church and economists.

A further route to promote dialogue is to make explicit the underlying ethical principles that drive the two perspectives and to demonstrate that Christian leaders' worldviews are more likely to be influenced by a different ethical principle than are economists' worldviews.

## 6.4 TWO ETHICAL PRINCIPLES: AUTONOMY AND JUSTICE

The dominant philosophical principle that guides ethics and law in the West today is the principle of autonomy. This principle states that an autonomous

[15] Juliette Koning and Heidi Dahles, "Spiritual Power: Ethnic Chinese Managers and the Rise of Charismatic Christianity in Southeast Asia," *The Copenhagen Journal of Asian Studies*, vol. 27, no. 1 (2009), pp. 5–37.

person possesses critical faculties and reflective ability and so is able to consciously accept or reject preferences and desires. This person is able to exercise self-determination. Thus, the principle of autonomy in law introduces constraints on individuals' actions because such actions might infringe someone else's right to self-determination. In medicine, for instance, the ethical principle of autonomy leads to the practice of medical care providers needing to acquire the informed consent of (typically poorly informed) patients before proceeding with treatment.

But autonomy is not the only governing principle in ethical debates. The principle of social justice takes a societal view of problems and so privileges the fair adjudication between competing claims. Justice is associated with fairness, equality, and entitlement. Through its consideration of competing claims, justice is the ethical principle that most restrains autonomy.

Entrepreneurship is legitimized above all by reference to the principle of autonomy. The individual entrepreneur exercises creative judgment, makes a specific investment to exploit an opportunity, and, if successful, enjoys a profitable return on that investment. Moreover, this privileging of autonomy is reinforced because of the way that economic theory undermines the restraining influence of the principle of social justice.

The revolution in economic thought introduced by Adam Smith's concept of the invisible hand legitimized the pursuit of self-seeking motives as being beneficial to society as a whole. As the Skidelskys have recently expounded, in Smith's scheme, "gain was the release of motives that promoted economic growth. Acquisitiveness was licensed on condition it served the social good. What was lost was the idea of the social good as a collective achievement. It became a result of individuals pursuing their self-interest in markets."[16] Because Smithian specialization and trade with free competitive entry benefited all, so justice became submerged in the clamor for individual self-determination. In modern economics, justice has become relegated to insignificance, its requirements deemed to be fully met in what economists call Pareto efficiency.

Many economists remain deeply ambivalent about the implications of such casuistry. The Skidelskys are clear about Keynes' reservations of the effects of capitalism on civilization, for example. But in the absence of strong countervailing arguments, the triumph of autonomy in economics, as in medical ethics and law, justifies privileging the interests of individuals over other concerns.

The force of autonomy as an ethical principle is derived from Kant's emphasis on the significance of each and every individual human being. If

[16] Robert Skidelsky and Edward Skidelsky, *How Much Is Enough? The Love of Money and the Case for the Good Life* (London: Allen Lane, 2012), p. 52.

each man and woman is made in the image of the Creator God, then each individual man and woman does indeed have intrinsic inalienable rights. But Christian ethical teaching does not only emphasize autonomy. The principle of justice is also hardwired into the church's interpretation of the world's ills. And this is where the apparent conflict with much economic thinking occurs. For the principle of justice is assumed to be wholly satisfied in modern economics through the masterful and mysterious outcome of the sum of market activities, of what Adam Smith called the invisible hand. This, as we have seen, suggests that all participants in market exchange will end up being better off than they otherwise would. The theory of the market therefore satisfies both autonomy *and* justice. Even technological disruptions, which clearly privilege the autonomous rights of the entrepreneur but which may be thought to be unjust because innovation may lead to some people losing jobs as their skills become redundant, are defended because the net gain to society from innovation is still positive. For theologians and church leaders, by contrast, justice is a far more powerful driving force in pursuing the church's mission.

How might constructive dialogue between church leaders and economists be promoted when each party is driven by a different ethical principle? I am proposing in this chapter that a more rigorous examination – using the principle of autonomy – of how markets actually function will allow a common approach to emerge and so a dialogue to develop. Here the key question is: How universal in reality are the underlying assumptions of Smithian economics? Do markets generally exhibit the properties of being, first, subject to the forces of competition and, second, featuring well-informed buyers and sellers?

In the area of competition policy considerable progress has been made in Western nations in the last thirty years. The ideological switch from corporatism to competition informed by Hayek and Friedman has become lampooned by antiglobalization protesters as neoliberalism, or as the intellectual framework to defend some sort of conspiracy of the commercial elite. These impressions can only possibly emerge from reading none of the writings of such scholars. Competition commissions police big businesses largely well, and within-jurisdiction monopoly profits have been much reduced compared with the 1970s, especially within Europe. Senior managers of large firms are well-aware of such constraints on their freedom of action.[17]

[17] We should also note that jurisdictional differences can lead to unethical outcomes. Regulatory arbitrage ranging from taxation to employment practices in international business is one currently prominent example. These are self-evidently ethical problems they are but problems about jurisdictional differences of markets rather than the economic theory of markets.

The criticisms of the apparent problem of market forces have more traction in exposing the difficulties posed to the autonomy principle by the asymmetries of information in many markets. As the complexity of market transactions increases, the volume of transactions where buyers are at a significant disadvantage in their information about or understanding of the properties of the transaction has increased dramatically. In complex markets, consumers are increasingly at risk of suffering from the effects of moral hazard and adverse selection.[18] Consumers are increasingly unable to give their informed consent to the sellers, and so instead simply take a product or service on trust. Consumer autonomy is, by definition, being undermined as consumers are increasingly unable to exercise their critical faculties in the absence of clear and unambiguous information about the properties of the transaction.

In complex markets, the asymmetric distribution of information means that consumers need to take suppliers on trust. Complex products and services may mean that the terms of the contract go beyond what ill-informed consumers would appreciate as their responsibility under the principle of *caveat emptor*, or buyer beware. Ill-informed consumers in such markets may believe that the contractual terms of exchange are one thing, while the reality may be different. Their autonomy has been undermined. Thus, small businesses and households are outraged when banks persuade them to buy expensive, complex insurance products with hidden costs to which, had the buyers been made aware, they would never have consented. In complex markets, such cases are the equivalent of doctors giving patients treatments to which they have not consented.

The information properties of many products and services make the autonomous rights of one party to the transaction susceptible to being trampled on by the other. Because sellers are able to profit from such transactions, the accumulation of reward becomes unjust. It is, in other words, the relative complexity of markets that introduces the prospect of ethical failings.

It follows that the risk of entrepreneurial activity being unethical is minimized in those markets where moral hazard or adverse selection effects are low. But in markets sufficiently complex that information asymmetries give rise to both high likelihoods of adverse selection and moral hazard, entrepreneurs may exploit uninformed consumers, and – whether intentionally or not – in doing so undermine consumer autonomy in the transaction. There is a risk,

[18] Andrew Godley, "Entrepreneurial Opportunities, Implicit Contracts and Market Making for Complex Consumer Goods," *Strategic Entrepreneurship Journal*, vol. 2013 (December 2013), pp. 273–287; Andrew Godley and Mark Casson, "'*Doctor, Doctor…*' Entrepreneurial Diagnosis and Market Making," *Journal of Institutional Economics*, vol. 11, no. 3 (2015), pp. 601–621.

then, that such markets may give rise to unethical behavior. What kinds of markets share the characteristics so described? Above all they would include specialized, complex, open-ended services such as financial, legal, or medical services, as well as novel high-tech consumer durables and services.

## 6.5 DISCUSSION AND CONCLUSION

The church's mission is to extend God's economy on earth. The properties of God's economy include redemption and regeneration, which in turn imply reducing spiritual and material poverty throughout society. As the section outlining a theology of entrepreneurship concludes, enterprise can and does contribute to this mission. Yet it is largely misunderstood in many sections of the church. This chapter contends that much of the church's confusion about the costs and benefits of entrepreneurship arises, first, because the theology of entrepreneurship is underdeveloped, and, second, because of a misunderstanding of the societal contribution of economic exchange, the role of profit, and the potential consequences of different kinds of market structures in a modern economy. These misunderstandings are easy to make and getting easier; the world is increasingly complex in many areas, so market exchange is veering further and further away from the underlying textbook assumptions of informed buyers and sellers. In addition, there is the ever-present impact of sin exacerbated by inequality, leading to ever more exploitative human behavior.

The correct response, however, is not to reject the remarkable benefits to the world that entrepreneurial activity in modern economies has brought about. Rather, it is to better understand the theological and ethical underpinnings of market exchange, and then to analyze how many markets have begun to deviate from these acceptable underlying structural and ethical principles. This chapter has suggested that redeemed work, markets, and entrepreneurship are all going to be present in heaven. To answer the question posed in the chapter's title, redeemed entrepreneurship is fully Christian.

Entrepreneurship in the fallen world is, however, susceptible to exploitative behavior. Individual Christian entrepreneurs may intuitively be alert to the need to avoid exploitative behavior through operating dualistically, cover their costs through the price mechanism, and bless their consumers through the blessing mechanism. For church leaders and theologians, the difficulty of differentiating ethical from unethical entrepreneurial behavior is more problematic, however, and complicated by the differences in ethical principles that guide church leaders and economists in their judgments.

The suggestion here is that, by prioritizing the principle of autonomy, at least theologians and economists will be able to engage more constructively in identifying ethical and unethical market behavior. For almost all entrepreneurial activity, the framework elaborated here leads to a presumption that the outcomes of market exchange are ethical. But in some markets – where the information asymmetries are sufficiently difficult to overcome and where the risks of both adverse selection and moral hazard effects are sufficiently great – the presumption ought to be that consumer autonomy will be undermined. Entrepreneurial activity in these markets runs the risk of being unethical. Church leaders and Christian entrepreneurs in these complex markets will benefit from assisting potential consumers to find fuller information about the product or service. The level of ethical responsibility shouldered by entrepreneurs in complex markets is commensurately greater and analogous to the obligations of medical professionals to their patients.

Concerns about justice in entrepreneurial activity remain. But for the purpose of opening a dialogue with economists and policymakers on the theological and moral underpinnings of entrepreneurship, it seems more sensible to begin by focusing on the principle of autonomy in complex markets. In situations where autonomy alone suggests unethical outcomes are likely to emerge, justice then demands that a wider ethical framework be consulted to guide decision-making.

# 7

# Subsidiarity and the Role of Regulation in the Financial Sector

PHILIP BOOTH

## 7.1 INTRODUCTION

Catholic social teaching has often suggested that markets need to be regulated by the government. This position has been articulated most recently in the letter from the Vatican entitled *Oeconomicae et pecuniariae quaestiones* published in May 2018. Of course, this perspective is not unique to the Catholic tradition, though Catholic social teaching is articulated more formally than are its equivalents in other Christian denominations.

In the Catholic tradition, it is often suggested that economic activity needs to be regulated by the state because of human imperfection and that, without regulation, markets will fail to promote the common good and human dignity.[1] Pope Francis has been particularly vocal on the need for markets to be restrained. In his apostolic exhortation, *Evangelii Guadium* (56), for example, he states: "This imbalance is the result of ideologies which defend the absolute autonomy of the marketplace and financial speculation. Consequently, they reject the right of states, charged with vigilance for the common good, to exercise any form of control.... In this system, which tends to devour everything which stands in the way of increased profits, whatever is fragile, like the environment, is defenseless before the interests of a deified market, which become the only rule." However, Pope Benedict XVI made similar comments in milder language.[2] It is specifically argued in Catholic social teaching that markets do not self-regulate and that they therefore need direction to ensure that they serve the common good[3] and

[1] See, for example, paragraphs 5 and 21 of *Oeconomicae et pecuniariae quaestiones*, Congregation for the Doctrine of the Faith and Dicastery for Promoting Integral Human Development, 2018. For more on the common good, see Chapter 2.

[2] For example, *Caritas in Veritate*, Encyclical Letter of Benedict XVI, 2009, para. 65.

[3] *Oeconomicae et pecuniariae quaestiones*, para. 21.

to guarantee that greed and corruption do not lead markets to serve inappropriate ends.

There is certainly some merit in these arguments. More generally, it can be argued that at least part of the need for a state to have authority arises from the Fall. Because the Fall means that people will not automatically live in peace and harmony, a state needs the power to coerce and to back this coercion up with the authority to impose punishment. People need to be protected against murder, theft, fraud, and so on. Following from this logic, it could reasonably be argued that the state should protect people against greed, recklessness, sharp practice, and people generally not behaving ethically in financial markets. This could be done by prohibiting certain forms of behavior through regulation.

However, the state does not exist to solve all problems, or to prohibit everything that is immoral. The reason the state cannot and should not resolve all problems also lies in the Fall. As Madison put it: "If men were angels, no government would be necessary. If angels were to govern men, neither external nor internal controls on government would be necessary." This is not entirely consistent with a Catholic view of the purpose of the state. Yet it serves as an important warning of the dangers of government trying to solve every problem. Any regulation will involve the governing of the imperfect by the imperfect. Other principles have to be applied in a spirit of prudence and in the context of a Christian understanding of our human nature to determine whether government should act in particular cases.

In this context, it is interesting to note that the Catholic Church has often been welcoming of a broadly free economy, even if the Church has favored a degree of regulation. This was expressed as follows by Saint John Paul II in an encyclical letter *Centesimus Annus* published in 1991 when answering the rhetorical question of whether capitalism was the model that should be followed after the failure of communism:

> If by "capitalism" is meant an economic system which recognizes the fundamental and positive role of business, the market, private property and the resulting responsibility for the means of production, as well as free human creativity in the economic sector, then the answer is certainly in the affirmative, even though it would perhaps be more appropriate to speak of a "business economy," "market economy" or simply "free economy."[4]

However, he also pointed out that an economy needed restraints:

4 *Centesimus Annus*, Encyclical Letter of John Paul II, 1991, para. 42.

> But if by "capitalism" is meant a system in which freedom in the economic sector is not circumscribed within a strong juridical framework which places it at the service of human freedom in its totality, and which sees it as a particular aspect of that freedom, the core of which is ethical and religious, then the reply is certainly negative.[5]

And, elsewhere in the document – referring to, for example, *Rerum Novarum*, published in 1891 – it was made clear that the state could have a role in the economy in certain situations. However, the role suggested for the state was not a particularly wide one:

> Economic activity, especially the activity of a market economy, cannot be conducted in an institutional, juridical or political vacuum. On the contrary, it presupposes sure guarantees of individual freedom and private property, as well as a stable currency and efficient public services. Hence the principle task of the State is to guarantee this security, so that those who work and produce can enjoy the fruits of their labors and thus feel encouraged to work efficiently and honestly.[6]

In neither case is a strong regulating role for government being proposed. There is a difference between strong governmental institutions such as the rule of law and the protection of private property, on the one hand, and the direct and detailed regulation of business by government bureaus, on the other hand.

The reason these documents suggest a limited role for governments is that Catholic social teaching, in accordance with the principle of subsidiarity, puts great importance on the institutions of society resolving problems without necessarily giving recourse to the state. This approach can resolve the paradox arising from simultaneously holding the beliefs that financial markets need strong mechanisms to ensure restraint but also that the power of the state should be limited.

Indeed, John Paul II specifically mentioned the role of societal institutions in regulation in the context of the protection of human rights in employment when he argued: "Another task of the State is that of overseeing and directing the exercise of human rights in the economic sector. However, primary responsibility in this area belongs not to the State but to individuals and to the various groups and associations which make up society."[7] This socio-cultural sphere, which does not seem to be mentioned to any great degree in

5 Ibid.

6 Ibid., para. 48.

7 Ibid.

Catholic Church pronouncements on the financial sector, is prominent also in the writings of Michael Novak,[8] as well as, of course, in the work of Alexis de Tocqueville.

The Church has developed the principle of subsidiarity, which recognizes the difficulty of the state being involved in all aspects of society and the economy. It also recognizes the ability – if not the right – of human persons to work purposefully, through the institutions of civil society, to resolve problems that they might face.

In an encyclical letter published shortly after the financial crisis, *Caritas in Veritate*, Pope Benedict XVI was careful not to criticize modern financial instruments in and of themselves but he did criticize their misuse.[9] He pointed out the importance of a financial system with ethical underpinnings. He also suggested that developments in regulation that safeguarded weaker parties and discouraged speculation were welcome and should be further explored and encouraged.[10] The encyclical referred to the importance of the cultural space, to businesses that pursued ends other than profits (or profits alone), and it reinforced, again and again, the importance of ethical behavior in the economy. However, the encyclical did not really develop the idea of institutions arising within society or from within the market to regulate activity in financial markets. The same is true of the recent letter *Oeconomicae et pecuniariae quaestiones*. Indeed, both documents explicitly stated that the state and state regulation should be used to direct the economy toward the promotion of the common good.[11]

In recent discussions of economic issues, the Catholic Church has also called for more regulation of financial markets at an international level. For example, *Towards Reforming the International Financial and Monetary Systems*, a letter published by the former Pontifical Council for Justice and Peace[12] suggests that the financial crisis resulted from the absence of regulation and that global regulation of the financial sector was needed, including a system for bailing out banks on a global basis.

8 See especially Michael Novak and Paul Adams, *Social Justice Isn't What You Think It Is* (New York: Encounter Books, 2015).

9 *Caritas in Veritate*, para. 36.

10 Ibid., para. 65.

11 It is worth noting that *Quadragesimo Anno*, Encyclical Letter of Pope Pius XI, 1931, also suggested that the role of the state was to regulate society to promote the common good. However, it also put significant emphasis on the concept of susbsidiarity.

12 *Towards Reforming the International Financial and Monetary Systems*, Pontifical Council for Justice and Peace, 2011.

The current Pope, Francis, is generally regarded as highly critical of unregulated markets. Indeed, in his encyclical on the environment, he seemed to suggest that those who did not believe in state regulation of markets were akin to those who justified modern slavery and the sexual exploitation of children:

> The culture of relativism is the same disorder which drives one person to take advantage of another, to treat others as mere objects, imposing forced labor on them or enslaving them to pay their debts. The same kind of thinking leads to the sexual exploitation of children and abandonment of the elderly who no longer serve our interests. It is also the mindset of those who say: Let us allow the invisible forces of the market to regulate the economy, and consider their impact on society and nature as collateral damage. (Laudato si 123[13])

Though Pope Francis proposed global institutions to direct the economy, including in the wake of the crash, he did on a number of occasions express skepticism of the state's ability to play this role, and reiterated the importance of civil society institutions and ethical renewal.[14] But this is certainly an undeveloped theme in recent pontificates, especially when referring to economic activity in financial markets. In his apostolic exhortation *Evangelii Gaudium*, Pope Francis twice criticized those who believed in what he termed the "absolute autonomy of markets" and also criticized those who rejected state control.[15] He argued that those who argued in favor of the autonomy of the market rejected ethics and God.

This analysis is too simple. It is possible to start from a position of understanding human fallibility and the need for ethical principles to guide finance (indeed, not just finance, but all economic and other social activity) but still, prudently, as a result of considering the underlying nature of the human person, believe that the imperfect human person, acting through the institution of the state, cannot perfect, or, indeed, improve upon, the outcome of an imperfect market.

Secondly, it does not make sense to think of a market as "autonomous." A market is neither a created order with a single specific purpose, nor do the participants in a market act in isolation from each other or from other institutions. A market order should be understood as an enlarged order of voluntary social cooperation in which people are able to control and govern their own behavior as well as develop institutions that create rules to govern behavior in

[13] *Laudato si*, Encyclical Letter of Pope Francis, 2015.

[14] See, for example, LS, 211.

[15] *Evangelii Gaudium*, Apostolic Exhortation of Pope Francis, 2013, para. 56. See above for full quotation.

concrete ways.[16] Indeed, the importance of ethics as an important guiding force within markets is the key theme of *Oeconomicae et pecuniariae quaestiones*, especially in section two. To simply dismiss markets as autonomous and conclude immediately that they therefore need state regulation is to avoid the question of whether regulatory institutions that arise within civil society and within markets themselves can be more effective in promoting the common good than can state regulation.

Furthermore, markets are not governed by "invisible" forces, as Pope Francis suggests. Markets develop as institutions governed by human action. And such human action can develop sophisticated regulatory structures that promote the common good, as we shall see subsequently. Such regulatory structures are not only very human, but also very visible, sometimes in the literal sense. The stock exchanges and other market institutions that regulate behavior are not only bustling hives of human activity but they are often also imposing and impressive architecturally.

The remainder of this chapter will look at the relationship between our understanding of human nature and the need for regulation. It will then consider the failure of financial regulation before the 2008 crisis. After examining the problems of global financial regulation, historical and modern examples of financial regulation that evolve within society will be discussed.

## 7.2 HUMAN NATURE AND REGULATORY STRUCTURES

In the earlier discussion, some reference has been made to human nature. Modern economics is often criticized for making unrealistic assumptions about human behavior and human nature.[17] The same criticism could also be leveled at recent Catholic social teaching on issues related to the regulation of economic life. When making prudential judgments about how we should regulate financial markets, it is important to begin by trying to understand human nature and behavior. As has been noted, the frailty of human nature is an important reason why we have government and also an important reason why government's power is limited. Social, economic, and political constructs are there to serve human persons and to help promote the common good and human dignity. Therefore, they must be compatible with a realistic view of human nature.

For example, Aquinas's view about private property was based on his analysis and understanding of human nature and the requirements for a

[16] This is essentially the Hayekian view of a market order.
[17] See, for example, the vast literature on behavioral economics.

peaceful society given what we know about human nature.[18] Using the same reasoning, what can we say about financial regulation?

The typical way of thinking about financial regulation in recent Church documents tends to follow the "neoclassical" approach of economics textbooks that, in other respects, the Church often criticizes. This approach involves making particular assumptions about human behavior and then identifying where markets might "fail" to maximize welfare. Imperfections in markets that lead to welfare not being maximized should, it is argued, be rectified by regulation. In this approach, which is criticized in Booth (2020),[19] the study of regulatory institutions that evolve within markets is limited.

As far as banks are concerned, for instance, the difficulty of systemic risk has been identified in Church documents, including *Oeconomicae et pecuniariae quaestiones*. Systemic risk is the problem of when the failure of one bank brings down the whole financial system. In a global financial system, this can happen on a worldwide scale; and, because individual banks do not bear the full costs of their mistakes, this leads to what economists call a "market failure." The problem can be exacerbated because those contracting with banks do not have perfect information about the solvency of individual banks. Furthermore, individuals might be incentivized to behave recklessly, especially if banks have limited liability.[20] It has also been suggested that what are known as "principal–agent problems" lead agents (managers, in this case) to behave more recklessly than principals (owner-shareholders) would like when it comes to, for example, taking risks with trading. Andrew Haldane, then Executive Director for Financial Stability at the Bank of England (at the time of writing, Chief Economist at the Bank of England), wrote: "Principal-agent problems crop up in all aspects of economics. But it is questionable whether there is any event in recent history where these agency problems have been exposed so frequently and extensively as during the current financial crisis."[21] It is this kind of analysis that has led to the view that international regulation is necessary to ensure that the financial system serves the common good.

[18] See, for example, Rodger Charles, *Christian Social Witness and Teaching: The Catholic Tradition from Genesis to Centesimus Annus* (Leominster: Gracewing, 1998).

[19] Philip M. Booth, "Ethics in Economics – Lessons and Themes for Further Development in the Vatican's 2018 Letter," in *Journal of Catholic Social Thought*, vol. 17, no. 2 (2020), pp. 325–346.

[20] A powerful critique of this way of thinking, both from the point of view of theory and practice, can be found in George Selgin, *Financial Stability without Central Banks* (London: Institute of Economic Affairs, 2017).

[21] See Andrew Haldane, "Why Banks Failed the Stress Test," *Speech to the Marcus Evans Conference on Stress Testing* (2009).

This is a typical approach to regulatory issues in modern economics. Economists start by making unrealistic assumptions about human nature in their models, such as the existence of perfect information. When those assumptions do not hold they argue that there has been what they call a "market failure." They then ascribe a role to government regulation in correcting such "market failures."

It should be noted that all these problems have ethical aspects. If individuals operated with greater ethical discernment, they may well react differently in situations where they are aware that their decisions have implications for the stability of the financial system as a whole. Furthermore, principal–agent problems would not arise because managers would not only act in their own interests, and so on.

Economists, in the neoclassical paradigm, tend to assume that government regulation can resolve these problems and assume, at least implicitly, that governments act in the general public interest and that government regulatory agencies have the perfect information lacked by market participants. The Catholic Church seems to take the same approach, while considering the problem from an ethical perspective. For example, *Oeconomicae et pecuniariae quaestiones* (21) states: "Such regulation is made even more necessary in view of the fact that among the major reasons for the most recent economic crisis was the immoral behavior of agents in the financial world." But unless we are willing to assume away human imperfection and the lack of perfect knowledge within government institutions, we cannot know in advance whether regulation will improve outcomes. What if the regulatory agencies are corrupt or make the same mistakes in assessing risks as those acting within markets?

Once, however, we recognize human imperfection in a government regulatory system, this approach takes us to an intellectual dead end. All we know is that government regulators cannot necessarily solve all the problems we hope they will solve, nor necessarily even improve upon the outcomes of a market. It is not that we know that regulation will not improve outcomes; we simply do not know what the implications will be of an approach that assumes that human imperfection necessarily requires regulatory intervention.

A better starting point would be to make realistic assumptions about human nature in whichever institutional context it operates.

Three principles about human nature that Christians – and perhaps non-Christians – would accept are:

- Human persons are inclined to do good but tempted by evil.
- No human person is omniscient; that is, there are limits to human knowledge.

- Human persons can use their reason to act purposefully to achieve their objectives, which will include cooperation with others.

The first and third principles should give us confidence that human persons, acting with social justice properly understood,[22] should be able to develop institutions within markets that help improve their functioning. The first and second principles should make us skeptical of the idea that markets can or should be centrally controlled by government bureaus with significant degrees of discretionary power. In other words, it could be considered imprudent to give power to the state for the regulation of markets unless it is absolutely necessary. This is because man's vices may bring about greater evils, such as the abuse of power, corruption, the lessening of individual responsibility, the growth of impersonal bureaucracies remote from the problems they are trying to solve, and the capture of regulatory processes by elites. In a Thomistic framework, we would consider it necessary for the state to develop positive law only where it is necessary for the political common good of the whole society.

Such a way of thinking does not demonstrate for certain that statutory regulation of financial markets is always and everywhere a bad thing. However, it does provide a prima facie case for carefully considering alternatives. In the past, though perhaps not so much in the recent past, Catholic social teaching has done this. This way of thinking might also make us skeptical of international institutions that attempt to regulate the global financial system.

## 7.3 THE FAILURE OF REGULATION IN THE FINANCIAL CRISIS

The financial crisis is often seen as a failure of markets, not least, as has been noted, amongst those responsible for producing Catholic social teaching documents. Putting aside whether this was the case, the crisis provides little evidence for the efficacy of statutory regulation. The experience of the financial crisis provides prima facie evidence for the preceding narrative that human imperfection exists in all economic and political structures. Such human imperfection is not necessarily a simple tendency to evil, but also relates to our inability to fully foresee the consequences of our actions.

[22] It is rare that this term is used in a way that embraces its richness in Catholic social teaching. However, it encapsulates the virtues that we should exhibit in the social and economic sphere, including in developing social and civil society institutions. See, for example, Philip M. Booth and Matías Petersen, "Catholic Social Teaching and Hayek's Critique of Social Justice," *Logos: A Journal of Catholic Thought and Culture*, vol. 23, no. 1 (2020), pp. 36–64.

It is sometimes argued that the financial crisis took place in an environment of deregulation. For example, Pontifical Council for Justice and Peace (2011) was critical of what it described as liberal approaches to finance and blamed them for the failure of Lehman Brothers. A similar argument was also made in secular circles. Senior figures in the British Labour Party, who were in government at the time of the crisis, also blamed it on what they described as "light touch" regulation.[23] In the United States, the repeal of the Glass–Steagall Acts, which had required the separation of retail and investment banking, has also been cited as a cause of the crisis. But the fact that none of the institutions that seriously contributed to the crisis had significant combined retail and investment business provides a prima facie case against the idea that the repeal of Glass–Steagall was the problem.

As far as the United Kingdom is concerned, it is difficult to identify a relevant process of deregulation, certainly not in the ten years before the financial crisis. In fact, it is difficult to exaggerate the extent of regulation in the United Kingdom at the time of the financial crisis and its growth in recent decades. Haldane and Madouros have pointed out that in 1980 there was roughly one financial regulator for every 11,000 people employed in finance and that by 2011 that figure was one for every 300 people employed in finance.[24] In the United States, Fannie Mae and Freddie Mac, two mortgage securitization warehouses whose failures were an important event in the crisis, had 236 regulators all to themselves.[25]

Furthermore, it would appear that government regulation not only did not prevent the crisis, it encouraged the very behavior that caused the crisis. Compulsory statutory deposit insurance encouraged risk-taking.[26] Lending to risky counterparties (sub-prime lending) was not only encouraged by US regulators through the Community Reinvestment Acts, it was required. Moreover, federal backing for Fannie Mae and Freddie Mac provided incentives to create complex mortgage-backed securities and encouraged banks to

[23] www.bbc.co.uk/news/uk-politics-14888933

[24] A. Haldane and V. Madouros, "The Dog and the Frisbee," *Speech to the Federal Reserve Bank of Kansas City's 366th Economic Policy Symposium, "The Changing Policy Landscape," Jackson Hole, Wyoming, August 31, 2012.*

[25] See Eamonn Butler, "The Financial Crisis: Blame Governments, Not Bankers," in *Verdict on the Crash: Causes and Policy Implications*, ed. Philip M. Booth, Hobart Paperback 37 (London: Institute of Economic Affairs, 2009), pp. 51–58.

[26] Deposit insurance is a long-standing feature of the US banking system, but is relatively recent in the UK.

undertake riskier lending and reduce the monitoring of risks. Various forms of bank regulation also encouraged the proliferation of complex financial instruments. Indeed, it was widely thought – both inside and outside regulatory bodies – that the securitization of bank lending would make the financial system safer. For example, speaking just a few months before a large British bank, Northern Rock, failed as a result of its use of the securitization model, Paul Tucker (at the time Executive Director for Market Operations at the Bank of England and later Deputy Governor for Financial Stability) said: "So it would seem that there is a good deal to welcome in the greater dispersion of risk made possible by modern instruments, markets and institutions."[27] Other actions by central banks, both in relation to monetary policy[28] and in relation to their support for the banking sector[29] may also have contributed to, or maybe even caused, the financial crisis.

This narrative is not intended to suggest that misguided regulation necessarily caused the financial crisis, though that is certainly a plausible hypothesis. Nor should it be thought that individuals working within the financial system who behaved recklessly or otherwise unethically are not culpable. The point is that we cannot assume ex ante that governments and government institutions will develop approaches to regulation that will reduce, rather than increase, the likelihood of poor outcomes. This may be because of special interests affecting government policy, such as bureaucracies that value writing rules more than producing good regulation, or large banks that believe complex and opaque regulation reduces competition or reduces their own moral responsibility. Alternatively, it may be because human ignorance simply prevents regulators from knowing in advance the approaches that will reduce the risk of bad outcomes. If power is centralized in a single regulatory body, it will make it more likely that the whole system will be affected by mistakes at the same time. The neoclassical idea that "market failures" can be solved by pulling regulatory levers seems to have failed in practice. Given a Christian understanding of human nature, we should not be surprised.

27 See speech given to Merrill Lynch Conference A *Perspective on Recent Monetary and Financial System Developments*, April 2007, www.bankofengland.co.uk/-/media/boe/files/speech/2007/a-perspective-on-recent-monetary-and-financial-system-developments.pdf?la=en&hash=C41CD782B2D3E37F04B580D4CA8EE9D52D6D7638

28 See Anna Schwartz, "Origins of the Financial Market Crisis of 2008," in Booth, ed., Verdict on the Crash.

29 See the Federal Reserve Bank of Richmond, "Feature Essay: Should the Fed Have a Financial Stability Mandate?," in *Annual Report of the Federal Reserve Bank of Richmond* (Virginia: Richmond Fed., 2013), pp. 4–25.

## 7.4 GLOBAL REGULATION OF THE FINANCIAL SYSTEM

It is often suggested in Catholic social teaching, including in Pontifical Council for Justice and Peace (2011) and in *Oeconomicae et pecuniariae quaestiones* (21), that the response to the failings of national financial regulation should be to have global regulation of the financial system. In arguing for global regulation, the Catholic Church follows the intellectual lead of many experts in the secular world. For example, the economist John Eatwell proposed a world financial authority in 1998, around the time of the Asian banking and currency crises.[30]

However, the financial crisis of 2008 occurred in an era when there was, in fact, global banking regulation. The Bank for International Settlements operates by consensus, but regulates capital requirements for internationally diversified banks. In addition, there has been a range of other initiatives to promote the international regulation of insurance and securities markets. Superimposed on this is the system of European Union financial regulation that the Union describes as follows: "The European System of Financial Supervision (ESFS) was created as a decentralised, multi-layered system of micro- and macro-prudential authorities in order to ensure consistent and coherent financial supervision in the EU."[31] It should be noted that, though the process of supervision is decentralized, the process of regulation is not. The European Securities and Markets Authority (ESMA), for example, states that it fulfills its role by "assessing risks to investors, markets and financial stability, completing a single rulebook for EU financial markets."

There are many other such supranational bodies and systems: the European Union's Solvency II regime for regulating insurance companies, International Accounting Standards (IAS), the International Organization of Securities Commissions (IOSC), and the European Union financial markets directives such as the Markets in Financial Instruments Directives (MiFID I and II).

So, does statutory international financial regulation help rectify the problems of national financial regulation in an era of globalization – as the Catholic Church and many economists would like to assume – by matching the jurisdiction of the regulator to the scope of the market? We certainly cannot be confident that it will in the future. Again, the reason lies in the

30 The timing was coincidental. See Eatwell and Taylor, *International Capital Markets and the Future of Economic Policy*. Paper prepared for the Ford Foundation project – International Capital Markets and the Future of Economic Policy (New York: Center for Economic Policy Analysis; London: IPPR, 1998).

31 See www.europarl.europa.eu/atyourservice/en/displayFtu.html?ftuId=FTU_3.2.5.html

imperfection of human nature, which makes it impossible to be sure that regulation will resolve problems that arise within markets. And there are some specific characteristics of international regulation that make the challenges all the greater.

Firstly, by its nature, regulation becomes more complex when it has to cope with a wider variety of situations. German banks are very different from British banks, for example, and a regulatory standard that can cope with both is necessarily more complex than a regulatory standard designed to deal with banks in either of the two countries separately.

The Basel Accord of 1988 was the first international prudential regulatory agreement for banks. It was just thirty pages long. Because the accord had to deal with so many different complex situations across diverse banking systems and because it could therefore be gamed, it became unsustainable. Its successor, Basel II, was 347 pages long. This clearly did not avert the financial crisis; indeed, it probably contributed to it. Basel III was agreed upon in 2010, following the crisis, and counted in at 616 pages – twenty times the length of Basel I.

Complexity tends to beget more complexity. Once a regulatory system becomes highly complex, the situation can be reached whereby only experts in the subject can understand the regulation. It is therefore not possible for regulators to be held to account by politicians, by the democratic process, by academics, or indeed by anybody other than those being regulated or else private sector consultants who work full-time on the subject. Some of the strongest supporters of complex regulation, then, become those big businesses that are able to spend large amounts of money on lobbyists and who play an active part in the process of developing regulation or are regulators themselves. Regulation can then serve interest groups rather than the common good.

A further problem with international regulation relates to man's lack of omniscience. Regulators do not get everything right. They come from the same strain of humanity as the rest of us. People want harmonization of financial regulation around the "right" rules. However, our human nature means that we cannot know the "right" rules in advance with any certainty. Practical wisdom and reasoning can help us discern features of regulatory systems that might be better or worse than other features. However, those who design regulatory systems are in a world of radical uncertainty where they cannot know in advance the flaws that may be exposed. And, if a single system of international regulation is badly designed, it could lead to the whole world's financial system experiencing similar problems at the same time.

Indeed, we had an element of this in the 2008 financial crisis. The Basel bank-capital-setting regime provided relatively high capital weights for mortgages, even if the mortgages were not especially risky. But it had lower capital weights for securitized mortgages, especially if they had a strong credit rating. Sovereign bonds were also favorably treated. This distorted the activities of ratings agencies and banks. It encouraged securitization (which was already encouraged by US government guarantees through the mortgage securitization agencies Fannie Mae and Freddie Mac), and it encouraged opacity. There were serious flaws in the Basel approach, though flaws, of course, can be expected in any regulatory regime. However, these were flaws that simultaneously affected many countries as well as a huge number of institutions in the United States because of the international nature of regulation. Indeed, it is notable that one country – Canada – did not follow the Basel approach to regulating banks and was relatively unscathed by the financial crisis of 2007–2008.

Developing good regulation, like any other human activity, is a process of trial and error. We often get things wrong. Different approaches in different markets and contexts allow things that do not work to be discarded and things that do work to be copied. Given the tendency of humans to err, perhaps it is better if they are limited to erring on a more local scale and not through an international system of regulation.

## 7.5 ALTERNATIVES TO GOVERNMENT REGULATION: THE EARLY EXCHANGES AND PROFESSIONS

If, given what we know about human nature, government regulation in general and international regulation in particular cannot be assumed to resolve the problems we might hope they will solve, it leads to the question of whether there is an alternative. The Catholic Church's social teaching has discussed alternatives. However, the ideas have not generally been applied to finance, and they have perhaps not been given sufficient emphasis in recent years.

The Catholic social encyclical tradition began with *Rerum Novarum*, which was published in 1891. In this encyclical and then more formally forty years later in *Quadragesimo Anno*, the importance of civil society institutions, professional organizations, and other related bodies in civil and economic life was emphasized. Their importance became embedded within the principle of subsidiarity, which was defined in *Quadragesimo Anno* (79):

> Just as it is gravely wrong to take from individuals what they can accomplish by their own initiative and industry and give it to the community, so also it is an injustice and at the same time a grave evil and disturbance of right order to

assign to a greater and higher association what lesser and subordinate organizations can do. For every social activity ought of its very nature to furnish help to the members of the body social, and never destroy and absorb them.

*Centesimus Annus*, published in 1991, was similarly supportive of non-state institutions in the economy and in society in general. As it happens, such nongovernmental bodies were prominent in the regulation of financial markets during the period when the development of modern finance was at its zenith in many different countries.

In Britain, modern stock exchanges first developed in coffee shops. One of these coffee shops developed into the first formally (and privately) regulated exchange. When the exchange first had an independent home at the beginning of the nineteenth century, it had restrictions on membership, but no comprehensive rule book. In the early years, the exchange was regulated by convention, reputation, and informal rules. For example, when delayed settlement was introduced to increase liquidity, those who did not settle their accounts would be labeled "lame duck" on a board and could be prevented from acting as brokers.[32]

In both London and Amsterdam, the respect for the exchanges was such that they could ensure the orderly enforcement of transactions that were unenforceable in courts of law.[33] Reputation was crucially important in governing business on these markets,[34] and there was encouragement toward virtuous behavior because of the need for participants to develop a reputation for probity.

Although regulation by reputation was important, exchanges developed codified rules over time. These included rules for those who traded on the exchanges and rules for companies that wished to be listed on the exchanges. It was in the interest of companies for rule-making to be robust because an orderly exchange would enable companies to raise capital at a lower cost.[35] It was also in the interest of members of the exchange that trade be regulated

[32] The history of exchanges as well as other market-emergent regulatory structures is discussed further inter alia in Terry Arthur and Philip M. Booth, *Does Britain Need a Financial Regulator?* (London: Institute of Economic Affairs, 2010), and Edward Stringham, *Private Governance: Creating Order in Economic and Social Life* (New York: Oxford University Press, 2015).

[33] See David Kynaston, *City of London – The History* (London: Vintage, 2012), p. 14; and Edward Stringham, "The Extra-Legal Development of Securities Trading in Seventeenth Century Amsterdam," *Quarterly Review of Economics and Finance*, vol. 43, no. 2 (2003), pp. 321–344.

[34] Edward Stringham and Peter J. Boettke, "Brokers, Bureaucrats and the Emergence of Financial Markets," *Managerial Finance*, vol. 30, no. 5 (2004), pp. 57–71.

[35] This is because a well-ordered exchange would make the trading of shares easier and fraud less likely and so make investors more inclined to invest in the securities that could be traded.

because it would reduce the costs of monitoring, reduce losses to fraud, and so on. Informal rules governing behavior were developed from the earliest days of the exchanges, as noted above. A codified rule book covering default and settlement, arbitration, and bad debts was introduced in the London exchange in 1812. There were rules relating to the quotation of prices and general behavior. These rules were designed to increase transparency; for example, partnerships among members had to be listed publicly. The exchange also dealt with problems relating to the use of insider information, and the quotation of securities was regulated from 1844 onward.

Statutory regulation of companies was limited. Government regulated information provision to some extent. However, the stock exchange maintained an entirely independent set of rules and control over its members until 1986. The London Stock Exchange was essentially a club or society that could determine its own rules for membership and for the behavior of its members. Sometimes these rules were stringent, such as those that prevented conflicts of interest by prohibiting members from both trading on their own book (jobbing) and providing advice (broking).

The effectiveness of this system of regulation by market-developed, club-like institutions was itself verified by a parliamentary inquiry. In 1877–1878, a Royal Commission held an inquiry into the stock exchange and concluded that the exchange's rules "had been salutary to the interests of the public" and that the exchange had acted "uprightly, honestly, and with a desire to do justice." It further commented that the exchange's rules were "capable of affording relief and exercising restraint far more prompt and often satisfactory than any within the read of the courts of law."

There are many non-UK examples of market-based regulation through stock exchanges. They developed in Amsterdam even earlier than in London. The New York Stock Exchange evolved later than that in London, but, like its London counterpart, it had rules both for companies that sought listings and for members trading in stocks. By 1914, companies with their shares listed on the New York exchange had to maintain a transfer agency and registrar approved by the exchange. The exchange's Governing Committee had the power to suspend dealings or remove a company's shares from trading. By the 1920s, the New York Exchange also had various reporting and disclosure requirements.[36]

Stock exchanges are not the only examples of private rule-making institutions in British financial markets. It is impossible to describe comprehensively all

[36] See Stringham, Private Governance.

such institutions and the various ways in which market orders and conventions restrained behavior. However, one further example will be given of a different type of regulating body that emerged within society itself.

Professional bodies blossomed in mid-to-late nineteenth-century financial markets. For example, in the United States from 1875 to 1930, there was very little regulation of accounting. Indeed, publicly quoted firms did not have to be audited, though many were. By 1926, 90 percent of companies quoted on the New York Stock Exchange had audited accounts, and there were self-governed professional bodies of accountants who were responsible for auditing in many cases.[37] The American Institute of Certified Public Accountants had codes of conduct for its members.[38] It was the profession – and not a statutory regulator – that proposed the adoption of tentative uniform standards. It is true that the accounting profession was not flawless in its operation. There were scandals. However, it is notable that many of those scandals arose after the government prohibited the profession from imposing regulations on its members (specifically, for example, the government prevented the professional body from banning advertising).

Over time, the accounting profession in the United States became regulated by various state actors, which imposed highly detailed accounting standards on all accountants and the companies they audited, thus removing professional judgment and independent regulation.[39] A very similar trend is evident in the United Kingdom. Independent professions were a mainstay of the processes that ensured financial probity, but regulation has now been taken over by state bodies, often on an international basis.[40]

As with banking regulation, the regulation of accounting has become an international activity. Although the body that develops international accounting standards is independent, its standards are imposed by governments and, indeed, are imposed by the European Union on all European Union listed companies.[41]

As it happens, the statutory imposition of uniform international accounting standards has been implicated in both the Enron scandal and in exacerbating

[37] See Stephen A. Zeff, "How the U.S. Accounting Profession Got Where It Is Today: Part I," *Accounting Horizons*, vol. 17, no. 3 (2003), pp. 189–205.

[38] Indeed, A. C. Ernst resigned from the Institute because of the rule book and never rejoined. His firm was later to become Ernst and Young.

[39] See Zeff, "How the U.S. Accounting Profession Got Where It Is Today."

[40] See David R. Myddelton, *Unshackling Accountants*, Hobart Paper 149 (London: Institute of Economic Affairs, 2004).

[41] Though the US government imposes different standards.

the financial crisis.[42] Andy Haldane, while serving as Executive Director of the Bank of England, argued that international accounting standards applied to banks added fuel to the boom-and-bust cycle by leading assets to be overvalued in the boom phase and undervalued at times of stress – thus exacerbating the cycle.[43] The problem here is not so much that the national or international government regulator may impose the "wrong" standards, but that the centralization of regulatory power and the removal of professional discretion and responsibility mean that the same standards will be imposed on all institutions. When mistakes are made, they will be made on a bigger scale so long as experimentation is not possible, nor differences allowed.

Further consideration of the role of professions is worthwhile – partly because professional associations are specifically mentioned in Catholic social teaching – but also because they are vehicles for fraternity as well as regulation. The evolution of the actuarial profession at the end of the nineteenth century and the beginning of the twentieth century provides an interesting contrast between the United States and the United Kingdom. The actuarial profession is very small. However, its particular area of interest (insurance) comprises a large proportion of the financial sector.[44]

Teece, commenting on the regulation of insurance in the United Kingdom, said:

> America in effect declared that the people could not be trusted to discriminate for themselves; England, on the contrary, said, "give the people the information necessary to enable them to judge, and leave everything else to the force of public opinion, moulded by the criticisms of a free and unfettered press."[45]

This view of the difference between the United States and the United Kingdom is not credibly disputed.[46] Hardy, in the discussion of

42 See David R. Myddelton, "Accounting Aspects of the Financial Crisis," in Booth, ed., *Verdict on the Crash*. Accounting standards are implicated both in allowing companies to overstate their capital in the first place and also in creating illiquidity in markets after the crash, thus exacerbating distress.

43 www.telegraph.co.uk/finance/newsbysector/banksandfinance/9311004/UK-accounting-like-trying-to-pin-tail-on-boisterous-donkey-says-BoEs-Andy-Haldane.html

44 Total assets in the life insurance sector in the United Kingdom are about equal to annual national income.

45 R. Teece, "State Supervision of Insurance," Paper presented to the Insurance Institute of New South Wales and reproduced in Abstract in *Journal of the Institute of Actuaries*, vol. 25 (1885), pp. 350–365.

46 See Philip M. Booth, "'Freedom with Publicity' – The Actuarial Profession and Insurance Regulation from 1844–1945," *Annals of Actuarial Science*, vol. 2, no. 1 (2007), pp. 115–146 for a much wider discussion.

King,[47] points out the much greater failure rate of US insurance companies as compared with UK companies, the former being much more heavily regulated by government.[48] The first president of the American Society of Actuaries, Sheppard Homans, was not against state regulation of insurance in general, but he was strongly critical of its manifestation in the United States, commenting, "On the other hand, we have the stupendous interests of the life insurance companies – that is to say of policyholders and their future widows and orphans – which are hampered, perhaps even endangered, by numerous conflicting, discriminating, and unstable laws."[49]

Thus, it seems that institutions can develop within society itself to regulate the financial sector. A further key question is whether government regulation actually crowds out private, market, and civil society institutions while providing a less effective, less personal, and more bureaucratic alternative. It is at least plausible that government regulation crowded out alternative private forms of regulation by professional bodies. Referring to the United Kingdom, Nicholl writes:

> It is really very doubtful whether the policy of non-interference is not, in most circumstances, the best for a Government to pursue; and, as regards the Institute of Actuaries, it is very questionable if it would have been so vigorous, or so surely founded as it is at the present day if it had depended, at its inception, on assistance or support in any form from the State. It is at least to the credit of our government that they have not at any time willingly put obstacles in the way of the progress of societies or associations for legitimate purposes ... and, in this respect they compare favourably with the Governments of many other countries.[50]

Nicholl went on to quote a fellow actuary's description of the position in the United States, where the existence of state supervision led to the diminution of the reputation and status of the actuarial profession.

It might be thought that these regulatory institutions that develop within markets are irrelevant to the banking crisis, which has been the spur for much of the recent comment from the Catholic Church on regulation in the

47 G. King, "On Legislation Affecting Life Assurance Companies, More Especially with Reference to the Life Assurance Companies Acts, 1870 to 1872, and Their Amendment," *Journal of the Institute of Actuaries*, vol. 29 (1892), pp. 481–540.

48 In the 100 years after the 1870 Life Insurance Companies Act in the United Kingdom, there were only two life insurance failures and neither had any substantial impact on policyholders.

49 Sheppard Homans, "On Government Regulation of Life Insurance Regulation in the United States of America," *Journal of the Institute of Actuaries*, vol. 33 (1897), p. 335.

50 John Nicoll, "The Relation of the Actuarial Profession to the State," *Journal of the Institute of Actuaries*, vol. 34 (1898), p. 170.

financial sector – though the documents that have been produced refer to finance more generally. But, in the field of banking, Selgin shows how, historically, there are examples of stable banking systems without government regulation or central banks because there is a strong and immediate discipline on the banks within the system if one of them stretches its balance sheet or liquidity position too far.[51] Bedard in Selgin (2017)[52] also shows how such disciplines within markets and without central banks may well make the development of systemic risk (specifically cited as a problem in *Oeconomicae et pecuniariae quaestiones*) less likely.

It is not possible to conduct a study that will show definitively whether government regulation is less effective than alternatives that arise from within markets. Market-based regulation does have specific problems.[53] For example, private regulatory systems have often been characterized by restrictive practices that kept outsiders out of markets. Despite this, private financial regulatory institutions have rarely had statutory monopolies. Investors can choose to trade and invest outside the regulated system. However, the overarching point is that the debate within Catholic social teaching should not be so much about whether to regulate but about who regulates. Certainly it should not be assumed that the answer to that question should be the state or international regulatory institutions. It should certainly not be assumed that regulatory institutions cannot develop within society or within markets.

## 7.6 NONGOVERNMENT REGULATION IN THE TWENTY-FIRST CENTURY

The club-like institutions described no longer exist as the main regulators in financial markets. Nevertheless, there are examples of private regulators that remain important. Although governments have tended to take over regulatory functions that previously developed within markets, private institutions still develop to fulfill a need, either filling in gaps or operating in new innovative markets.

For example, there are available exemptions from EU regulations on the trading and listing of securities. In this context, the Alternative Investment Market (AIM) has established as a market that is not directly regulated by

[51] Selgin, Financial Stability.

[52] Mathieu Bédard, "On Chain Gangs in Financial Stability – A Commentary on George Selgin's Lecture," in Selgin, *Financial Stability*.

[53] See Philip M. Booth, "Stock Exchanges as Lighthouses," *Man and the Economy*, vol. 1, no. 2 (2014), pp. 171–188.

government agencies and on which securities can be issued and traded without typical government regulation. Statutory regulation on market abuse applies to trading in companies listed on the market, but, otherwise, the market develops its rulebook independently of government. AIM requires that companies must produce half-yearly reports and annual audited accounts. Where a company is located outside a jurisdiction that applies specific accounting standards, AIM still requires accounts to be produced according to recognized standards, but allows some discretion. There are also policies related to dealing in shares by directors and similarly high-level employees of AIM-listed companies. Many other sets of rules dealing with disclosure, conduct, and trading also exist.[54]

This market is not a trivial, bit-part player. In November 2019 there were 745 UK companies traded on the exchange, in addition to 127 companies domiciled in other countries. The total market capitalization of all the companies traded on AIM was over £100 billion. In 2018, total trades came to nearly £69 billion.[55] While there are some companies with trivial market capitalization, sixteen companies have a market capitalization of over £1 billion.

A number of studies suggest that fraud on AIM is no greater than on other markets.[56] Indeed, incidents of fraud are rare. This system shows how intermediary institutions are able to develop their own regulatory approaches that are appropriate to the contexts in which they are operating, even where finance is heavily regulated by government.

Another example of nongovernmental regulation arises in derivatives markets. For example, derivatives exchanges have comprehensive rules to prevent fraud and reduce risks, such as the requirement to keep cash in a "margin account," in case contracts incur losses.

The over-the-counter derivatives business is almost wholly the preserve of wholesale investors. But, interestingly, these markets do not go unregulated even though they do not attract the same regulatory interest from governments as do consumer-facing markets. These markets are regulated by a private body, the International Swaps and Derivatives Association (ISDA). ISDA's mission is "[to foster] safe and efficient derivatives markets to facilitate effective risk management for all users of derivative products." It achieves this in a number of ways, all of which involve regulatory functions, such as "[d]eveloping standardized documentation globally to promote legal

[54] The rule book can be found here www.londonstockexchange.com/companies-and-advisors/aim/advisers/aim-notices/aimrulesforcompaniesjan16.pdf

[55] See www.londonstockexchange.com/statistics/markets/aim/aim.htm

[56] See Stringham, *Private Governance*, pp. 95–98.

certainty and maximum risk reduction."[57] Members have to apply to join and can have their memberships revoked.

ISDA members can choose to use the ISDA master agreement, which applies to over 90 percent of over-the-counter derivatives transactions in the world. At the end of November 2019, this amounted to almost $0.6 quadrillion.[58] In addition, as part of its regulatory function, ISDA also has a dispute resolution procedure (thus circumventing the need to use courts in most instances) and a Credit Derivatives Determinations Committee. The latter uses a set of rules to determine, for example, whether a credit default event has taken place and, thus, whether counterparties to a derivative contract need to settle. In many respects, this is similar to the juridical functions of stock exchanges praised by the 1877–1878 Royal Commission mentioned earlier.

It might be argued that the financial crisis demonstrated the failure of private regulation, especially as credit derivative swaps were at the heart of some of the big-name failures. However, it is not the purpose of ISDA to prevent banks and insurance companies from making bad investments or from taking derivative positions without adequate collateral. These regulatory functions – rightly or wrongly – were taken over by government agencies at various times in the last century. Rather, it is ISDA's role to regulate the market itself. In fact, ISDA oversaw the orderly settlement and unwinding of trillions of dollars of derivatives contracts upon the failure of Fannie Mae and Freddie Mac.[59]

Of course, no regulatory mechanism, private or state, is foolproof. The LIBOR scandal is an example of a private regulatory process that went very wrong.[60] This is a generally sorry tale, in which banks provided misinformation that was then used to compile an important index of short-term interest rates against which contracts were priced. As it happens, it appears that the regulators knew about the irregularities for many years before taking action and also that the Bank of England might have encouraged some of the questionable practices. As such, nobody comes out well from the incident. Even so, as an example of private regulation, it clearly fell short of what should have been expected. In this context, though, it is worth repeating the message that the purpose of studying alternative approaches to regulation is not to find

57 See www2.isda.org/about-isda/mission-statement/

58 See Bank for International Settlements statistics at www.bis.org/publ/otc_hy1911.htm

59 For a more detailed discussion of the problems in different aspects of the regulatory systems in the credit derivatives market, see Stringham, *Private Governance*, chapter 11.

60 This scandal was mentioned in *Oeconomicae et pecuniariae quaestiones* in the slightly odd context of the taxation of bank loans.

perfection. The purpose is to find the institutional approaches to restraining markets that best deal with the imperfection of the human person.[61]

## 7.7 CONCLUSION

Catholic social teaching has long been critical of what are sometimes described as "unfettered" markets. In some contexts, the discussion has been a nuanced one, with the respective roles of individuals exercising moral restraint as well as professions and other civil society regulatory institutions being proposed as restraining features of markets. However, in recent years, Catholic social teaching documents have proposed a greater role for the state in the regulation of the economy. This is especially true in the financial sector.

Experience with financial markets suggests that regulation has often been either a shared responsibility or else a function undertaken by market institutions entirely. It is demonstrably false that, if the state does not regulate financial markets, those markets will not be restrained and regulatory institutions would not exist at all. When Catholic social teaching is applied to the specific area of the regulation of the economy, the question is what the appropriate respective roles of the state and market institutions are. Even today, there is a considerable role for market institutions in regulating financial activity, and there are good reasons for reviving that tradition of thinking within Catholic social teaching.

For reasons that should be understandable to Christians, allowing the state alone to regulate financial markets is likely to be problematic. The same flawed human nature that leads to fallibility in markets is likely to lead to fallibility amongst regulators. Certainly, the extension of international regulation, for which the Church has often called, should be concerning. Among other things, it is likely to increase systemic risk in the financial system by compounding the effects of human error on an international scale. The fact that participants in markets can be fallible, that this can give rise to serious problems, and that we cannot be confident that such problems can be resolved by regulation might suggest that we cannot say anything about the matter with much confidence at all.

However, history and prior theory suggest that private regulatory institutions ought to be able to make an important contribution to restraining behavior in financial markets. Parallels can also be drawn with the work of Elinor Ostrom,

[61] The actions in relation to LIBOR were in any case illegal and can be (and were) dealt with through appropriate criminal or civil procedures.

the 2009 Nobel laureate in economics, whose work examined the management of natural resources. She discovered that regulation could take place in several layers, with the governmental layer often simply supporting the others through enforcement or the provision of information. There is much in common here with the principle of subsidiarity in Catholic social teaching. And there are many parallels between these contexts and the various regulatory institutions in financial markets,[62] although regulatory institutions in financial markets have often been effective without any government structures or assistance at all.

It is interesting that a process in the United Kingdom that is often described as "deregulation" of financial markets involved the state's prohibition of regulatory powers by an entirely private body, the stock exchange. There are many other examples where the state has restricted the activities of market-based regulators and independent professional bodies in the name of promoting competition. Catholic social teaching in general would suggest the opposite approach. The principle of subsidiarity would suggest that the state might need to play a part in regulation,[63] but that it should not be the primary actor. Rather, it should support other regulatory institutions that have evolved to deal with human imperfection in finance.

It seems that recent Catholic social teaching has fallen into the trap of accepting the state–individual nexus, whereby the state sets the rules of the game and individuals work within them. However, a richer interpretation of the tradition would involve important roles for all institutions in society, whether civil society institutions, professional bodies, or institutions arising within markets. This would not only be a richer interpretation of the tradition of Catholic social teaching, but would also be a realistic response to human frailty within the market and within government.

[62] In a conversation with Elinor Ostrom not long before she died, We discussed the early stock exchanges and compared them with her work on environmental and property rights regulation. She was not aware of the history of financial regulation at all and was fascinated by the parallels.

[63] This may be through codes of law, bankruptcy procedures, and so on rather than directive regulation.

# 8

# Christianity and Bankruptcy

DAVID SKEEL

The term "bankruptcy" is nowhere to be found in the Bible. It seems to have first emerged in the late sixteenth century as a concoction of "banca" and "rotta," which together mean "broken bench."[1] According to a common historical account, lenders in late medieval Italy set up benches in the market square – the equivalent of hanging out a shingle – and made their loans on their benches. If a lender defaulted, his bench was broken, thus preventing him from continuing to do business. Default ended his lending career.[2]

Although these developments came long after Christ, debt and the consequences of default have always been with us. They are a major theme both in the Hebrew Bible and in the New Testament. In Israel, as in the ancient Near East generally, a debtor who defaulted on his obligations was often sold into slavery or servitude. Biblical law moderated the harshness of this system by prohibiting Israelites from charging interest on loans to one another, thus diminishing the risk of default, and by requiring that slaves be released after seven years of service. Jesus alluded to the lending laws at least once,[3] and he frequently used economic illustrations in his teaching, linking forgiveness of sins to debt relief both in the Lord's Prayer and in one of his parables.[4]

Thanks to Daniel Crane, Sam Gregg, Jonathan Master, Ruth Okediji, Scott Pryor, Jesse Schupack, Robert Thrasher, Alvin Velazquez, and Professor Ruth Okediji's Christian Legal Perspectives class at Harvard Law School for helpful comments, and to Robert Thrasher for excellent research help.

1 See, for example, Vern Countryman, "Bankruptcy and the Individual Debtor – And a Modest Proposal to Return to the Seventeenth Century," *Catholic University Law Review*, vol. 32 (1982–1983), p. 809.

2 Ibid.

3 In Luke 6:35, Jesus says "love your enemies, and do good, and lend, expecting nothing in return, and your reward will be great." All Bible quotations are from the Revised Standard Version.

4 Matthew 18:21–35 (Parable of the Unforgiving Servant).

Banca rotta was neither the first word nor the last in the evolution of bankruptcy in the centuries after Christ. Under Roman law, a debtor who defaulted could be dismembered and his body parts delivered to creditors, although scholars are skeptical whether this punishment was ever seriously enforced.[5] In the eighteenth and nineteenth centuries, debtors who defaulted on their obligations could be thrown into a debtors' prison, with release only when the debtor repaid his obligations. The risk of imprisonment for debt was very real.[6] Robert Morris, one of the financers of the American Revolution, spent time in debtors' prison,[7] as did Charles Dickens's father. Dickens's father's imprisonment in London's notorious Marshallsea prison inspired Dickens's novel *Little Dorrit*.[8]

Although I will touch on these developments briefly, since they shed light on historical understandings of the Biblical passages on debt and financial distress, I will focus in this chapter on modern bankruptcy law, especially American bankruptcy law. The past century has seen a significant expansion of personal bankruptcy law, the emergence of corporate bankruptcy, and most recently a debate over whether over-indebted countries should have access to bankruptcy relief. I will consider the extent to which each of these developments could be seen as reflecting Christian principles, and what a more fully Christian vision of bankruptcy law might look like.

## 8.1 THE BIBLICAL CONTEXT

Other than sex, almost no other feature of daily life figures so prominently in Scripture as debt. The Mosaic Law, the prophets, the Psalms, Proverbs, and Jesus himself all devote considerable attention to lending and debt. Moses exhorts God's people to lend freely, and without charging interest, to a brother in need.[9] Ezekiel includes two separate references to lending and debt in his description of righteous behavior: a righteous man "restores to the debtor his pledge" and "does not lend at interest or take any profit."[10] Jesus refers to debt

5 See, for example, Alan N. Resnick and Henry J. Sommer, eds., *Collier on Bankruptcy*, 16th ed., 20.01[1] (2009 update).

6 The classic work is Bruce Mann, *Republic of Debtors: Bankruptcy in the Age of American Independence* (Cambridge, MA: Harvard University Press, 2002).

7 Ibid., pp. 100–102.

8 Dickens's father's experience is recounted in the editor's introduction to *Little Dorrit*. Charles Dickens, *Little Dorrit*, eds. Helen Small and Stephen Wall (New York: Penguin Classics, 2004 [1857]).

9 For example, Deuteronomy 15:8–10; 23:19–20. See also Nehemiah 5:1–13 (condemning the nobles and officials for charging interest and urging loans without interest).

10 Ezekiel 18:7, 8.

in the Lord's Prayer and in several of his parables.[11] Ever since Adam and Eve were expelled from Eden, debt and the consequences of default have been a familiar feature of economic life.

Nearly all of the Old Testament's debt passages either impose restrictions on its scope or call for adherence to those restrictions. The restrictions are important, and interpretations of their implications have shaped lending laws for centuries. But a crucial implication of the debt restrictions is too often neglected: The frequent reference to debt necessarily implies that debt is beneficial, despite its risks. Overall, debt must be good. If debt were always undesirable, the Mosaic Law could simply have banished it. The law could have instructed God's people to make gifts to struggling members of their community, while forbidding any repayment obligation. But that's not what the law did, even within the community of God's people. The debt passages seem to envision that a righteous person will make interest-free loans to his struggling neighbor.

It is not hard to imagine why this might be so. The debtor might need funds today that she is likely to be capable of repaying later. Historically, farmers have often been in this position. They do not have sufficient funds to buy the necessary seeds, fertilizer, and equipment at the outset of the growing period, but they expect to be able to repay the funds when the harvest comes in. If debt were not an option, a farmer who did not already have large amounts of funds, and who was unable to wheedle gifts from friends or relatives, might be stranded. Loans are a very attractive alternative. Loans can ensure that the debtor has funds when she needs them and has a productive use for them, which is especially important if the debtor's business is volatile or seasonal. Debt thus gives the borrower access to funds at times when she has good use for them but would not be able to repay, and enables her to repay at a later time, or in increments that she is able to repay. Borrowing the money rather than relying solely on gifts may also be preferable from the perspective of the debtor's dignity.[12]

In contrast to the benefits of debt, which it leaves implicit, the Bible is quite explicit about the risk of defaulting on one's obligations. In Israel, and in the ancient world generally, a debtors who were unable to repay what they owed might be forced into some form of indentured servitude – that

[11] Matthew 6:9–13 (Lord's Prayer).

[12] For a popular book making this point, see Steve Corbett and Brian Fikkert, *When Helping Hurts: Alleviating Poverty without Hurting the Poor . . . and Yourself* (Chicago: Moody Publishers, 2009).

is, slavery.[13] Debt was like two other ubiquitous features both of the ancient and moderns worlds, sex and fire. Each is good in its proper domain, but dangerous if misused.

The most prominent Biblical constraint on lending transactions is the prohibition on charging interest.[14] The anti-usury rule is referred to dozens of times in the Old Testament,[15] and had a long, at times fraught, history in the centuries after the Biblical canon was complete. The prohibition on usury was construed in many Jewish communities as barring interest on loans to fellow Jews, but not on loans to outsiders.[16] In Catholic canon law, the distinction between appropriate compensation for a loan and usury underwent a long evolution.[17] Although usury prohibitions do not guarantee that debtors will never default on their loans, they make default less likely. Like strict restrictions on sexual intimacy or the use of fire, they mitigate risk. The most obvious objectives of the prohibition are preventing predatory lending, and reducing the burden of a debtor's repayment obligations. The most obvious cost of a strict prohibition is that lenders may be less willing to lend if they cannot ask for interest on the loan. This may be why the Biblical writers extol lenders who are willing to lend money without charging interest.[18]

In addition to prohibiting usury, Biblical law restricted loan transactions in another important way. Biblical law limited the use of certain kinds of collateral for what we would now call secured loans. Even if the debtor agreed to pledge his grinding stone to the lender as security for repayment of a loan, the Bible prohibited this.[19] The Bible imposed a more nuanced restriction when a debtor pledged his cloak as collateral. Although lenders were allowed to take the cloak as collateral, they were required to give the cloak back to the debtor before sunset.[20]

13 See, for example, Michael LeFebvre, "Theology and Economics in the Biblical Year of Jubilee," *Reformed Presbyterian Theological Journal*, vol. 1, no. 2 (Spring 2015), pp. 13–32, 20.

14 For additional perspective on the treatment of usury in the Bible, see Stephen M. Bainbridge, *Christianity and Corporate Purpose*, this volume.

15 See, for example, Exodus 22:25; Leviticus 25:35–37; Deuteronomy 23:19–20.

16 Some theologians contend that it applied only to loans to the poor, not to ordinary business loans. See, for example, LeFebvre, "Theology and Economics," pp. 23–24.

17 The classic modern study construed the church as having changed its theology of usury. John T. Noonan, Jr., *The Scholastic Analysis of Usury* (Cambridge, MA: Harvard University Press, 1957). For an argument that the current theology is consistent with its antecedents. Brian M. McCall, *The Church and the Usurers: Unprofitable Lending for the Modern Economy* (Ave Maria, FL: Sapienza Press, 2013).

18 See, for example, Ezekiel 18:8.

19 Deuteronomy 24:6.

20 Exodus 22:26–27.

These limitations on the collateral a debtor could pledge are similar to what we now call "exemptions." Modern law often restricts the right of creditors to seize a debtor's house or the tools of her trade if the debtor defaults on their obligations, much as Biblical law prohibited the pledge of a grindstone and required lenders to return the debtor's cloak at the end of each day.[21] These Biblical restrictions are both narrower and broader than exemptions in contemporary law. They cover only a limited number of assets, whereas the range of modern exemptions is broader. But the Biblical restrictions were absolute. Under modern American bankruptcy law, debtors generally are not prevented from pledging otherwise exempt assets; the assets are only exempt if they have not been pledged to a particular creditor.[22]

The Biblical constraints on lending would have significantly reduced the risk of default. A debtor who does not need to pay interest on a loan, and whose grinding stone and cloak cannot be taken, is less likely to fall into financial distress than he would in the absence of these strictures. But default is still quite possible. If a debtor's crop was destroyed or his business suffered a setback, he might be unable to pay even a no-interest loan. Even if debt is restricted and every lender obeys these restrictions, some debtors will inevitably default.

Biblical law anticipates and responds to the consequences of default – which in the ancient world often meant slavery – with two sets of debt relief provisions. The first called for the release of a debt after seven years, and of a Jewish slave after he had served seven years.[23] The forty-ninth year brought an even more sweeping release. God's people were instructed to blow a trumpet after counting "seven weeks of years, seven times seven years," and to "proclaim liberty throughout all the land to all of its inhabitants" for the coming year.[24] For the Jubilee year, they were to leave their land fallow, to return to their family homestead, and to release every slave and financial obligation. Their debts were entirely erased.

[21] For a similar point, see Paul B. Rasor, "Biblical Roots of Modern Consumer Credit Law," *Journal of Law and Religion*, vol. 10 (1993), pp. 157, 179–180. In the United States, debtors are permitted to choose either the exemptions provided by federal bankruptcy law, or the exemptions provided by the debtor's state of residence, although the state is permitted to require its debtors to use the state law exemptions. State exemptions vary considerably. These rather convoluted rules are set forth in section 522 of the Bankruptcy Code. 11 U.S.C. § 522.

[22] See generally 11 U.S.C. § 522(f) (removing most judicial liens, but not liens arising from consensual pledges, from property to the extent of a debtor's exemption).

[23] Deuteronomy 15:1–12.

[24] Leviticus 25:8, 10.

The most striking feature of debt relief in the Hebrew Bible is that it is unconditional. The debt release contained a partial exception: a debtor who had sold himself or was sold into slavery for debt received his relief only after serving for seven years.[25] But the release after seven years was unconditional, as were the release for ordinary debts and the release in the Jubilee.

One concern with generous access to debt relief is that it may reduce lenders' willingness to lend. The seven year release and Jubilee rules in the Hebrew Bible anticipate this effect. With the seven year release, Israelites are admonished not to stop lending to and otherwise helping poor fellow Israelites when the seven year release was near.[26] With land transactions, by contrast, the Jubilee instructions not only permit, they instruct – buyers and sellers to take the number of years until the Jubilee into account.[27]

Modern bankruptcy laws often limit relief to debtors who especially need relief and are in some sense worthy of the assistance they receive. In American law, this inclination is captured in the statement, memorialized in an early twentieth-century Supreme Court decision, that bankruptcy is intended for "honest but unfortunate" debtors.[28] Biblical law is not indifferent to the risk of debtor misbehavior. The Psalms describe a debtor who "borrows but does not pay back" as "wicked,"[29] and a debtor who shirks his financial obligations would be seen as violating two of the Ten Commandments, the prohibition against stealing and (because he had promised by contract to repay) against false witness. These are serious offenses. But they are not the focus of the Biblical relief laws. Those laws do not distinguish between worthy and unworthy debtors; they call for forgiveness of everyone's debts.

Jesus devoted as much attention to debt and financial distress as the Hebrew Bible did. Indeed, debt figures even more prominently in his parables and other teachings than marital fidelity. In the Lord's Prayer, Jesus instructed his disciples to ask God to "forgive our debts, as we forgive our debtors."[30] The importance of debt forgiveness recurs elsewhere in Jesus' teachings as well. In one parable, a servant who is unable to pay his obligations begs his master to give him more time to pay his debt; moved by the plea, the master agrees to forgive the debt altogether.[31] When the servant is asked by a fellow servant for more time to pay a much smaller debt, however, the first servant refuses,

25 Deuteronomy 15:12–13.
26 Deuteronomy 15:9–10.
27 Leviticus 25:15–16.
28 *Local Loan Co.* v. *Hunt*, 292 U.S. 234, 244 (1934).
29 Psalm 37:21.
30 Matthew 6:9–13.
31 Matthew 18:21–35.

insisting that his own debtor pay everything he owes. The first servant is condemned for his lack of mercy, and in the parable the master rescinds his promise to forgive the servant's debts and throws him in prison.

Because Jesus is using debt to make a spiritual point about our need for forgiveness and about forgiving others, these passages need to be handled carefully in an essay about financial distress. They are not necessarily a blueprint for legislation, both because the economic implications are often secondary and Jesus is speaking primarily to his followers, not speaking directly about secular law. Yet it would be odd if these teachings had no relevance. Here and elsewhere, Jesus seems to imply that charging interest for a loan is legitimate.[32] Jesus also assumes that his hearers will understand debt and its potentially ruinous consequences. On multiple occasions, in several different contexts, he praises those who respond favorably to pleas for forgiveness of debt or condemns those who insist on strict adherence to the terms of a credit contract. This seems to have implications for a Christian understanding of financial distress.

## 8.2 AN ESSAY UPON PROJECTS: OF BANKRUPTS

A famous signpost on the road to modern bankruptcy law was a political tract called *An Essay upon Projects* published in 1697 by Daniel DeFoe, who later wrote *Robinson Crusoe* and several other classic early English novels.[33] In *An Essay upon Projects*, DeFoe, who was a Protestant dissenter from the established Anglican Church, outlines a variety of proposals for social reform. In a chapter called "Of Bankrupts," DeFoe lamented that while most English laws were "temper'd with Mercy, Lenity, and Freedom," the bankruptcy law had "something in it of Barbarity."[34] DeFoe proposed an alternative approach that would, he believed, leave both debtors and their creditors better off.

The English bankruptcy law of the time authorized creditors of a debtor to obtain a judgment if creditors failed to repay them. The debtor could be put in prison for the failure to satisfy the judgment, and while the debtor was in prison, the creditors were entitled to any money he earned, until the debts were repaid. DeFoe insisted that the law "tend[ed] wholly to the Destruction of the Debtor, and yet very little to the Advantage of the Creditor."[35] Although

32 See, for example, Luke 19:11–27 (interest on bank deposit in Parable of the Ten Minas).

33 Daniel DeFoe, *An Essay upon Projects*, eds. Joyce D. Kennedy, Michael Seidel, and Maximillian E. Novak (New York: AMS Press, 1999 [1697]).

34 Ibid., p. 75.

35 Ibid.

dishonest debtors might evade their creditors, he argued, the law gave honest debtors no incentive to work. They could not earn a living if they were locked up in prison, and any assets they obtained outside of prison could immediately be seized by creditors. This did not seem to be in anyone's interests, since it humiliated the debtor and did nothing to improve the creditors' prospects for recovery.

What was needed, according to DeFoe, was a law that would provide suitable treatment for four types of people, the "Honest Debtor," the "Knavish, Designing, or Idle, Extravagant Debtor," the "Moderate Creditor," and the "Rigorous Severe Creditor." Under the framework that DeFoe proposed, the debtor would file a petition stating that:

> [Y]our Petitioner being unable to carry on his Business, by reason of great Losses and Decay of Trade, and being ready and willing to make a full and entire discovery of his whole Estate, and to deliver up the same to your Honors upon Oath, as the Law directs for the satisfaction of his Creditors, and having to that purpose entered his Name in the Books of your Office . . . [y]our Petitioner humbly prays the Protection of this Honorable Court.[36]

The debtor would thus turn over all of his assets to the court. If the debtor made a "fair and just Surrender of all his Estate and Effects," Defoe goes on to suggest, 5 percent of the value of his assets would be returned to the debtor, and his obligations would be erased – "discharged," in bankruptcy parlance.[37] The other 95 percent of the value of the debtor's assets would be "fairly and equally divided among the Creditors." If the debtor hid some of his assets from his creditors, by contrast, he would be punished with life in prison.

The author of "Of Bankrupts" was not exactly a dispassionate observer of the insolvency laws of the time. A few years earlier, DeFoe had been arrested for failing to pay debts he had incurred as a merchant, and he spent a short time in prison as a result. He took a keen interest in the treatment of debtors throughout his life, and was in precarious financial straits at various points, in part because of his criticism of the established church.[38]

In one respect, DeFoe's proposed bankruptcy law reflected the realities of his time. His reference to the "Decay of Trade" suffered by a debtor assumes that the debtor would be a merchant or trader, rather than an ordinary citizen. The insolvency laws of the time made the same assumption, and this would hold true for another two centuries. The earliest English (and the first

36 Ibid., p. 83 (italics removed).
37 Ibid., p. 84.
38 Ibid., pp. xix–xx (editors' introduction).

American) bankruptcy laws applied only to merchants and traders. In other respects, however, DeFoe's framework called for a radically different conception of bankruptcy. In DeFoe's era, creditors were the ones who invoked the laws, not debtors, and a debtor's obligations were not discharged even if the debtor turned over all of his assets to the court. If the assets were not sufficient to pay the debtor's creditors in full, the debtor was still liable for the unpaid amount. DeFoe's proposal that the debtor himself file the petition, that he receive a 5 percent living stipend, and that his obligations be fully discharged if he turned over all of his assets to the court called for strikingly new approach to the regulation of financial distress.

Although many of the social reform proposals in *An Essay on Projects* are justifiably forgotten, DeFoe's bankruptcy proposal was remarkably prescient, at least from the long view of history. Less than a decade after DeFoe wrote the Essay, England enacted insolvency reforms that provided for a complete discharge of the debtor's obligations for the first time in England's history.[39] Only creditors could invoke the law, but if they did, and the debtor's assets were turned over to the court, the debtor received a discharge. Truly voluntary bankruptcy – a bankruptcy law that the debtor could invoke – would not come for another century and a half. After enacting a short-lived bankruptcy law based on then-current English law in 1800, American lawmakers passed the law permitting voluntary bankruptcy filings in 1841.[40] The Bankruptcy Act of 1841 was remarkably similar to the framework that DeFoe had proposed, although it was as short-lived as its predecessor.

## 8.3 CHRISTIANITY AND US BANKRUPTCY LAW

The American approach to bankruptcy, which emerged in halting steps during the nineteenth century,[41] is closely linked to the concept of a "fresh start" for struggling debtors. Under American bankruptcy law, a debtor who is overwhelmed by her debts can file a bankruptcy petition, discharge all

39 A 1705 reform, the Statute of Anne, provided the first discharge. See, for example, Lawrence Shepard, "Personal Failures and the Bankruptcy Reform Act of 1978," *Journal of Law and Economics*, vol. 27 (1984), pp. 419, 421–422.

40 See, for example, Charles Jordan Tabb, "The History of the Bankruptcy Laws in the United States," *The American Bankruptcy Institute Law Review*, vol. 3 (1995), pp. 5, 17.

41 During this same period, states also began to abolish debtors' prisons, and the Thirteenth Amendment barred involuntary servitude for debt after the Civil War. Recent patterns of imprisonment for nonpayment of criminal fees and costs have been widely condemned as creating new debtors' prisons. For an excellent analysis of the history and current developments, see Christopher D. Hampson, "The New American Debtors' Prisons," *The American Journal of Criminal Justice*, vol. 44 (2016), p. 1.

of her debts, and receive a fresh start. Although the debtor is required to turn over their property to the court, they are permitted to retain property that is defined as "exempt" in their state, such as tools of trade or some of the value of their house. For Protestant evangelicals especially, this narrative sounds as if it came straight from the pages of the New Testament. The Bible teaches that each of us is a sinner who has rebelled against God and is utterly hopeless on our own. We are "dead in [our] trespasses and sins."[42] Yet if we seek forgiveness in Christ, we are offered a categorical absolution from all of our past mistakes.[43] Bankruptcy and the Christian story both promise a new beginning. One is temporal, the other spiritual, but the trajectory of the narratives is the same.

It is important to recognize how sharply the American fresh start differs from other countries' insolvency laws. Until very recently, many countries did not provide for a discharge at all. In countries that did offer a discharge for financially distressed debtors, the discharge often required the debtor first to make payments for a period of years, and it could be denied for misbehavior or a failure to pay.[44] Even in England, the source of America's earliest insolvency regulation and the home of Daniel DeFoe, many debtors are not given a discharge.

America is of course known as far more religious, and far more Christian, than most other similarly developed nations. This and the deep similarities between the bankruptcy fresh start and the Christian narrative suggest an obvious hypothesis: Perhaps Christian influence shaped the emergence of the fresh start principle in American bankruptcy. It did, but in more subtle and complex fashion than the parallel narratives might seem to suggest.

Early on, many Christian pastors seem to have been more likely to preach about a debtor's moral obligation to repay his debts than to call for debt forgiveness.[45] To be sure, attitudes toward debt were shifting during the eighteenth century. According to the leading historian of the bankruptcy and insolvency laws of this era, the widespread belief that financial obligations

[42] Ephesians 2:1.

[43] An influential recent study of American bankruptcy law, one of whose authors is now a prominent politician, was entitled *As We Forgive Our Debtors*. Teresa A. Sullivan, Elizabeth Warren, and Jay Lawrence Westbrook, *As We Forgive Our Debtors: Bankruptcy and Consumer Credit in America* (New York: Oxford University Press, 1989).

[44] For discussion of the European approach to consumer insolvency and bankruptcy law, see, for example, Iain Ramsay, "Comparative Consumer Bankruptcy," *The University of Illinois Law Review*, vol. 2007 (2007), pp. 241, 250–251.

[45] Mann, *Republic of Debtors*, pp. 36–44 (recounting writings of Samuel Moody and Cotton Mather in the early eighteenth century).

were an absolute moral obligation began giving way to broader acceptance of commercial life as entailing calculated risks.[46] The latter perspective – that risks were inevitable in commercial life – suggested that default was not necessarily a moral failure. But this view was initially confined to commercial life. There does not seem to have been a Christian consensus that debtors who are overwhelmed by debt should be given a fresh start.

The next complexity is that explicit appeals to Christianity diminished in the legislative debates over bankruptcy during the period when the fresh start concept emerged. Although legislators made occasional references to the Bible and more frequent claims about the morality or immorality of proposed bankruptcy legislation, they did not explicitly articulate a Christian perspective on the appropriate contours of bankruptcy law. But Christian principles figured prominently in a lively popular debate over the expectations of "commercial morality" during the early and mid-nineteenth century especially.[47] Henry Ward Beecher, one of the nation's most famous pastors and the brother of the author of *Uncle Tom's Cabin*, "implored creditors to act 'with the lenity of Christian men,' and debtors to demonstrate a 'manly honesty' that will work a 'sustenance of religion.'"[48] This meant that creditors should treat debtors charitably, and that debtors should be forthright and disclose all of their assets.[49]

The fresh start and American bankruptcy more generally emerged from a remarkable pas de deux between pro-creditor lawmakers in the Northeast, who saw bankruptcy as essential to the quest to create a commercial economy, and pro-debtor lawmakers in the South and West, who feared that creditors would use any federal bankruptcy law to displace farmers from their farms when the farmer had a bad crop or other misfortune.[50] The Bankruptcy Act of 1841, which permitted debtors to file for bankruptcy voluntarily for the first time, was promoted and enacted by the creditor-oriented Whig Party, which was strongly associated with evangelicals during this period.[51] Although other evangelicals, especially those outside the Northeast, opposed bankruptcy, their

46 Ibid., p. 77.

47 For discussion of conceptions of commercial morality during this period, see Edward J. Balleisen, *Navigating Failure: Bankruptcy and Commercial Society in Antebellum America* (Chapel Hill: University of North Carolina Press, 2001), pp. 70–72.

48 Quoted in ibid., p. 72.

49 Ibid., p. 70.

50 See, for example, David A. Skeel, Jr., *Debt's Dominion: A History of Bankruptcy Law in America* (Princeton, NJ: Princeton University Press, 2001), pp. 26–28.

51 See C. Scott Pryor, "The Missing Piece of the Puzzle: Perspectives on the Wage Priority in Bankruptcy," *American Bankruptcy Institute Law Review*, vol. 16 (2008), pp. 121–160, 151–159.

views influenced many of its features. Starting with the 1867 bankruptcy law, debtors were permitted to exempt any property that would be exempt under state law, and the 1898 law made it more difficult to throw a debtor into bankruptcy involuntarily.[52]

My claim that Christianity shaped the distinctive American approach to bankruptcy should not be pressed too strongly, given the complexity of the interaction between pro-debtor and pro-creditor advocates. Moreover, then as now, many Christians questioned the morality of bankruptcy, emphasizing the Biblical warning that the "wicked [person] borrows but does not pay back."[53] Although these complications are significant, the evidence of Christian influence remains striking. And the framework that emerged is remarkably consistent with Christian principles.

Some might question – and some do – whether the American fresh start truly is consistent with the Biblical pattern of debt and relief from financial distress. I have already hinted at the long tradition of emphasizing the Biblical call to make good on our promises, financial and otherwise.[54] The contention that bankruptcy is never appropriate still is widely held, including by some evangelical consumer finance experts.[55] In my view, this position cannot easily be reconciled with elaborate provision for debt relief in the Jubilee passages of the Hebrew Bible.[56] To be sure, the Jubilee was closely linked to Israel's unique relationship with the Promised Land, and thus looks quite different through the lens of the New Testament. But there is little reason to believe that Christ's fulfillment of the old covenant rendered Jubilee principles obsolete. To the contrary, Jesus called for

[52] See, for example, Skeel, *Debt's Dominion*, pp. 24–43.

[53] Psalm 37:21.

[54] In addition to Psalm 37:21, Christian critics of bankruptcy also point to the command in Romans 13:7 and 8 to "[p]ay to all what is owed to them" and "[o]we no one anything, except to love one another." See also 2 Kings 4 (Elisha miraculously provides oil to indebted widow, and tells her to sell the oil and use the proceeds to repay her debts, rather than calling for debt forgiveness).

[55] Larry Burkett, a leading evangelical financial counsellor, taught that using bankruptcy to "start afresh ... reflects a lack of trust and a deceitful attitude," and is thus inherently sinful. Larry Burkett, *How to Manage Your Money* (Chicago: Moody Press, 1971), p. 27. Similarly, Howard Dayton says that Christians generally should not file for bankruptcy, and if there is no other realistic option, they should try to repay what they owe after bankruptcy. Howard Dayton, *Your Money Counts: The Biblical Guide to Earning, Spending, Saving, Investing, Giving, and Getting Out of Debt* (Carol Stream, IL: Tyndale House Publishers, 2011), pp. 44–45.

[56] For a similar conclusion, see John R. Sutherland, "The Ethics of Bankruptcy: A Biblical Perspective," *Journal of Business Ethics*, vol. 7 (1988), pp. 917–927. Sutherland bases his conclusions on the Hebrew Bible passages on debt and for some reason does not give any consideration to New Testament teaching.

creditors to forgive the debts of their financially overwhelmed debtors in several of his most familiar teachings.[57]

These same teachings also call another potential objection into question. According to this objection, even if Jubilee principles are still relevant, the Jubilee did not give debtors the right to ask for relief, as American bankruptcy law does. The relief was available only because it was commanded at regular intervals. Once again, Jesus's teachings provide a perspective that looks remarkably like the American fresh start. Jesus condemned the ungrateful servant who asked for forbearance from his creditor – and master – while refusing to show mercy on the debtor who asked the ungrateful servant for relief.[58] The parable suggests that it is appropriate for a debtor who is incapable of repaying his obligations to ask for relief.

Although American bankruptcy law is remarkably congruent with Christian principles,[59] several of its features deviate in important respects. The first is a set of provisions, often referred to as "exceptions to the discharge," that forbid the debtor from erasing debts she incurred as a result of morally problematic behavior.[60] A century ago, debtors could not discharge debts for "criminal conversation" – that era's delicate term for adultery.[61] In addition to debts that arise through fraud or willful and malicious injury to persons or property, which have long been excepted from the discharge, today's list includes damages caused by drunk driving.[62] The desire to punish these behaviors is understandable and in many cases justifiable. What is far less clear is whether prohibiting a debtor from discharging these debts is consistent with fresh start principles. In one respect it might be. If the prohibited behavior is evidence that the debtor has hidden assets or is otherwise capable of repaying what he or she owes, delaying or withholding the discharge is the right response. But why should the fresh start be withheld from debtors who are not hiding assets and who are not capable of repaying what they owe? By withholding the fresh start,

57 See, e.g., Matthew 18:21–35 (Parable of the Unforgiving Servant).

58 Matthew 18:35.

59 Another, more technical feature of American bankruptcy law that accords with Christian principles is the debtor's right to choose whether to seek an immediate discharge (under chapter 7 of the current bankruptcy law) or to propose a three to five year payment plan (under chapter 13). A debtor who is genuinely incapable of repaying can choose chapter 7, whereas those who are able to pay some of what they owe can choose chapter 13. The process is messier in practice, but the basic framework is quite defensible from a Christian perspective.

60 The exceptions to the discharge are found in section 523(a) of the Bankruptcy Code. 11 U.S.C. § 523(a).

61 See *Tinker* v. *Colwell*, 193 U.S. 473 (1904), which upheld the denial of the discharge of a $50,000 judgment against the debtor for criminal conversation.

62 The drunk driving exception is section 523(a)(9). 11 U.S.C. § 523(a)(9).

American bankruptcy law conflates the penal role of the secular law with the fresh start that bankruptcy is meant to provide. A more consistent approach would be to put debtors in jail or otherwise punish their misbehavior as warranted, but to permit them to discharge their debts in bankruptcy.

I need to acknowledge that I am calling into question, at least in a limited sense, a central theme of American bankruptcy law – that it is designed for the "honest but unfortunate debtor." The concern for a debtor's honesty is a legacy of early bankruptcy history. Making sure the debtor isn't hiding assets remains relevant today, although it is more difficult for a dishonest debtor to evade detection. Whether a debtor is "unfortunate" and fell into bankruptcy due to events beyond her control and did not act rashly or ill-advisedly, by contrast, should not be the concern of bankruptcy law, at least from a Christian perspective. Jesus did not teach that only those who were essentially well-intentioned should be forgiven. To the contrary, he called for forgiveness – and offers forgiveness – for everyone who earnestly repents. This principle also seems relevant to bankruptcy.[63]

I do not mean to suggest that Christian teachings on debt should simply be incorporated into secular bankruptcy law. Jesus' teachings on these issues are intended primarily for interactions among his followers. But the logic translates to secular bankruptcy law in this context. If a debtor is trying to manipulate the bankruptcy process – and is acting in bad faith – she should not be given the bankruptcy fresh start. But if she is acting in good faith, her need for a fresh start may be as great if her obligations are problematic as it would be if the obligations were less problematic.

The nature of forgiveness brings us to a second shortcoming of the American bankruptcy system. Nowhere does American bankruptcy law provide an opening for debtors to apologize and seek the forgiveness of their creditors. In Jesus' teachings centered on relief from debt, debtors seek the forbearance or forgiveness of their creditors. In the parable of the Ungrateful Servant, for instance, the ungrateful servant and his debtor each beg for more time to repay what they owe, and the Lord's Prayer uses terms that translate either as debt forgiveness or forgiveness of sin. These teachings suggest that repentance is the essential prerequisite for forgiveness. Once again, their logic seems relevant to bankruptcy. To be sure, they do not translate neatly into the context of secular bankruptcy law. The debtors in Jesus' teachings usually have one main creditor, and the creditor is an individual lender. Contemporary

63 Bill Stuntz made a similar argument some years ago, describing bankruptcy as a "form of legal amnesty." William J. Stuntz, "Law and the Christian Story," *First Things* (December 1997), pp. 1–2.

debtors may have numerous creditors, many of which are institutions such as credit card companies that the debtor has never dealt with face-to-face. Yet, even if the debtor apologizes to a representative of the institution whom she has not previously met, the apology would still play a valuable role in the debtor's reconciliation process.[64]

Here, I am implicitly taking a position on a much debated issue, whether acknowledging our wrongdoing is a prerequisite to being forgiven. Some writers argue that repentance – acknowledging our failure or misdeed – is not required. From a Christian perspective, these writers seem to me mistaken, as repentance lies at the heart of Jesus' teachings on how we can be reconciled with God.[65] Even if repentance, in the form of an apology, were not essential to forgiveness, it still can make possible a more complete healing and reconciliation than would be possible in its absence.

The most serious concern with introducing apology into the bankruptcy process is that debtors will feel coerced to apologize, and that creditors will feel compelled to accept the apology. These concerns significantly complicate reconciliation whenever the reconciliation has legal consequences.[66] The reality of current bankruptcy law magnifies these concerns. There is considerable evidence that debtors are pressured to comply with the expectations of particular bankruptcy courts – expectations that vary dramatically from court to court – on key issues such as whether to seek an immediate discharge or to propose to pay creditors a portion of what they are owed.[67] Jurisdictions that pressure debtors to repay some of their obligations would be likely also to signal that they expect debtors to apologize. Apology might quickly become the norm in these courts. Some debtors might apologize not from genuine repentance, but because their lawyer nudged them to do so.

Despite these concerns – and despite the fact that we would never know for sure whether any particular apology is feigned or real – apology remains

64 My former colleague and now Judge, Stephanos Bibas, has advocated extensively for incorporating apology into the criminal justice system. See Stephanos Bibas, *The Machinery of Criminal Justice* (New York: Oxford University Press, 2015).

65 For a careful philosophical defense of the view in the text, see Nicholas Wolterstorff, *Justice in Love* (Grand Rapids, MI: Eerdman's Publishing Company, 2011), p. 173.

66 Martha Minow has written extensively and eloquently about these issues. See, for example, Martha Minow, *When Should the Law Forgive?* (New York: W.W. Norton, 2019); Martha Minow, "Forgiveness, Law, and Justice," *California Law Review*, vol. 103 (2015), p. 1615; Martha Minow, *Between Vengeance and Forgiveness: Facing History after Genocide and Mass Violence* (Boston: Beacon Press, 1998).

67 Jean Braucher drew attention to the divergence of cultures in her work. Jean Braucher, "Lawyers and Consumer Bankruptcy: One Code, Many Cultures," *The American Bankruptcy Law Journal*, vol. 67 (1993), p. 526.

essential. Most of us insist that our children apologize when they hurt someone else, hoping that they will experience at an early age the restorative powers of apology and forgiveness. Not every apology is sincere, but some are, and sincere apology makes true forgiveness possible. Although debtors should not be forced to apologize, and the presence or absence of an apology should not affect the debtor's legal treatment, a bankruptcy framework that more fully reflected Christian principles would give them an opportunity to do so.

## 8.4 THE "NO BANKRUPTCY" ALTERNATIVE

Although the American fresh start is remarkably congruent with Christian principles, the Bible does not provide a single blueprint for secular regulation of financial distress. It is quite possible that other approaches also fit the Biblical pattern. One obvious candidate would be to limit debt or banish it altogether, thus making bankruptcy unnecessary. As I have already noted, this perspective has strong support in some Christian circles.

One set of "no bankruptcy" advocates – including some Christian financial counsellors – tend to emphasize the obligations of an individual believer. The Bible calls us to make our yes, yes and our no, no, the reasoning goes, and condemns those who borrow and do not repay. Each of us should therefore avoid debt unless we are certain we can repay it. If we borrow money to buy a house, for instance, we should borrow much less than the value of the house, so that the lender would be fully repaid even if we were unable to make the payments. These financial counsellors strongly discourage Christian believers who do fall into financial distress from filing for bankruptcy.[68]

One very practical difficulty with the financial counsellors' call for Christians to control their financial destiny is that it may be impossible to avoid major financial obligations, even if a Christian believer is extremely careful not to borrow money. If a debtor loses her job, she may need to borrow money for basic living expenses or may incur debt as a result of a medical crisis that is not covered by insurance. In countries with a broader safety net than the United States, these risks would be much less likely to materialize. In the United States, by contrast, they affect a substantial number of people.

For Christian believers who do find themselves in financial crisis, the admonition to forgo bankruptcy is very hard to defend in Biblical terms. The Hebrew Bible and New Testament both seem to contemplate that debt will sometimes be forgiven. It is possible that debt relief for those who are

[68] See, for example, Burkett, How to Manage Your Money, p. 27.

incapable of repaying was an accommodation to the conditions of the time, much as the acceptance of polygamy and slavery was.[69] But there is little evidence that debt relief was a temporary accommodation, particularly given that Jesus incorporated it into his pronouncements about the forgiveness of sin that lies at the very heart of the Christian faith.

A second set of "no bankruptcy" advocates, Christian finance scholars (or, more precisely, a small number of Christian finance scholars) focus on the Biblical restrictions on debt and the virtues of these restrictions for Christian community. According to this view, the Old Testament calls for Israelites to lend money to anyone who was in need, and not to charge interest on the loans, were designed to promote dignity and strengthen communal bonds. "[I]f one cannot lend at interest," as one scholar puts it, "the options are either to make an outright gift, to lend interest-free, to rent/lease property, or to make an equity-based investment. The ban on interest pushes the lender toward sharing risk with the borrower."[70]

Here, too, the call for permitting only interest-free loans is both practically and Biblically problematic. Practically, it would significantly constrain access to financing. Lenders often prefer to lend money rather than to take an equity interest in the debtor's project, and thus serve as a joint-venturer with the debtor. A loan ordinarily provides more certainty and requires less direct commitment to the debtor's enterprise. To be sure, the distinctions are malleable, and equity interests can often be structured in a way that gives them many of the same characteristics as debt. But forbidding traditional debt, even when this is the preferred form of investment, creates unnecessary and unjustifiable costs, thus reducing access to credit. There also is no guarantee that the equity instrument will promote community. If the parties structure the "investment" like a loan, it will not provide any more community solidarity than a traditional loan.

Biblically, the ban on interest was always limited to loans by one Israelite to another.[71] This suggests that if the members of a church lend money to one another, they should not charge interest. But there is no Biblical basis for

69 For extensive discussion of polygamy and slavery, which are permitted but implicitly discouraged in the Bible, see Christopher J. H. Wright, *Old Testament Ethics for the People of God* (Downers Grove, IL: IVP Academic, 2004).

70 Jonathan Burnside, *God, Justice, and Society: Aspects of Law and Legality in the Bible* (Oxford: Oxford University Press, 2011), p. 227. Some Catholic scholars advocate a more nuanced view. Under this view, derived from Catholic natural law theory, lenders would be permitted to charge interest on loans, but the permissible interest would be limited by usury principles. See McCall, *The Church and the Usurers*. Although I am skeptical of these approaches on prudential grounds, I believe they are Biblically defensible.

71 Indeed, some interpret the lending restrictions to apply only to loans to needy Israelites, not to business loans, as noted earlier.

extending this principle to lending in every context. As noted earlier, Jesus implied that lending at interest is appropriate when he told a parable about a servant who is criticized for failing to find a productive use for money entrusted to him by his master.[72] The parable suggests that, at the very least, the servant should have deposited the money in a bank (thus, loaning it to the bank) so that it could earn interest.

Rather than avoiding either traditional debt or bankruptcy in all cases, a more consistently Biblical perspective would balance the obligation for Christian debtors to repay what they owe with the promise of debt forgiveness for those who are genuinely unable to repay. From this perspective, bankruptcy is appropriate only for those for whom repayment is no longer plausible. Even those who have seemingly crushing debts may nevertheless be capable of repaying. But if it becomes clear that the debtor is genuinely unable to repay, it is entirely appropriate for her to discharge the obligations in bankruptcy.

## 8.5 DELAYED BANKRUPTCY RELIEF

The insolvency laws of European countries often provide for a conditional or delayed discharge of the debtor's obligations, rather than an immediate fresh start as in the United States. In England, a governmental officer examines a debtor who has requested bankruptcy relief, and then determines whether to grant unconditional relief, deny relief, or condition relief on the debtor's payment of some of its obligations over a period of years.[73] Other countries impose a mandatory payment period as a prerequisite for a discharge for all debtors.[74]

The European approaches, with their less fulsome access to bankruptcy relief, do not map as neatly onto a narrative of debt forgiveness as the American fresh start. Whereas the American fresh start offers the kind of debt forgiveness Jesus seems to gesture toward in his parables, the European approach is forgiveness "if." Yet the differences are not quite as stark as they initially seem. Even under the American approach, bankruptcy is only appropriate if the debtor is genuinely unable to repay her debts. Just as with the European approach, bankruptcy relief is therefore conditional.

[72] Luke 19:11–27.

[73] Douglass G. Boshkoff, "Limited, Conditional, and Suspended Discharges in Anglo-American Bankruptcy Proceedings," *University of Pennsylvania Law Review*, vol. 131 (1982), p. 69.

[74] See, for example, Ramsay, "Comparative Consumer Bankruptcy," pp. 250–251.

It's just that the condition is left to the debtor's conscience, rather than to a governmental official.[75]

Both approaches have limitations. Under an American-style fresh start, a few debtors may abuse the system by seeking bankruptcy relief when they do not actually need it. A debtor also might innocently misgauge their capacity to repay, thinking she can't when in actuality she can. Under a conditional discharge, the governmental official may mistakenly conclude that the debtor is capable of repaying when she cannot, or that she is not capable of repaying when they are.

In my view, the American fresh start more robustly embodies a Christian vision of bankruptcy relief than a conditional bankruptcy discharge. But the European approach also can be defended as consistent with Christian principles.[76] Indeed, it can be seen as mirroring the Hebrew Bible approach, where debtors who had been sold into slavery were released only after having served for seven years.[77]

## 8.6 CORPORATE BANKRUPTCY FROM A CHRISTIAN PERSPECTIVE

Corporations and business entities raise different questions from a Christian perspective than the financial distress of an individual. The question is how a collective should be treated in the event of financial distress. Although the implications for individuals – such as shareholders or employees of a corporation – are important, they are one-step removed.

The significance of this distinction is perhaps best seen with the question whether financially distressed corporations should be entitled to a fresh start. In the United States, a mechanism for restructuring troubled corporations emerged at roughly the same time as the fresh start for consumer debtors. The first corporations that benefited from this mechanism – which became known as equity receivership – were railroads. But the receivership strategy was subsequently used by other corporations as well, and is reflected chapter 11.[78] Like the fresh start, the American corporate bankruptcy framework can be seen as providing a second chance for financially distressed businesses.

75 Moreover, debtors' access to immediate fresh start in the United States has been limited slightly by a 2005 amendment that foreclosed chapter 7 to debtors that fail a new means test that is designed to determine whether they are capable of repaying some of what they owe. 11 U.S.C. § 707(b)(2). Only a small number of debtors fail the means test, but a few do.

76 For an analysis concluding English insolvency law accords with natural law principles, see John Finnis, *Natural Law and Natural Rights* (Oxford: Clarendon Press, 1980), pp. 188–193.

77 Deuteronomy 15:12–13.

78 The history is discussed in Skeel, *Debt's Dominion*, pp. 24–43.

The equity receivership was a remarkable achievement, and it has bequeathed an effective mechanism for resolving the financial distress of private corporations. It does not, however, have any special claim of fidelity to Christian principles. The Bible's jubilee and debt relief passages are concerned with the dignity of individuals, not with the question whether a particular business shuts down or continues. A bankruptcy law that attempts to reorganize troubled businesses is not inherently superior from a Christian perspective to a law that requires them to be liquidated or sold to the highest bidder.

Although Christian principles do not dictate any particular approach to corporate bankruptcy, they do offer insight into particular features of the approach that is selected. An issue that has become increasingly salient in the largest American bankruptcy cases is the overall fairness of the process to ordinary individuals who are affected by it. The terms of reorganization are negotiated by the lawyers representing each of the major constituencies, with little input by the people who will be most directly affected by the outcome. Biblical principles of justice, which call for evenhandedness and universal access to justice, suggest that the absence of voice even in cases where ordinary individuals have a great deal at stake is problematic. In several recent cases, bankruptcy judges have attempted to provide opportunities for affected individuals to voice their concerns.[79] It is possible that these initiatives influenced the outcomes in the cases; even if they did not, the opportunity to be heard enhances the perceived fairness of the bankruptcy process.

## 8.7 SOVEREIGN DEBT CRISES

Biblical bankruptcy principles have been voiced quite explicitly in recent decades in a very surprising context – the financial distress not of individuals or even corporations, but countries. Countries in financial distress seem to have little in common with the individual debtors with whom the jubilee and debt relief passages are concerned. Yet there are surprising similarities between the two.

The application of Biblical principles of debt relief to countries can be traced to the work of a nongovernmental organization called Jubilee in the 1990s. The founders of Jubilee sought to galvanize support for debt relief for debt-burdened countries in Africa and elsewhere by linking the Bible's call for

[79] For discussion of the bankruptcy judge's efforts to include ordinary citizens and individual retirees in the Detroit bankruptcy, see Melissa B. Jacoby, "Federalism Form and Function in the Detroit Bankruptcy," *Yale Journal on Regulation*, vol. 33 (2016), pp. 55, 94.

debt relief every forty-nine years to the coming of a new millennium in 2000.[80] The Jubilee movement proved highly effective, especially in the United Kingdom. Jubilee and related organizations continue to actively call for debt relief for financially distressed countries and territories such as Greece and Puerto Rico.[81]

The relevance of the Jubilee passages, which were designed for individuals and families, to the financial obligations of sovereign countries is often asserted and rarely explained. It might easily be dismissed as a clever rhetorical move. After all, if Jubilee principles are not relevant for corporations, they seem even less fitting for countries. Yet this is one place where transitivity does not apply. Consumer and sovereign debtors are remarkably similar – and quite different than corporations – in two important respects. First, they are subject to very similar decision-making biases. Ordinary individuals tend to focus heavily on the benefits of current purchases, and to underestimate the long-term costs. Credit card companies take advantage of this bias by charging stiff fees and high interest rates to consumers who fail to pay their bill in full or miss a payment. A country's political decision-makers have a very similar bias, though for somewhat different reasons. They are tempted to borrow money to finance current projects, because they enjoy the benefits of the spending in the short-run, but do not have to bear the costs until later. In each case, these decision-making biases can increase the risk of financial distress. Second, unlike with corporations, which can be liquidated when they default if they are no longer viable, individuals and countries cannot be liquidated, no matter how hopeless their plight.[82] This distinction is far starker today than in the past. Historically, individuals could be enslaved or executed if they failed to pay their obligations, and countries might face "gunboat diplomacy," but these alternatives are no longer viewed as legitimate.

Consumer and sovereign debtors also differ in highly significant ways, of course. As long as their taxing authority has not completely atrophied, sovereign debtors have a continuing source of revenue. A financially distressed consumer, by contrast, may not have access to any source of income. But both can be overwhelmed by debt, and with potentially severe humanitarian

80 See, for example, LeFebvre, "Theology and Economics," p. 14 n.4.

81 Others, such as Bono, lead singer of the band U2, have also invoked Biblical principles in their advocacy for debt relief and aid for developing countries.

82 For discussion of the similarities between individual debtors and US states in these terms, see David A. Skeel, Jr., "States of Bankruptcy," *University of Chicago Law Review*, vol. 79 (2012), pp. 677, 687–689. It is also harder to change the decision-maker with an individual or country than with a corporation.

consequences, in the absence of a debt relief option.[83] Sovereign bankruptcy may be impractical in many contexts; but to the extent it is administratively feasible, it can be defended as consistent with Christian principles.

In some of the recent debt crises, advocates for the financially distressed nation have pointed to odious debt doctrine as justifying debt relief. Under odious debt doctrine (which has not yet been endorsed as a feature of international law), a country whose citizens did not benefit from money borrowed by a corrupt former regime can disavow the ostensible obligations.[84] The logic of odious debt doctrine is quite different than debt relief or bankruptcy. Odious debt doctrine declares an obligation to be illegitimate; the debtor is not responsible for paying it. Bankruptcy, by contrast, provides relief from obligations that are fully legitimate, but which the debtor is unable to pay.

***

Unlike the poor, bankruptcy has not always been with us. But it is an increasingly central feature of commercial life around the world. In my view, personal bankruptcy relief is consistent with Christian principles, although no current bankruptcy system fully honors those principles. Perhaps more surprisingly, sovereign debt relief or bankruptcy is – or would be – consistent with Christian principles too.

83 Note too that the Bible often analogizes nations to people, and emphasizes the distinct personalities that nations have.

84 For an overview and history, see Lee C. Buchheit, G. Mitu Gulati, and Robert B. Thompson, "The Dilemma of Odious Debts," *Duke Law Journal*, vol. 56 (2007), pp. 1201–1262.

# 9

# Patents, Access to Health Technologies, and Christianity

MARGO A. BAGLEY AND DANIELLE C. LLOYD

## 9.1 INTRODUCTION

"Beloved, I Wish Above All Things That You May Prosper and Be In Health" The desire for others to enjoy good health reflected in the Apostle John's wish for his friend Gaius[1] is one that Christians have embraced since New Testament times. Christ instructed his disciples to "heal the sick . . . freely you have received; freely give."[2] The vast networks of religiously affiliated hospitals in countries across the globe exemplify one way Christians seek to follow this command.[3]

However, well-staffed hospitals alone are rarely enough to restore good health when serious diseases are involved; effective medication and medical devices also are often required. And the costs of prescription medications are skyrocketing and increasingly out of the reach of many who need them in both low- and, increasingly, high-income countries. According to the World Health Organization (WHO), 90 percent of people who need assistive products such as wheelchairs, low-vision devices, and hearing aids do not have access due to high costs, among other factors.[4] Moreover, for up to 90 percent of the population in developing countries, medicines comprise the largest

Special thanks to Samuel Bagley II, Daniel Crane, Samuel Gregg, and Ruth Okediji, Audra Savage, John Witte, and the Harvard Law School students in Professor Okediji's Christian Legal Perspectives seminar for helpful comments, and to Clover Ding, Eric Pettis, Gregory Sefian, and the research librarians at the MacMillan Law library for excellent research assistance. Some of the material in this Chapter first appeared in Margo A. Bagley, "The Morality of Compulsory Licensing as an Access to Medicines Tool," *Minnesota Law Review*, vol. 102 (2018), p. 2463.

1. 3 John 1:2 (NIV).
2. Matthew 10:8 (NIV).
3. Ann-Kathrin Seemann et al., "Are Religiously Affiliated Hospitals More Than Just Nonprofits? A Study on Stereotypical Patient Perceptions and Preferences," *Journal of Religion and Health*, vol. 54 (2015) 1028 (noting that, in the US alone, "approximately 58 % of hospitals are nonprofits, of which approximately 30 % are church-owned").
4. "Improving Access to Assistive Technology," *World Health Organization*, 2016, p. 6.

family expenditure after food, as pharmaceuticals are often purchased through out-of-pocket payments.[5] According to polls in 2015 and 2013, respectively, approximately one in four Americans had not filled a prescription in the prior year because of the high cost of the drug, and one in four cancer patients had either not filled a prescription or had reduced their prescribed dosage due to the drug's cost.[6]

Of course, drug cost is not the only factor impacting access to medicines. According to the WHO, obtaining access to essential medicines requires three different types of access: therapeutic access (the creation of drugs and treatment), supply access,[7] and financial access (the ability to pay for needed medicines).[8]

Intellectual property protection, in the form of patents, is often the tool that allows pharmaceutical and medical device companies to charge exorbitant prices and garner supra-competitive profits. As maximizing shareholder value is generally the key driver of pricing decisions for corporations,[9] setting a drug

5 "Addressing the Global Shortage of, and Access to, Medicines and Vaccines," *World Health Organization*, 2018, p. 50.

6 "Poll: Nearly 1 in 4 Americans Taking Prescription Drugs Say It's Difficult to Afford Their Medicines, Including Larger Shares Among Those with Health Issues, with Low Incomes and Nearing Medicare Age," *The Henry J. Kaiser Family Foundation* (blog), March 1, 2019, www.kff.org/health-costs/press-release/poll-nearly-1-in-4-americans-taking-prescription-drugs-say-its-difficult-to-afford-medicines-including-larger-shares-with-low-incomes/; and S. Yousuf Zafar et al., "The Financial Toxicity of Cancer Treatment: A Pilot Study Assessing Out-of-Pocket Expenses and the Insured Cancer Patient's Experience," *The Oncologist*, vol. 18, no. 4 (2013), pp. 381–390, https://doi.org/10.1634/theoncologist.2012-0279.

7 There are several factors that impact whether drugs actually reach the people who need them. Lucie White, "Getting Real about Essential Medicines: The Last Kilometer," *Maryland Journal of International Law*, vol. 31 (2016), p. 79 (exploring the complex barriers that may exist to getting drugs the last mile, or last kilometer, to the patients who need them); Ellen F. M. 't Hoen, "Public Health and International Law: TRIPS, Pharmaceutical Patents, and Access to Essential Medicines: A Long Way from Seattle to Doha," *Chicago Journal of International Law*, vol. 3 (2002), pp. 27, 28 (noting that "[u]navailability [of essential medicines] can be caused by logistical supply and storage problems, substandard drug quality, inappropriate selection of drugs, wasteful prescription and inappropriate use, inadequate production, and prohibitive prices").

8 Presentation, World Health Organization, Challenges to Securing Access to Essential Drugs (October 1998), cited in Margo A Bagley, "Legal Movements in Intellectual Property: TRIPS, Unilateral Action, Bilateral Agreements, and HIV/AIDS," *Emory International Law Review*, vol. 17 (2003); Judy Rein, "International Governance through Trade Agreements: Patent Protection for Essential Medicines," *Northwestern Journal of International Law & Business*, vol. 21, no. 2 (Winter 2001).

9 Jia Lynn Yang, "Maximizing Shareholder Value: The Goal That Changed Corporate America," *The Washington Post*, August 26, 2013, sec. Business, www.washingtonpost.com/business/economy/maximizing-shareholder-value-the-goal-that-changed-corporate-america/2013/08/26/26e9ca8e-ed74-11e2-9008-61e94a7ea20d_story.html.

price at a level that maximizes profit – even if it constricts financial access and thereby exacerbates human suffering – often makes good economic sense to pharmaceutical executives. But such pricing also, ostensibly, incentivizes the development of new treatments, thus facilitating therapeutic access to medicines.

There are a myriad of complex factors affecting access to health care and health technologies in the United States and abroad, a full analysis of which could fill volumes. This chapter explores the narrower questions of what Christian tradition can teach us about patents and financial access to health technologies[10] and whether the Biblical desire for all to enjoy good health suggests that constraints on drug and device pricing should be obligatory.

The chapter begins in Section 9.2 with an introduction to the Biblical principles that underlie the historical evolution of Christian approaches to care for the sick and access to health more broadly. Following that, Section 9.3 explores how patent protection can impact access to health technologies in particular. Section 9.4 then considers the interplay of patents and access to health technologies, as well as the tensions among modern Christian approaches to these topics. The chapter concludes that Christianity does have valuable teachings to contribute on the topic of patents and access to health technologies, although these teachings may not be voiced with sufficient force and clarity by believers today.

## 9.2 CHRISTIAN TRADITION AND ACCESS TO HEALTH TECHNOLOGIES[11]

The report of the U.N. Secretary General's High-Level Panel on Access to Medicines gives a succinct description of the problem of access to health technologies:

[10] The phrase "health technologies" as used in this chapter refers to pharmaceuticals, assistive devices, and medical devices. A medical device is, among other things, an "instrument, apparatus, implement, machine . . . or other similar or related article . . . which is intended for use in the diagnosis of disease . . . or in the cure, mitigation, treatment, or prevention of disease . . . or intended to affect the structure or any function of the body . . . and which does not achieve its primary intended purposes through chemical action within or on the body." 21 U.S.C. 201(h).

[11] Until the early twentieth century, which saw a dramatic rise in the patenting and regulation of medicines and a concomitant increase in the cost of medicines and other health technologies, Christian thought regarding the sick focused on the provision of health care more generically. As such, the following historical overview focuses on access to health care holistically, as opposed to being limited to access to health technologies per se. However, the principles described are, nonetheless, fully pertinent and applicable to that issue.

> Cost is one of the key determinants of access . . . According to the WHO and the World Bank, 400 million people worldwide lack healthcare, including access to medicines, vaccines and diagnostics and medical devices. Those who lack access are disproportionately poor, and three-quarters of them live in so called "middle-income" countries. Individuals in many wealthy countries face challenges in accessing treatment for many diseases.[12]

Facilitating access to health technologies can be viewed as a strand in a larger tapestry of Christian traditions relating to the poor that grew out of Christ's ministry and example. Recognizing and valuing the humanity in each person – including one's physical, mental, emotional, and spiritual health and material body as essential to human identity – was fundamental to Christ's earthly ministry. In His first documented sermon in the book of Luke, Jesus publicly recognized that the Spirit of the Lord anointed Him "to bring good news to the poor . . . to proclaim release to the captives and recovery of sight to the blind, to let the oppressed go free."[13] Both the Old and New Testament affirm a concern for the physical well-being of the poor, a concern that has evolved through the centuries and is still evident in Christian thought and action today.

### 9.2.1 An Old Testament Example: Pe'ah

It is worth noting at the outset that care for the health of the poor is not solely a New Testament concept. The gleaning laws in Deuteronomy and Leviticus explicitly allowed the poor, foreigners, and widows to come onto another person's property and gather the crop gleanings without it being considered trespass or theft. These laws, embodied in the Jewish concept of *pe'ah*, can be seen as a form of promoting access to health, as nutritious food is critical to health and wellness.[14] The descriptions of *pe'ah* are found in Leviticus 19 and 23, and in Deuteronomy 24:

[12] "Report of the U.N. Secretary General's High Level Panel on Access to Medicines: Promoting Innovation and Access to Health Technologies," September 2016.

[13] Luke 4:18 (NRSV).

[14] In Hebrew, *pe'ah* means "corner" or "side." See *Strong's Concordance*, Bible Hub, http://biblehub.com/hebrew/6285.htm. As Jeffrey Spitzer explains: "The Bible's model of tzedakah (social justice and support) included a variety of agricultural gifts. Grain and produce that were left or forgotten during the harvest were available for the poor to glean. The corners of the fields (pe'ah) were also designated for the poor." Jeffrey Spitzer, "Pe'ah: The Corners of Our Fields," *My Jewish Learning* (blog), May 8, 2020, www.myjewishlearning.com/article/peah-the-corners-of-our-fields/.

"When you reap the harvest of your land, do not reap to the very edges of your field or gather the gleanings of your harvest. Leave them for the poor and for the foreigner residing among you. I am the LORD your God." "When you reap the harvest of your land … Do not go over your vineyard a second time or pick up the grapes that have fallen. Leave them for the poor and the foreigner. I am the Lord your God."[15]

In these examples, the poor have the *right* to enter onto the land of a property owner and harvest the remnants of the crop. These are not leftovers after the workers have cleaned every scrap of salvageable fruit or grain. The property owner is instructed not to do too good of a job in harvesting the crop so that he leaves some portion of the crop for the poor and the foreigner.[16] In fact, these examples illustrate that loving one's neighbor is so important that not only are the poor *not* stealing (nor even trespassing), the landowner is *enjoined* from harvesting to the edges of his field. What is left does not belong to the landowner, *and it will not harm him to let the poor have it.* Gleaning laws required this access even though one could imagine how it could affect the market price. A continuous refrain throughout the entire Hebrew Bible that can be read in the laws, psalms, proverbs, and narrative accounts is that the Lord cares about relieving oppression and correcting neglect of strangers, widows, orphans.[17] Justice and righteousness (*mishpat* and *tsedaqah*) are important aspects of God's character, and a righteous society is measured by how well it cares for those the Lord cares for – the most vulnerable. Even as God knows that there will always be poor people among them, it seems that God wanted people to trust Him and not wealth to supply their needs, and wanted the entire community to love and have compassion for the poor and play a role in justice-seeking to meet their basic needs.

### 9.2.2 New Testament Teachings

Because the same God inspired both sacred testaments, it is not surprising that this theme is repeated and expanded upon in the New Testament. Many

[15] Leviticus 23:22 (NIV) and Leviticus 19:9–11 (NIV). The instructions apply not only to vineyards but to other crops as well: "When you beat the olives from your trees, do not go over the branches a second time. Leave what remains for the foreigner, the fatherless and the widow" (Deuteronomy 24:20, NIV). "When you are harvesting in your field and you overlook a sheaf, do not go back to get it. Leave it for the foreigner, the fatherless and the widow, so that the LORD your God may bless you in all the work of your hands" (Deuteronomy 24:19, NIV).

[16] Tzvi Novick, "Social Justice in Rabbinic Judaism," *Oxford Handbooks Online*, November 2019.

[17] Several verses reflect this concept; some examples include Exodus 22:21–24; Leviticus 19:34, 25:35; Isaiah 1:17; Micah 6:8.

within Christian tradition refer to the communal configuration Jesus offered as God's (upside-down) Kingdom: a kingdom where the last shall be first, where those who hunger and thirst will be filled, where the weak and poor are beneficiaries of an eternal reward, where loving one's neighbor (and one's enemy) as oneself is the norm, and where the Prince gave up His heavenly throne to become the human sacrifice that would forever satisfy the need for a sin offering.[18] Essentially, God's priorities are in opposition to those of the world; living with His guidance often leads Christians – in order to realize an equitable society – to embody morals that the secular culture may regard as counterintuitive and even disadvantageous.

In fact, Jesus' harshest criticisms while ministering on earth were aimed at those who claimed to be religious (diligently following God's kingdom-law) but showed little concern for others' suffering in their daily lives. There were leaders whose burdensome, man-made laws and personal interpretations of the faith completely contradicted the God of justice and mercy Jesus wanted to show the world. Christ modeled how caring for people's practical needs is foundational – and sometimes even a prerequisite – for sustaining a spiritual ministry: each model of engagement is enhanced by depending on or interlocking with the other.

Carrying concern for the needy into the tradition of the nascent New Testament Church, James sheds light on the question of receiving salvation by faith versus earning salvation by works, explaining that:

> Believers in our glorious Lord Jesus Christ must not show favoritism. . . . [I]f a person with gold rings and in fine clothes comes into your assembly, and if a poor person in dirty clothes also comes in, and if you take notice of the one wearing the fine clothes and say, "Have a seat here, please," while to the one who is poor you say, "Stand there," or, "Sit at my feet," have you not made distinctions among yourselves, and become judges with evil thoughts? Listen, my beloved brothers and sisters. Has not God chosen those who are poor in the eyes of the world to be rich in faith and to inherit the kingdom he promised those who love him? But you have dishonored the poor. Is it not the rich who are [exploiting] you? . . . For judgment without mercy will be shown to anyone who has not been merciful. Mercy triumphs over judgment.[19]

*James* goes on to instruct that faith *without* works (charitable activities resulting from said faith[20]) is actually meaningless. He suggests that only

[18] Matthew 5:3–12 (NIV).

[19] James 2:1–7; 13 (NIV).

[20] H. W. Attridge et al., eds., "The Letter of James," in *New Revised Standard Version (NRSV) The HarperCollins Study Bible*, revised (San Francisco: HarperSanFrancisco, 2006).

offering prayers or blessings for someone starving and naked will render little comfort for that person's present situation; instead, a literal provision of food or clothes would be a much more useful expression of concern. He further notes that both the Jewish patriarch Abraham and the Gentile convert Rahab were justified by God because of their deeds. The Biblical message advises that one's actions in response to others' needs are the natural outpouring of one's Christ-like faith.[21]

### 9.2.3 The Evolution of Charitable Health Care

Early Christian tradition was immediately fashioned after Jesus' teachings on the interpretation of the law (such as caring for one's neighbor *and* enemy) and His emphasis on attitudes of the heart as well as one's outward actions. Early Christian apologists referenced Christ's ministry as their moral orientation, which consisted of adopted Jewish moral teachings as well as parallel and rival contemporary philosophies.[22] They also recognized that alienation from God was the most significant human problem; therefore, while subordinating (even miraculous) physical healing "to the deeper spiritual healing given in Jesus' redemptive act," early Christians still prioritized the sick, hungry, homeless, and ostracized.[23] Physical problems like sickness and poverty were symptoms and expressions of the brokenness that sin's effects create in the human race, and living the gospel message was to bring healing and wholeness to spiritually and physically sick souls.

A special focus on charity for the poor was a representative attribute of the emerging theology and culture: "The strong sense of brotherhood brought a corresponding sense of obligation to alleviate the physical needs of other believers."[24] This contributed to early Christians beginning to call each other "sister" and "brother" instead of just "friend."

Community-centered benevolence was viewed as "an imitation of God's philanthropy for human beings" and was not at the discretion of the donor,

[21] James 2:14–26 (NIV).

[22] Everett Ferguson, *Church History, Volume One: From Christ to the Pre-Reformation: The Rise and Growth of the Church in Its Cultural, Intellectual, and Political Context*, 2nd ed., vol. 1 (Grand Rapids, MI: Zondervan, 2013), p. 153. Christian Apologists even considered honesty in business, caring for the poor, and family solidarity in their arguments.

[23] M. Therese Lysaught and Joseph J. Kotva, Jr., "Christianity and the Social Responsibility of Health Care," in *On Moral Medicine: Theological Perspectives in Medical Ethics*, ed. M. Therese Lysaught, Joseph J. Kotva, Jr., Stephen E. Lammers, and Allen Verhay, 3rd ed. (William B. Eerdmans, 2012), p. 21.

[24] Ferguson, *Church History*, vol. 1, p. 155.

nor did benevolence create corresponding obligations, for there were to be no strings attached.[25] Justin and Tertullian reported church collections being used to provide for the sick, elderly, widows, orphans, prisoners, and travelers as well as the burial of the poor.[26] Clement of Alexandria counseled fellow believers that "it was better to do good to the unworthy than, by guarding against the unworthy, to fail to do good to the worthy."[27] In addition, the churches' efforts sometimes received secular support: Emperors Theodosius and Honorius issued an edict in the fifth century requiring prison wardens to allow entry to bishops so that they might, among other things, "heal the sick."[28]

For the early Church, ministering to the physically sick was important in itself but even more because it furthered the spread of the good news about Jesus Christ the healer and savior. "The analogy between physical and spiritual health provided Christians with an opportunity to convey symbolically through concrete deeds of service their message of life … [People] will be able to understand how God reaches out to sinful humanity."[29] This was Augustine's reason for calling Jesus the "Great Physician," and the sacraments a form of "medicine."[30]

As the early church missionaries traveled across Europe, Africa, Asia, and eventually the Americas, the moral instruction and focus on right-living also spread and posed a radical challenge to live counterculturally to the pagan norms of the day. New Christian groups learned to rely on each other for physical, financial, and spiritual communion with a particular eye on reaching the "least of these" through both health care and evangelism.[31] The centuries-long movement toward establishing health care centers led the Catholic Church to found hospitals throughout the world as early as AD 370. Bishop Basel of Caesarea's construction of the Basiliad, a combination hostel/hospice outside Caesarea, served as a model and inspiration for similar facilities throughout Cappadocia.[32] The roles of nurses developed from Catholic monastery hospitals, and spread through migrating missionaries' desire to take the Gospel to the ends of the earth.

25 Pheme Perkins, *First and Second Peter, James, and Jude*, Interpretation, A Bible Commentary for Teaching and Preaching (Louisville, KY: John Knox Press, 1995), p. 109.

26 Ferguson, *Church History*, vol. 1, p. 155.

27 Ibid.

28 Maria E. Doerfler, "Social Justice in Early Christianity," in *The Oxford Handbook of Biblical Law* (2019), p. 527 (citing the *Codex Theodosianus* 9.3.7).

29 George Khushf, "Illness, the Problem of Evil, and the Analogical Structure of Healing: On the Difference Christianity Makes in Bioethics," in Lysaught, et al. *On Moral Medicine*, p. 22.

30 Ibid.

31 Matthew 25:40 (NIV).

32 Doerfler, "Social Justice in Early Christianity," p. 521.

### 9.2.4 Contributions of Catholic Thought

A key principle and contribution of Catholic social doctrine to the evolution of charitable health care is the universal destination of goods, particularly as it relates to the preferential option for the poor.[33] The principle holds that "God destined the earth and all it contains for all men and all peoples so that all created things would be shared fairly by all mankind under the guidance of justice tempered by charity."[34] Pope John Paul II describes the preferential option for the poor:

> [It is]a special form of primacy in the exercise of Christian charity, to which the whole tradition of the Church bears witness. It affects the life of each Christian inasmuch as he or she seeks to imitate the life of Christ.... [This preference] cannot but embrace the immense multitudes of the hungry, the needy, the homeless, those without medical care and, above all, those without hope of a better future.[35]

Catholic concern for the dignity of every human person is a deeply held element in its outlook on human rights and suggests that there are positive entitlements owed to people by society at large.[36] Aligning with the United Nations' Universal Declaration on Human Rights, Pope John XXIII named health care as a fundamental human right in 1961.[37] It should be noted,

[33] This discussion is, of necessity, abbreviated, providing just a glimpse of the rich history of Catholic teachings and actions regarding care for the sick and poor. Beginning with Thomas Aquinas and continuing through the array of medieval institutions of care, shelter, and healing, then continuing through important encyclicals from Leo XIII onward, much more could be said about the Catholic church's teachings on our obligations to the sick, poor, and needy. And of course, there have been and continue to be many Catholic hospitals, clinics, hospices, and other emergency relief organizations facilitating access to care and health technologies even today. Of course, much more could be written regarding Protestant teachings and initiatives in the next subsection as well. However, a fuller discussion is beyond the scope of this short chapter.

[34] "Universal Destination of Goods," Catholic CEO, www.catholicceo.net/universal-destination-of-goods.

[35] *Sollicitudo Rei Socialis*, "On the Social Teaching of the Church" by John Paul II, December 30, 1987, in Richard W. Rousseau, ed., *Human Dignity and the Common Good: The Great Papal Social Encyclicals from Leo XIII to John Paul II* (Westport, CT: Greenwood Press, 2002), p. 419.

[36] Philip S. Keane, *Catholicism and Health-Care Justice*, Problems, Potential and Solutions (Paulist Press, 2002), p. 8.

[37] Lysaught and Kotva, "Christianity and the Social Responsibility," p. 118. "The UN's Universal Declaration on Human Rights was heavily influenced by the tradition of Catholic social thought." United Nations, "Universal Declaration of Human Rights," October 6, 2015, Article 25, www.un.org/en/universal-declaration-human-rights/.

however, that while Catholic social teaching does identify health care as a right, it does not mandate any particular way of *realizing* that right.

The classic Catholic term *distributive justice* was first given systematic expression in Catholic teaching in the Middle Ages, most notably in Aquinas's *Summa Theologiae*.[38] The phrase refers to "the obligation of society to provide all of its citizens with a means to ensure that all can have access to a sufficient level of basic human goods."[39] In this vein, Catholic social thought continues to prioritize a preferential option for the poor – "the idea that [Christians] have a strong obligation to provide in a special way for those who cannot speak for themselves," which might even require prioritizing their needs over the private property rights of others.[40]

Regarding health care, some Catholic scholars argue that "the poor" encompasses far more than just the economically poor and that this definition must also be extended to groups that may face significant challenges when seeking suitable access to health technologies – for example, racial minorities, immigrants and nonnative English speakers, "chemically addicted persons," and those with mental health challenges.[41] Thus, from a Catholic social doctrine perspective, access to health care can be seen as not only a personal challenge but also a matter of justice and human rights.[42]

### 9.2.5 Protestant Perspectives

Protestant theologians' teachings are largely consistent with Catholic social doctrine on this topic. According to Martin Luther, "Man … should be guided in all his works by this thought and contemplate this one thing alone, that he may serve and benefit others in all that he does, considering nothing except the need and advantage of his neighbor.… This is a truly

[38] "*Summa Theologiae*: The Parts of Justice (Secunda Secundae Partis, Q. 61)," www.newadvent.org/summa/3061.htm.

[39] Keane, *Catholicism and Health-Care Justice*, p. 7.

[40] Ibid., p. 14.

[41] Ibid. One contemporary challenge that is beyond the scope of this chapter involves deciding what is the baseline level of care required of society. Religious ethicist Gene Outka's perspective on the model of distributive justice for health care "rejects merit, social worth, and ability to pay as grounds for healthcare decision making," a view widely accepted by justice scholars. His next two principles – distributing health care according to need versus doing so in a way that assures that all people are treated the same in their basic health care – are more readily contested, especially considering that health care is considered only one of several basic human goods that society should provide; ibid., p. 7.

[42] Ibid., p. 6.

Christian life."[43] And Karl Barth, whose work is considered key to the revitalization of Protestant theology in the twentieth century, puts it well:

> The Church is witness of the fact that the Son of man came to seek and to save the lost. And this implies ... the Church must concentrate first on the lower and lowest levels of human society. The poor, the socially and economically weak and threatened, will always be the object of its primary and particular concern, and it will always insist on the State's special responsibility for these weaker members of society.[44]

John Wesley, one of the founders of the Methodist church, is known for also embracing a preferential option for the poor in addition to the view that any excess that one has should not be saved for oneself, but rather given to assist the poor.[45] In his sermon *The Character of a Methodist* (1746) he writes:

> A Methodist is one, who has the love of God shed abroad in his heart ... as he has time, he does good unto all men; unto neighbours and strangers, friends and enemies ... not only to their bodies by feeding the hungry, clothing the naked, visiting those that are sick or in prison; but much more does he labour to do good to their souls.... And he is willing to spend and be spent herein, even to be offered up on the sacrifice and service of their faith, so they may all come unto the measure of the stature of the fullness of Christ. These are the principles and practices of our sect, these are the marks of a true Methodist.[46]

This view is also reflected in the teachings of the Seventh-day Adventist church, a denomination with more than 650 hospitals and clinics worldwide,

[43] Martin Luther, "On the Freedom of a Christian," in *Luther's Works: Career of the Reformer I*, eds. Harold J. Grimm and Helmut T. Lehmann (1520), p. 31, www.spucc.org/sites/default/files/Luther%20Freedom.pdf. However, some of Luther's contemporaries promoted the primacy of civil authority and the subjugation of personal conscience in relation to the needs of others if necessary. See W. Bradford Littlejohn, *The Peril and Promise of Christian Liberty: Richard Hooker, The Puritans, and Protestant Political Theology* (Grand Rapids, MI: W. B. Eerdsmans, 2017), pp. 63–66 (discussing views of Henrician theorists Thomas Starkey and Stephen Gardiner).

[44] George Hunsinger, "Karl Barth (1886–1968)," in *The Teachings of Modern Christianity on Law, Politics and Human Nature*, vol. II, eds. John Witte and Frank Alexander (New York: Columbia University Press, 2006), p. 296.

[45] Randy L. Maddox, "'Visit the Poor': John Wesley, the Poor, and the Sanctification of Believers," in *The Wesleys and the Poor: The Legacy and Development of Methodist Attitudes to Poverty, 1729–1999*, ed. Richard Heitzenrater (Nashville, TN: Kingswood Books, 2002), p. 62 (noting Wesley "renounced accumulation of anything above what meets one's basic needs, directing it instead to meet the needs of our neighbors").

[46] John Wesley, *The Character of a Methodist. By John Wesley, M.A. Late Fellow of Lincoln College, Oxford.; [One Line of Text]* (1742), 2011, 6, 11, http://name.umdl.umich.edu/N20188.0001.001.

that states as a fundamental belief: "[A]s Christians, we are concerned with both the spiritual and the physical aspects of people's lives. Jesus, our pattern, healed 'every disease and sickness among the people' (Matthew 4:23, NIV)."[47] Ellen White, one of the founders of the church, wrote in the book *The Ministry of Healing* that:

> During His ministry, Jesus devoted more time to healing the sick than to preaching. His miracles testified to the truth of His words, that He came not to destroy, but to save.... He passed by no human being as worthless, but sought to apply the healing remedy to every soul.[48]

Other Protestant denominations also reflect, theologically, a strong commitment to care for the sick as a Christian duty. As Baptist theologian Gary Gunderson notes: "At the core of every major faith tradition stands an explicit commitment to be with the sick, the poor, the alienated, the marginal, the wounded, and the dying. The commitments are very old, but the implications are forever new and increasingly radical because of remarkable changes in health science."[49] The greater society seemingly recognizes these commitments, as researchers have found that "for reasons related to Christianity, patients expect to receive hope and support to better handle serious medical conditions during a stay in a religiously affiliated hospital."[50]

Twenty-first-century Christianity models its continued practice of offering healthcare after how Christ cared for people who were poor, oppressed, and unclean, striving to be "at the forefront of efforts to alleviate human suffering, cure disease, and advance knowledge and understanding."[51] Jesus' offering of

[47] General Conference of Seventh-Day Adventists, *Seventh-Day Adventists Believe ... A Biblical Exposition of 27 Fundamental Doctrines* (Hagerstown, MD: Review and Herald Publishing Association, 1988), p. 280. We have no quantitative assessment of Christ's time spent healing but White's assertion can be seen as consistent with both John 21:25 and Matthew 11:4–5 (e.g., John queried Jesus because while John only preached, Jesus spent so much time healing) where in answering John the Baptist, Jesus summed up his own ministry as "The blind receive sight, the lame walk, those who have leprosy are cured, the deaf hear, the dead are raised, and the good news is preached to the poor." Nevertheless, as noted by Maragh, "The healing ministry of Jesus as recorded in the synoptic gospels shows Jesus' commitment to restore the whole person to God and not focus on a single dimension of healing." Alvin Lloyd Maragh, "The Healing Ministry of Jesus as Recorded in the Synoptic Gospels," Loma Linda University Electronic Theses, Dissertations & Projects, 2006, p. 457. http://scholarsrepository.llu.edu/etd/457.

[48] Ellen G. White, *The Ministry of Healing* (Washington: Review and Herald Publishing Association, 1905), pp. 2–3.

[49] Gary Gunderson, *Deeply Woven Roots: Improving the Quality of Life in Your Community (Rhetoric and Society)* (Minneapolis, MN: Fortress Press, n.d.), p. 5.

[50] Seemann et al., "Are Religiously Affiliated Hospitals More Than Just Nonprofits?," p. 1030 (citations omitted).

[51] Rosie Beal-Preston, "The Christian Contribution to Healthcare," Triple Helix (Spring 2000), www.cmf.org.uk/resources/publications/content/?context=article&id=827.

life more abundant implies not only that we learn to care for each person in our community according to their needs, but even more so that the type of care given be of *quality* and as our best unto God.[52]

## 9.3 PATENTS AND ACCESS TO HEALTH TECHNOLOGIES

The previous section discussed the framework underlying Christian approaches to care for the sick and, by extension, access to health technologies. The following explores the role of patent protection in facilitating or hindering financial and therapeutic access, as patents are the key form of intellectual property protection for pharmaceuticals and other health technologies.

Patents and drug products seem to go hand-in-hand.[53] Through the patent mechanism, a government grants an inventor the right to exclude others from making, using, selling, offering to sell, or importing a patented invention into a country for the patent term, typically twenty years from the filing date.[54] Patent rights are territorial, so inventors must apply in each country or region where they desire protection, and the resulting patent is only valid in that country.[55] Moreover, because patent laws differ by country, an inventor may obtain a patent in one country and not in another on the same invention. Patent infringement is a strict liability offense; no particular mental state is required to violate a patent owner's rights. Nevertheless, enhanced damages may be awarded for willful infringement, and, controversially, some countries even provide criminal remedies.[56]

### 9.3.1 Patents and Drug Prices

The right to exclude granted by a patent is widely considered essential to pharmaceutical investment and development. Moreover, the deadweight losses that patents create are generally considered justifiable for

[52] 1 Corinthians 10:31; 2 Timothy 2:15; Matthew 5:48.

[53] Rebecca S. Eisenberg and W. Nicholson Price, "Promoting Healthcare Innovation on the Demand Side," *Journal of Law and the Biosciences*, vol. 4, no. 1 (April 17, 2017), pp. 3–49, https://doi.org/10.1093/jlb/lsw062.

[54] TRIPS: Agreement on Trade-Related Aspects of Intellectual Property Rights, April 15, 1994, Marrakesh Agreement Establishing the World Trade Organization, Annex 1C, 1869 U.N.T.S. 299, 332–334, Articles 28 and 33 (1994) [hereinafter TRIPS].

[55] Paris Convention for the Protection of Industrial Property, Article 4, March 20, 1883, 828 U.N.T.S. 305 (1979).

[56] J. W. Baxter et al., *World Patent Law and Practice* (Matthew Bender, 2008), appendix 2A.00.

pharmaceuticals, as companies need to price above marginal cost to recoup significant fixed development expenses.[57]

However, these exclusionary rights translate to soaring drug prices in both rich and poor countries,[58] despite global calls for access to affordable medicines.[59] Moreover, the problem is exacerbated by the fact that biologics,[60] which can be covered by a web of "life" patents[61] and cost an average of twenty-two times as much as a small molecule drug[62] for treating the same condition,[63] comprise an increasing proportion of new drugs in development.[64] This has resulted in the United States alone spending "an estimated $3.6 trillion, or 17.6% of its $20.5 trillion gross domestic product, on health care, including $345 billion on prescription drugs sold in retail pharmacies" in 2018, with per-person prescription drug spending basically doubling between 1999 and 2017.[65]

57 Joseph A. Dimasi, Henry G. Grabowski, and Ronald W. Hansen, "Innovation in the Pharmaceutical Industry: New Estimates of R&D Costs," *Journal of Health Economics*, vol. 47 (2016), pp. 20–21, https://doi.org/10.1016/j.jhealeco.2016.01.012.

58 Sharon Begley, "Cancer Drugs Are Unaffordable in the Developing World," STAT, June 6, 2016, www.statnews.com/2016/06/06/cancer-drug-prices-developing-world/; Joanna Shepherd, "Biologic Drugs, Biosimilars, and Barriers to Entry," *Health Matrix: Journal of Law-Medicine*, vol. 25, no. 1 (2015), p. 159, https://doi.org/10.2139/ssrn.2403068; "Essential New AIDS Drugs Unaffordable for Developing Countries," The New Humanitarian, July 25, 2007, www.thenewhumanitarian.org/news/2007/07/25/essential-new-aids-drugs-unaffordable-developing-countries.

59 "Health – United Nations Sustainable Development," United Nations, p. 8, www.un.org/sustainabledevelopment/health/; United Nations, "Report of the United Nations Secretary-General's High-Level Panel on Access to Medicines," www.unsgaccessmeds.org/s/UNSG-HLP-Report-FINAL-12-Sept-2016.pdf.

60 "What Are 'Biologics' Questions and Answers," U.S. Food and Drug Administration (FDA), www.fda.gov/about-fda/center-biologics-evaluation-and-research-cber/what-are-biologics-questions-and-answers.

61 Cynthia Koons, "This Shield of Patents Protects the World's Best-Selling Drug," *Bloomberg News*, September 7, 2017, www.bloomberg.com/news/articles/2017-09-07/this-shield-of-patents-protects-the-world-s-best-selling-drug; Jayne O'Donnell, "Biologic Drugmakers Use Patents, Suits, to Thwart Generic Competition," *USA Today*, August 4, 2016, www.usatoday.com/story/news/politics/2016/08/04/biologic-drugmakers-patents-suits-generic-competition/879157347.

62 AZBio, "Small Molecules, Large Biologics and the Biosimilar Debate," AZBio, www.azbio.org/small-molecules-large-biologics-and-the-biosimilar-debate.

63 Anthony D. So and Samuel L. Katz, "Biologics Boondoggle," *New York Times*, March 7, 2010, A23.

64 Ameet S. Sarpatwari, Jerry S. Avorn, and Aaron S. Kesselheim, "Progress and Hurdles for Follow-on Biologics," *New England Journal of Medicine*, vol. 372, no. 25 (June 18, 2015), pp. 2380–2382, https://doi.org/10.1056/nejmp1504672.

65 Olivier J. Wouters, "Lobbying Expenditures and Campaign Contributions by the Pharmaceutical and Health Product Industry in the United States, 1999–2018," *JAMA Internal Medicine*, vol. 180, no. 5 (March 1, 2020), https://doi.org/10.1001/jamainternmed.2020.0146.

The costs of bringing a drug or regulated medical device to market are high and often involve significant risk.[66] Thus, there is considerable pressure to allow pharmaceutical companies to charge high prices so that they will be incentivized to develop new treatments that society needs. As Professors Sachs and Frakt explain:

> The response from the pharmaceutical industry [to reduced price proposals] has been the same: Even if these proposals improve access to medicines today, they will have a negative effect on innovation in the future. If the government limits manufacturers' ability to recoup the costs of risky research and development ... they will simply reduce their investment in developing new drugs. This could harm all of us. The drugs we need in the future may not be available.[67]

But companies sell drugs so far above marginal cost that the prices more than make up for the costs of drug development, as their annual profits clearly show.[68] According to the United States Government Accountability Office:

> About 67 percent of all drug companies saw an increase in their annual average profit margins from 2006–2016. Among the largest 25 companies, the annual average profit margin fluctuated between 15 and 20 percent. For comparison, the annual average profit margin across non-drug companies among the largest 500 globally fluctuated between 4 and 9 percent.[69]

As described in a World Health Organization submission, "launch prices as set by companies are not based on R&D investment or production costs, but on the outcomes of economic calculations that aim to identify the highest possible profit margin the market will tolerate."[70] For example, a recently approved "breakthrough" drug, Trikafta, capable of helping 90 percent of people afflicted with cystic fibrosis, costs $311,503 a year, which is 34 percent

[66] Rhona Finkel, "The 5 Most Profitable Medications Ever Produced," May 23, 2014, www.drugsdb.com/blog/the-5-most-profitable-medications-ever-produced.html.

[67] Rachel E. Sachs and Austin B. Frakt, "Innovation–Innovation Tradeoffs in Drug Pricing," *Annals of Internal Medicine*, vol. 165, no. 12 (December 20, 2016), p. 871, https://doi.org/10.7326/m16–2167.

[68] James Bessen and Michael James Meurer, *Patent Failure: How Judges, Bureaucrats, and Lawyers Put Innovators at Risk* (Princeton, NJ: Princeton University Press, 2009), p. 88.

[69] United States Government Accountability Office, *Drug Industry Profits Research and Development Spending, and Mergers and Acquisition Deals* (November 2017), www.gao.gov/products/GAO-18-40.

[70] World Health Organization, "WHO Submission to the UN SG High Level Panel on Access to Medicines" (2006), p. 5, https://static1.squarespace.com/static/562094dee4b0d00c1a3ef761/t/56e746279f7266a586c2b893/1457997352055/WHO_HLP_Submission_7Mar2016.pdf.

more than the median list price of a house in the United States.[71] Similarly, a different study, published in March 2020 in the *Journal of the American Medical Association*, reported that between 2000 and 2018, the median net earnings for pharmaceutical companies were significantly greater than for non-pharmaceutical companies (13.8 percent versus 7.7 percent).[72]

Because most pharmaceutical companies are for-profit corporations with the goal of maximizing shareholder value,[73] they often are not interested in pursuing the development of drugs for conditions with low profit potential, even though a meaningful profit likely could be made. This has been evident with infectious diseases, Ebola, and now even COVID-19 before sufficient public pressure incentivized companies to begin working on a cure.[74] The current system leaves society to depend on the profit-motivated whims of pharmaceutical companies in deciding which diseases to research, as pharmaceutical companies are incentivized to develop drugs for conditions that afflict wealthy people, not poor people, and drugs for which they can charge exorbitant amounts, such as those that treat rare diseases.[75]

"Neglected tropical diseases" as well as more well-known diseases like malaria and tuberculosis affect more than one billion people each year.[76] Ten million people die from these diseases annually. Millions more are so incapacitated by the diseases that they cannot work, care for themselves, or care for their children. These diseases predominantly affect the poorest people

[71] Matthew Herper, "The Debate over America's Drug-Pricing System Is Built on Myths," STAT, December 23, 2019, www.statnews.com/2019/12/23/debate-over-us-drug-pricing-system-time-to-face-reality/.

[72] Fred D. Ledley et al., "Profitability of Large Pharmaceutical Companies Compared With Other Large Public Companies," *JAMA*, vol. 323, no. 9 (March 3, 2020), p. 834, https://doi.org/10.1001/jama.2020.0442.

[73] Yang, "Maximizing Shareholder Value."

[74] Josh Nathan-Kazis, "Some Drugmakers Are Racing to Develop a Coronavirus Vaccine. Why Big Pharma Isn't Rushing In.," Drugmakers Race to Develop a Coronavirus Vaccine – Barron's (Barrons, January 31, 2020), www.barrons.com/articles/drugmakers-race-to-develop-a-coronavirus-vaccine-51580485967; Ellen 't Hoen, "Time for New Pharmaceutical-Innovation Models," *Medicines Law & Policy*, February 7, 2020, https://medicineslawandpolicy.org/2020/02/time-for-new-pharmaceutical-innovation-models/.

[75] John Jenkins, "CDER Approved Many Innovative Drugs in 2014," *FDA Voice*, January 14, 2015, https://blogs.fda.gov/fdavoice/index.php/2015/01/cder-approved-many-innovative-drugs-in-2014/; Laura Fegraus and Murray Ross, "Sovaldi, Harvoni, And Why It's Different This Time," Health Affairs, November 21, 2014, www.healthaffairs.org/action/showDoPubSecure?doi=10.1377/hblog20141121.042908&format=full.

[76] "CDC – Global Health – Neglected Tropical Diseases," Centers for Disease Control and Prevention, January 29, 2020, www.cdc.gov/globalhealth/ntd/index.html.

in least developed countries.[77] Yet pharmaceutical research and development disproportionately focuses on chronic, noncommunicable diseases such as cancers, even though many more disability-adjusted life years (DALYs) are lost for infectious diseases like malaria and tuberculosis.[78] Thus it is perhaps not surprising that governments are looking for tools to reduce the costs of making necessary drugs available to needy patients at affordable prices.

### 9.3.2 Patents and Compulsory Licenses

One tool governments can use to reduce drug prices and increase access to health technologies for patented inventions is compulsory licensing. Through compulsory licensing, a nation allows a third party to practice a patented invention without the patent owner's permission and requires that third party to pay a government-specified royalty to the patent owner.[79] A compulsory license does not require the patent owner to *do* anything except sit back and receive the royalties from the third party. However, it does prevent the patent owner from stopping that third party from practicing the patented invention. In this sense, compulsory licenses can be analogized to the rights of the poor in the Old Testament *pe'ah* system, discussed earlier, to come onto the property of the landowner and glean from the fields in a way that did not harm the landowner.

A Malaysian report justifying a compulsory license on the Hepatitis C drug Sovaldi® (Sofosbuvir) provides an example of the potential financial impact of compulsory licensing:

> Sofosbuvir ... is patented in Malaysia, which means it must be sold at the originator companies' proposed Malaysian price (USD $12,000 for twelve weeks of treatment). Given that it is estimated that the drug can be produced at USD $171–360 for twelve weeks of treatment, at volume, pricing is likely to be based on maximization of profit margins rather than any rational stratification based on country developmental levels (as claimed by pharmaceutical companies).[80]

77 Suerie Moon, "Powerful Ideas for Global Access to Medicines," *New England Journal of Medicine*, vol. 376, no. 6 (February 9, 2017), pp. 505–507, https://doi.org/10.1056/nejmp1613861.

78 European Patent Office, "Scenarios for the Future" (2007), p. 77, http://documents.epo.org/projects/babylon/eponet.nsf/0/63A726D28B589B5BC12572DB00597683/$File/EPO_scenarios_bookmarked.pdf.

79 Cynthia M. Ho, "Compulsory Licenses under TRIPS: An Introduction," *Access to Medicine in the Global Economy*, May 2011, p. 127, https://doi.org/10.1093/acprof:oso/9780195390124.003.0006.

80 Malaysian AIDS Council, "At the Edge of a Miracle: The Hepatitis C Virus (HCV) Epidemic in Malaysia" (Fifa Rahman, 2017), p. 5, www.mac.org.my/v3/wp-content/uploads/2017/07/HCV_Report_A4_FA_23052017-web.pdf.

However, efforts by developing country governments to reduce costs, using mechanisms like compulsory licenses, routinely meet with censure[81] at the hubris of even considering harm to the patent "goose" that lays the golden eggs of new medical breakthroughs.[82] This is particularly troubling in view of the fact that pharmaceutical companies are not basing their research and development decisions on the possibility of generating profits in developing countries. They are basing them on the needs of the United States, Europe, and other highly developed markets where the bulk of their revenue originates. The ability to obtain US, European, and Japanese patent protection is what companies are considering in deciding whether to pursue the development of a particular drug, not whether patent protection is available in, say, Mozambique.

In fact, almost 80 percent of pharma revenue comes from North America, Europe, and Japan.[83] As such, whatever drug companies earn in poor countries is largely gravy. Bayer CEO Marijn Dekkers confirmed this when he stated, after the Indian government issued a compulsory license on a cancer drug that Bayer had priced so high in India that it was available to only 2 percent of the patients who needed it: "Is this going to have a big effect on our business model? No, because we did not develop this product for the Indian market, let's be honest. We developed this product for Western patients who can afford this product, quite honestly."[84]

In other words, allowing poor people in developing countries to access such drugs cheaply through compulsory licensing would not be expected to meaningfully affect drug development incentives for diseases that afflict people in wealthy countries. This is not to suggest that the relatively small percentage of

[81] "Letter from Livia Leu, Swiss Ambassador, to Dr. Carolina Gomez, Adviser, Colombian Ministry of Health and Social Protection," May 26, 2015, www.minsalud.gov.co/sites/rid/Lists/BibliotecaDigital/RIDE/VS/MET/patent-of-Imatinib-glive-closing-arguments.pdf; "Letter from Dr. Deborah Gleeson et al. to Juan Manuel Santos, President of the Republic of Colombia," May 16, 2016, www.keionline.org/wp-content/uploads/5-16-2016-letter-to-colombia-santos-imatinib-license.pdf.

[82] William W. Fisher III and Talha Syed, *Infection: The Health Crisis in the Developing World and What We Should Do About It* (Stanford University Press, forthcoming 2018), chapter 6, https://cyber.harvard.edu/people/tfisher/Infection_Regulations.pdf; Muhammad Zaheer Abbas, "Pros and Cons of Compulsory Licensing: An Analysis of Arguments," *International Journal of Social Science and Humanity*, vol. 3 (2013), pp. 254–255, https://doi.org/10.7763/ijssh.2013.v3.239.

[83] Matej Mikulic, "Worldwide Pharmaceutical Sales by Region," Statista, April 9, 2020, www.statista.com/statistics/272181/world-pharmaceutical-sales-by-region.

[84] Ketaki Gokhale, "Merck to Bristol-Myers Face More Threats on India Drug Patents," Bloomberg, January 28, 2014, www.bloomberg.com/businessweek/news/2014-01-21/merck-to-bristol-myers-face-more-threats-on-india-drug-patents.

revenue is not a meaningful sum that companies would not wish to lose. However, this potential loss of revenue does not justify pressuring countries to forego compulsory licensing. Unfortunately, when governments are threatened with economic sanctions by other countries (acting on behalf of pharmaceutical companies)[85] for issuing compulsory licenses, they may be reluctant to issue such licenses to alleviate access to medicines problems, and some people may die as a result.

### 9.3.3 Incentives and Pharmaceutical Innovation

Pharmaceuticals have been called the "poster child" for the patent system, and it has been argued that without strong patent protection and high prices, companies would not be incentivized to develop many of the drugs society needs.[86] That is undoubtedly true for some drugs. Moreover, as Professor Merges argues, "[T]he poor benefit so much from things covered by IP rights that the products covered by those rights more than make up for the excess distributional shares that wind up in the hands of rightowners."[87]

However, that does not mean that patents and high prices are the only way to obtain development of new needed drugs, especially in light of the fact that, as noted earlier, pharmaceutical companies already are not incentivized to develop many of the drugs needed in this global society. As Professors Hemel and Ouellette compellingly argue, in analyzing the necessity for monopoly pricing of drugs as simply the cost that must be paid for drug innovations, it is important to disconnect the innovation incentive from the allocation mechanism.[88]

85 Ketaki Gokhale, "Merck to Bristol-Myers Face More Threats on India Patents," Bloomberg, January 28, 2014, www.bloomberg.com/news/articles/2014-01-21/merck-to-bristol-myers-face-more-threats-on-india-drug-patents. See U.S. Department of State Report, U.S. Government Efforts to Negotiate the Repeal, Termination or Withdrawal of Article 15C of the South African Medicines and Related Substances Act of 1965 (February 5, 1999); Shubha Ghosh, "Pills, Patents, and Power: State Creation of Gray Markets as a Limit on Patent Rights," *Florida Journal of International Law*, vol. 14 (2002), p. 244; Robert Block, "Big Drug Firms Defend Right to Patents On AIDS Drugs in South African Court," *The Wall Street Journal* (Dow Jones & Company, March 6, 2001), www.wsj.com/articles/SB983836144503505217.

86 Jason Urbach, "State Will Undercut Itself with New IP Policy," BHF, February 28, 2014, http://ftp.bhfglobal.com/state-will-undercut-itself-with-new-ip-policy; Phil Kerpen, "Time to Get Tough on India Stealing Our Stuff," American Commitment, April 18, 2014, www.americancommitment.org/content/time-get-tough-india-stealing-our-stuff.

87 Robert P. Merges, *Justifying Intellectual Property* (Cambridge, MA: Harvard University Press, 2011), pp. 136, 270.

88 Daniel J. Hemel and Lisa Larrimore Ouellette, "Innovation Policy Pluralism," *Yale Law Journal*, vol. 128 (2019), p. 544.

There are IP (e.g., patent) and non-IP (e.g., prizes) innovation incentives and IP (e.g., monopoly pricing) and non-IP (e.g., patent buyout) allocation mechanisms that can be mixed, matched, and layered in a variety of ways to achieve both innovation and health technology access objectives. Hemel and Ouellette note that "on various occasions, governments have purchased patent rights from innovators and then placed those knowledge goods in the public domain … [Also,] government funding played at least an indirect role in the development of almost two-thirds of FDA-approved priority-review drugs" between 1988 and 2005.[89] They further explain that:

> [A] large swath of the market for pharmaceuticals in the United States involves two scenarios. Either (a) the government purchases patented products from the private sector and then distributes those products to patients for free or at deeply discounted prices, or (b) the government develops new drugs in-house or at federally financed laboratories and then allows firms to allocate access through proprietary pricing mechanisms.… [T]he pharmaceutical sector in the United States should not be seen as relying purely on IP either as an innovation incentive or as a mechanism for allocating access; a fair amount of matching between IP and non-IP innovation incentives and allocation mechanisms occurs in this sector.[90]

Moreover, almost forty-one million Americans are enrolled in Medicare Part D plans, accounting for more than 30 percent of all prescription drug spending in the United States. Under Medicare Part D, "access to prescription drugs is not entirely determined by monopoly pricing … access is allocated through a mix of market power and government assistance … [thus] for a very large swath of the population, pharmaceutical drugs are allocated neither fully on the basis of proprietary pricing nor through open access, but instead through a mix of IP and non-IP mechanisms."[91]

In other words, patents and monopoly pricing are not the only ways to incentivize pharmaceutical drug development. Moreover, limitations on patent rights such as compulsory licenses for public health purposes in developing countries are often both necessary and justifiable, as innovation decisions are not being made based on the possible revenue to be gained from patents in such countries in the first instance.

It is worth noting that patent rights are limited property rights, at best, and that their contours and scope are constantly being adjusted through judicial,

89 Ibid., p. 595.
90 Ibid., p. 595.
91 Ibid., pp. 598–599.

legislative, and administrative action. Governments grant patents to meet utilitarian societal goals, and governments decide the subject matter, scope, and duration of patents. Two inventors in the same country may independently work countless hours and develop the same invention; however, only one of them will receive a patent claiming that exact invention from that country's patent office.[92] In the United States, Article 1, Section 8, clause 8 of the Constitution authorizes, but does not require, Congress "to promote the progress of Science and the useful arts by securing to authors and inventors for *limited times*, the exclusive right to their respective writings and discoveries."[93]

Because governments create patent rights, governments can impose appropriate limitations on those rights. And facilitating access by the poor[94] to life-sustaining drugs in a way that does not harm the patent holder, such as through a compulsory license, should be viewed as part of the social bargain inherent in the patent system, a bargain that Christian believers should support.

More robust use of global price discrimination –where prices of drugs are lower in poorer countries and higher in richer ones – could be another way to improve access to health care technologies by poor people in developing countries.[95] Enabling poorer countries to pay close to marginal costs for drugs would likely increase access to necessary medicines for the poor. If, at the same time, drug companies can charge high prices in wealthy markets, they still can recoup sunk research and development costs. This arrangement would appear to contribute to both output maximization and distributive justice.[96] However, as proponents of such an approach admit, it also would likely increase the "already significant extent to which the cost of developing new drugs … is borne by the residents of the developed world, either as consumers purchasing patent-protected drugs or as taxpayers."[97]

So why should the residents of rich countries disproportionately bear the costs of drug development? Of course, as noted earlier, pharmaceutical

92 *Patent Act, U.S. Code* 35 (1952), §§ 291 et seq.

93 U.S. Constitution, art. 1, sec. 8, cl. 8.

94 As explained in Section 9.2, having low cost drugs produced does not guarantee patient access to those drugs, as there are several factors at play, beyond cost, that impact whether drugs actually reach the people who need them. For example, even if compulsory licenses were available or if pharmaceutical companies voluntarily reduced their prices, fair pricing in other areas of a country's health care system (e.g., insurance companies and medical providers) would still be necessary.

95 John A. Vernon and Joseph H. Golec, *Pharmaceutical Price Regulation: Public Perceptions, Economic Realities, and Empirical Evidence* (Washington, DC: AEI Press, 2009), p. 2.

96 Special thanks to Daniel Crane for illuminating this point.

97 William W. Fisher and Talha Syed, "Global Justice in Healthcare: Developing Drugs for the Developing World," *University of California Davis Law Review*, vol. 40 (2007), p. 585.

company drug development decisions generally focus on the noncommunicable diseases that tend to afflict wealthy countries. But Professors Fisher and Syed also point to another justification: historical equity. They note:

> The poverty of most Southern countries today is traceable in substantial measure (although not entirely, of course) to two major periods of modern history: (1) the period of encounter, coerced trade, conquest, imperial rule, and colonization by European countries with respect to much of the rest of the world, from, roughly, 1500 to the early 1900s; and (2) the post-World War II era of decolonization marked by an international system of unequal political, economic, and military relations, in which Western dominance has been anchored in the power of the United States.[98]

Nevertheless, while a price discrimination approach might help poor people in other countries, it does nothing to aid poor people in the United States who cannot afford their medications. It may be that the current drug development system is simply not fit for this purpose, and that without free rein to employ profit-maximizing strategies, including not developing drugs for the poor, today's pharmaceutical companies may provide even less of the breakthrough treatments society needs. While politically challenging, it may be that adoption of a universal health care system, which provides sufficient compensation to pharma companies while ensuring all members of society are able to access necessary health technologies, could be a way forward. Another, more-targeted approach could involve a de-linkage of the costs (and risks) of drug development from the prices charged for particular drugs, an elegant idea proposed by Jamie Love and others.[99]

Yet another and possibly even better approach would be the rise of more pharmaceutical companies structured as public benefit corporations (PBC). PBCs are designed to combine the best of for-profit and nonprofit approaches. As Eiser and Fields explain:

> Pressures for ever-higher profits are driving many pharmaceutical firms to push the pricing envelope beyond reasonable limits ... but the profit motive need not dictate endless price increases.... We propose the model of the benefit corporation for the pharmaceutical industry as a for-profit corporate structure that combines the best features of both sectors. These entities sell equity to private investors who expect a return on their investments, but they also promise to adhere to a social mission.... In the case of pharmaceutical

98 Ibid., p. 592.

99 James Love, "An Economic Perspective on Delinking the Cost of R&D From the Price of Medicines," WHO (2016). See also Hemel and Ouellette, "Innovation Policy."

> companies, the primary social mission would be to develop and sell life-sustaining therapies at prices that do not place an unsustainable burden on patients or society at large.[100]

In recent years, commentators have proposed a range of policy instruments to incentivize pharmaceutical innovation separate from, or as an adjunct to, the patent system. These include patent buyouts (involving reimbursement of R&D expenditures),[101] a global fund for drug development,[102] direct grants to compensate for R&D costs, patent pools,[103] "wild-card" patent term extensions,[104] prizes,[105] and more. As these are largely untested at scale, it is unknown how adopting any of these approaches would affect drug development incentives for good or ill.

Thus, there are, unfortunately, no easy answers to the question of how to maintain sufficient incentives for robust drug development (across a range of conditions) while achieving affordable US drug pricing. But as to the question of whether believers, in particular, should be pushing for the development of such solutions, the answer is a resounding "yes."

## 9.4 CHRISTIAN TRADITION, PATENTS, AND ACCESS TO MEDICINES

Religious views underlie several of our fundamental conceptions of intellectual property; in fact, there is a deep interweaving of faith with the secular pillars that animate IP theory today. For example, John Locke's theories

[100] Arnold R. Eiser and Robert I. Field, "Can Benefit Corporations Redeem the Pharmaceutical Industry?," *The American Journal of Medicine*, vol. 129, no. 7 (2016), pp. 651–652. See also Callie Davidson, "Strategies for Public Benefit Corporations in Pharmaceutical R&D," *UC Berkeley School of Law*, https://sites.law.berkeley.edu/sustainability-compliance/strategies-for-public-benefit-corporations-in-pharmaceutical-rd/ (exploring why PBCs are well situated to address certain diseases).

[101] Kevin Outterson, "Patent Buy-Outs for Global Disease Innovations for Low- and Middle-Income Countries," *American Journal of Law & Medicine*, vol. 32, no. 2–3 (June 1, 2006), pp. 159–173, https://doi.org/10.1177/009885880603200202.

[102] Thomas Pogge, "The Health Impact Fund: Boosting Pharmaceutical Innovation without Obstructing Free Access," *Cambridge Quarterly of Healthcare Ethics*, vol. 18, no. 1 (2009), pp. 78–86, https://doi.org/10.1017/s0963180108090129.

[103] "MPP-Home," Medicines Patent Pool, https://medicinespatentpool.org/.

[104] B. Spellberg et al., "Societal Costs versus Savings from Wild-Card Patent Extension Legislation to Spur Critically Needed Antibiotic Development," *Infection*, vol. 35, no. 3 (2007), p. 167, https://doi.org/10.1007/s15010-007-6269-7.

[105] James Love and Tim Hubbard, "Prizes for Innovation of New Medicines and Vaccines," *Annals of Health Law*, vol. 18 (2009), pp. 155–157; Michael Abramowicz, "Perfecting Patent Prizes," *Vanderbilt Law Review*, vol. 56 (2003), p. 115.

regarding the appropriation of private property were based on the view that the earth and its bounty were given by God to mankind for its common use.[106] Similarly, Georg Hegel posited a philosophy of personhood in relation to property against a backdrop of Christian thought regarding the human spirit and soul.[107] Lockean and Hegelian theories are the basis for two of the three dominant justifications for intellectual property protection.[108]

Religion, in addition to connecting us to Someone greater than ourselves, generally provides a moral context for our relationships to things (property) and to each other. As Professor Berg explains:

> Christian theology has generally taken an attitude toward property that is particularly suitable for IP: namely, that property rights, while important guarantors of both human industry and human dignity, also exist ultimately as instruments to serve the end of human dignity and may need to be limited in order to serve that end. This idea is reflected in a variety of religious doctrines, e.g., those of stewardship and (specifically in the Catholic context) the 'social mortgage on private property.'[109]

However, the problem of access to affordable health technologies is both urgent and real, and it requires not only thought but also action on the part of those who claim to be followers and disciples of Christ.

[106] See John Locke, *Two Treatises of Government, Second Treatise*, ed. Peter Laslett (Cambridge: Cambridge University Press, 1988), chapter V, section 24 ("it is very clear that God, as King David says (Psalm 115. 16), 'has given the earth to the children of men,' given it to mankind in common"). Of course, Locke was not alone in this view. As one commentator explains: "In Chapter V, Locke's premise, which he shared with most seventeenth century writers, was that God gave the earth and its fruits in common to men for their use. The problem he faced was to explain how commonly available resources can become legitimate private property, which excludes the right of other men." Karen I. Vaugh, "John Locke's Theory of Property: Problems of Interpretation," Libertarianism.org, March 1, 1980, www.libertarianism.org/publications/essays/john-lockes-theory-property-problems-interpretation. Locke further notes, in his famous Charity proviso, that "Charity gives every Man a Title to so much out of another's Plenty, as will keep him from extreme want, where he has no means to subsist otherwise." John Locke, *Two Treatises of Government, First Treatise*, ed. Peter Laslett (Cambridge: Cambridge University Press, 1988), chapter IV, section 42.

[107] Georg W. F. Hegel, *Elements of the Philosophy of Right*, ed. Allen Wood (Cambridge: Cambridge University Press, 1991).

[108] See Justin Hughes, *The Philosophy of Intellectual Property*, *Georgetown Law Journal*, vol. 77 (1988), pp. 287, 287–366 (the third being utilitarianism).

[109] Margo A. Bagley, "Inspired by the Word: Exploring Intellectual Property through the Lens of Religious Thought," in *Handbook on Intellectual Property Research*, eds. Irene Calboli and Maria Lilla Montagnani (Oxford University Press, forthcoming) (quoting Thomas Berg).

### 9.4.1 A Role for Christian Believers

Modern US politics looks very different from the sociopolitical context of the New Testament. As a Jew living under Roman occupation, Jesus did not focus his efforts on political reform or economic redistribution, and some theologians interpret that to mean that Christians should not get involved with politics. Others think that political activity is actually a distraction from the gospel message. At one point in his career, Reverend Jerry Falwell stated "[b]elieving in the Bible as I do, I would find it impossible to stop preaching the pure saving Gospel of Jesus Christ and begin doing anything else, including participating in civil rights reforms. . . . Preachers are not called upon to be politicians but to be soul winners. . . . We are here to serve Jesus."[110]

However, because physical and spiritual healing were clearly a priority to Jesus – and medicine is almost exclusively practiced through the modern health care system, in the United States at least – it is also important that the Church be involved in health care reform as a thoughtful advocate for those who cannot speak for themselves. This is not to imply that the Church needs to publicly support any specific candidate or policy, but Christians should at least collectively respond to the discussion of health care accessibility from the perspective and practice offered by Christ. Instead of banishing health care ethics to secular conversations, the Church should recognize its unique response to the "rampant medicalization of reality," and that its response is regulated by the "particular end it advances; namely, by fellowship with God [including renewal in God's image] which is manifest in the person of Jesus Christ."[111]

Interestingly, a recent article revealed that, from 1999 to 2018, the pharmaceutical and health products industry spent $4.7 billion – more than any other industry – on federal lobbying efforts.[112] The article concluded that "government efforts to lower drug costs and other legislative and regulatory initiatives may be counteracted by campaign donors and lobbyists in the pharmaceutical and health product industry."[113] But pharmaceutical company lobbyists are not the only ones with the ability to influence legislative and policy decisions. All Americans, including those who are Christians, have that right and can do

[110] Jerry Carrier, *The Making of the Slave Class* (Algora Publishing, 2010), , p. 107. We note, with irony, that Jerry Falwell founded the "Moral Majority," a political organization that "played a key role in the mobilization of conservative Christians as a political force." https://en.wikipedia.org/wiki/Moral_Majority.

[111] Lysaught and Kotva, "Christianity and the Social Responsibility," p. 23.

[112] Wouters, "Lobbying Expenditures and Campaign Contributions."

[113] Ibid.

so individually or collectively.[114] In writing about the need for Christians to actively engage in politics, John Danforth, a former US senator and ordained Episcopal priest, stated the following:

> I believe that there is much we can do that can make American politics better, and that what the faithful offer is uniquely religious. In other words, if religious people remain passive, if we don't do the work of fixing politics, the work simply won't be done. . . .What America needs is many more activists in politics-not activists who work for their own causes, but men and women who are committed to the higher calling of our republic . . . Inspiring such activists would be a great gift of religion to America. Faithful people have much to offer American politics . . . but to make this offering, we will have to show up and speak up. This may seem an unpleasant prospect for many of us, but nothing in religion says that we should be content with the pleasant.[115]

These words can and should also be applied to active engagement by Christians in the politics and policy arenas of patents and access to health technologies.

Active involvement by people of faith in social issues relating to patents is not new. When the United States Supreme Court held in *Diamond* v. *Chakrabarty*[116] that living organisms could be patented, and refused to consider the moral ramifications of its decision, churches sprang into action. The decision, which opened the floodgates to a seemingly illimitable array of biotechnology-derived subject matter, generated considerable criticism from religious individuals and organizations concerned about the commodification of life and the lessening of human dignity. As Daniel Kevles notes, "[I]mmediately following the Court's decision, the general secretaries of the National Council of Churches, the Synagogue Council of America, and the United States Catholic Conference joined in sending a letter to President Jimmy Carter urging a reexamination of the patent laws and a government inquiry into the moral, ethical, and religious questions raised by genetic engineering."[117] Moreover, the active, vocal, and organized participation of many Christians in the politics surrounding abortion in the United States is

[114] Constitution of the United States of America (1789), 1st Amendment ("Congress shall make no law . . . abridging . . . the right of the people . . . to petition the Government for a redress of grievances").

[115] John Danforth, *The Relevance of Religion: How Faithful People Can Change Politics* (Penguin Random House, 2015), pp. 244, 249–250.

[116] *Diamond* v. *Chakrabarty*, 447 U.S. 303, 316 (1980).

[117] See Daniel Kevles, "Ananda Chakrabarty Wins a Patent: Biotechnology, Law, and Society, 1972–1980," *Historical Studies in the Physical and Biological Sciences*, vol. 25 (1994), pp. 111, 135.

well known.[118] If anything, Christians' concern for an embryo's personhood potential, united with the reverence for all human life, should result in a decidedly pro-health posture in support of access to health care technologies. A greater involvement by people of faith in issues relating to patents and access to medicines could be a welcome extension of this kind of advocacy.

Of course, it takes more than just concerned individuals to truly address and affect inequitable systems. Some theologians even suggest that evangelism efforts ought to "incorporate a social agenda oriented toward redistributive economic policies" to add authenticity to the spirit-centered elements of the gospel "for evangelicals themselves, but [also to] eliminate the hypocrisy of wealthy evangelicals preaching the gospel in a poverty-stricken world."[119] This seems particularly true for Christians in the United States. As eloquently stated by Senator Danforth:

> For our founders, the future of America would depend on the virtue of its citizens. If the nation was to succeed, we would have to put the good of the whole above the interests of ourselves. The question, then is what moves us to be virtuous, what causes us to live not only for our own sakes but also for the good of others? In part it's how we are made.... Religion is the most persistent and effective teacher of virtue, because living beyond ourselves, for God and neighbor, is the heart of its message.[120]

Living beyond ourselves, for God, should involve advocacy on behalf of our neighbors who may not be able to adequately advocate for themselves, particularly in relation to access to health technologies.

### 9.4.2 Impediments to Action

Yet such advocacy is not readily apparent. Might aspects of selfishness be at play? A self-interested view might support patents that enable high pharmaceutical industry pricing as necessary to incentivize the development of the drugs society needs. Wealthy Christians may also benefit as shareholders from the profits such companies generate. Another type of self-interest may have contributed to the catastrophic loss of life on the African continent, due to HIV/AIDS drugs being priced out of the reach of millions of poor people in the late 1990s and 2000s. As vividly described in the documentary film *Fire in*

118 See, e.g., Monica Hesse, "'Jane Roe,' from *Roe v. Wade*, made a stunning deathbed confession. Now what?" *The Washington Post*, May 20, 2020.

119 Craig M. Gay, *With Liberty and Justice for Whom?: The Recent Evangelical Debate over Capitalism* (W. B. Eerdmans, 1991), p. 127.

120 Danforth, *Relevance of Religion*, p. 50.

*the Blood*, the entire continent of Africa counted for only 1 percent of originator pharma HIV/AIDS drug sales.[121] Yet the drug companies took a hard line, keeping their prices at $10,000–15,000/patient/year in Africa, just as in the United States, and fought against the introduction of generic drugs while millions of lives were lost.[122] The documentary notes that people in the United States, including most US HIV/AIDs activists, were seemingly unconcerned, in part due to the fear that if antiretroviral drugs were provided to Africans, resistant forms of the virus might develop that would later harm Americans.

Herman Bavinck, writing at the beginning of the last century, describes the problem thus:

> Today's Christianity is narrow-minded and selfish. One evil day it enlisted in the service of wealth and power, thus positioning itself over against the sick and the weak.... But original Christianity had an entirely different purpose. It opposed all competition between social classes. It wanted community and cooperation of its members. It recommended harmony and love such as exists between members of the same body. If the Christian religion of today wants to regain its lost influence and become a blessing to society, its attitude will have to change radically.[123]

Christians should be champions for the equitable distribution of life-saving and life-preserving medicine, insisting that everyone have equal access to options of care that can improve a patient's quality of life. Adopting such a stance would be one of the clearest reflections of the gospel, showing the capacity to love and care about other humans who are unable to afford access to the newest remedies, including those who might be considered enemies or foreigners.

Professors Amy Kapzynski and Greg Gonsalves provide a striking assessment of these issues in relation to the COVID-19 pandemic:

> Those hardest hit will be the most vulnerable – the elderly and those with chronic diseases, particularly those in nursing homes, crowded homeless shelters, and prisons. [The virus] will spread unchecked ... unless we create social immunity, woven of the ways we interact and care for one another. But what kind of social immunity can we build in a body politic that has been ravaged for decades by neoliberal policies?

[121] See www.fireintheblood.com.

[122] Ibid.

[123] Herman Bavinck, *Essays on Religion, Science, and Society*, ed. John Bolt (Baker Academic, 2008), p. 120 (originally published in 1908).

> Those policies have delivered us a rapaciously profit-driven health care system … [and] an austerity-ravaged state.… We have known [since] the mid-nineteenth century … that we create conditions that make people sick, and that those who lack economic, social, and political power typically bear the greatest burden of disease. But more recent work on the impact of inequality on health reveals another truth: inequality is itself associated with poorer health outcomes, including lower life expectancies.… [Many] Americans … seek a new order that, instead of perpetuating the virulent inequality and exploitation of late twentieth-century capitalism, makes justice a core feature of our health care system. Social mobilization is a key tool for achieving these goals. We must demand continuous and sustained reinvestments in our common good.[124]

The followers of Christ should be the first mobilizers in this cause, leading the call for justice in access to health technologies. As such, it is encouraging to see Christian leaders offering houses of worship to be COVID-19 vaccination sites and advocating for vaccine access for the neediest, not the wealthiest, among us.[125]

Unfortunately, Christians have not always, or even often, acted in accordance with the principles of love and care for the poor and sick, often due to the twin evils of greed and selfishness. After His encounter with the rich young ruler in Matthew 19, Jesus made it clear that an unhealthy relationship with money is one of the biggest obstacles to coming into a faith relationship with Christ in that the desire to gain wealth "drives us to do all sorts of things that drive us further and further away from God."[126]

Of course, wealth is not presented as being intrinsically evil in the Bible; rather, it is "the *love* of money" that is identified as the root of all kinds of evil.[127] This verse speaks judgment over insatiable greed, especially at others'

[124] Amy Kapczynski and Gregg Gonsalves, "Alone against the Virus," The Boston Review, March 13, 2020, https://bostonreview.net/class-inequality-science-nature/amy-kapczynski-gregg-gonsalves-alone-against-virus#.XmuloH4gEjQ.facebook.

[125] Rebecca Randall, "Christians Ready to Help COVID-19 Vaccine Go to Neediest First," Christianity Today, November 17, 2020, www.baynews9.com/fl/tampa/news/2021/01/10/florida-churches-join-covid-19-vaccination-effort ("With outbreaks resurging around the world and – finally – a likely COVID-19 vaccine on the horizon, Christian leaders are advocating for fair distribution to protect the neediest people and places, not just the richest."). See also Nadine Yanes, "Seminole County Health Officials Partner with Faith Organizations to Provide Vaccines in Churches," ClickOrlando.com, January 9, 2021, www.clickorlando.com/news/local/2021/01/08/seminole-county-health-officials-partner-with-faith-organizations-to-provide-vaccines-in-churches/ (noting forty-eight churches in Seminole County alone are vaccination sites).

[126] Matthew 6:25–34; "What Does the Bible Say about Greed?"

[127] 1 Timothy 6:10.

expense. Our heart's desire should be to "seek first [God's] kingdom and his righteousness, and all these things will be given to you as well," which includes trusting God to provide all of our needs when we live lives not focused on acquiring earthly treasure.[128]

The development of new drugs is important to human flourishing, and patents do facilitate drug development.[129] Moreover, as stated by Professor Berg:

> Intellectual property, like other forms of property, serves important purposes related to human dignity, productivity, and especially creativity.... But for a variety of reasons, limits on intellectual property are equally important: in particular, the full extension of IP rights may harm the poor, and certain limits on those rights are important to benefiting and empowering the poor.[130]

Today, many Christians run the risk of thinking that living one's faith is purely a private, individual, and internal matter. But Micah 6:8 is an exhortation to do justice, love mercy, and walk humbly with God. Believers are to create opportunities for equitable access (including being transparent about business decisions) and liberation from oppression, to embrace with loving kindness those deemed unworthy in our society, and to remember Christ's sacrifice individually and collectively. A reprioritization of purpose – as individuals, but also, importantly, as businesses and corporations – seems necessary for believers as participants in the public debate over access to health technologies. Societal-level policy shifts, in addition to individual generosity toward those in need, could truly impact and result in not simply equal but *equitable* access to health technologies for all.[131]

## 9.5 CONCLUSIONS

Jesus said, "I have come that they might have life, and that they may have it more abundantly."[132] It is God's desire for human beings to flourish in health and every other way. Jesus' ministry on earth was one of healing, not only of

[128] Matthew 6:25–34; "What Does the Bible Say about Greed?," GotQuestions.org, www.gotquestions.org/Bible-greed.html.

[129] As noted in Section 9.4, there are, however, a variety of other tools that may facilitate incentivizing drug development while providing affordable access.

[130] See Thomas C. Berg, "Intellectual Property and the Preferential Option for the Poor," *Journal of Catholic Social Thought*, vol. 5 (2008), p. 193 (advocating a "degree of skepticism toward broad IP rights," particularly in relation to pharmaceutical patents, as necessary to effectuate the Catholic principle of the preferential option for benefitting or empowering the poor among us).

[131] 2 Corinthians 8:13–14; 1 John 3:16–17 (emphasis added).

[132] John 10:10b (NKJV).

spiritual illnesses but especially of physical ones. Christians, those who claim to be His followers, should also seek physical healing and prosperity for their neighbors (defined by Christ as anyone who needs their help).[133] This duty is part of the fabric of Christianity and is a foundational tradition in both Catholic and Protestant faith communities.

With prescription drug prices soaring, the extension of these Biblical principles to medicines and other health technologies is needed now more than ever. To the extent patent protection hinders access to necessary medicines, the counsel from Christian tradition appears to include the obligation to impose necessary limits on such protection in a way that does not unduly harm the product manufacturers.

Greed is not a Christian virtue, but showing compassion certainly is. It also can be an economically sound course of action by enabling greater workforce productivity, higher educational attainment, and stronger families who are less reliant on handouts and social safety nets. Societies can and should, consistent with Christian tradition, make the wise choice to show compassion and affirm human flourishing in the economic regulation of access to health care technologies.

[133] Luke 10:25–37.

10

# Price Controls and Market Economies

ANDRÉ AZEVEDO ALVES AND INÊS GREGÓRIO

## 10.1 INTRODUCTION

Governments usually adopt price controls to impose restrictions on the price of goods and services by employing the appealing argument that they are protecting the groups who find it difficult to meet increasing prices. Since ancient times, regulators have set maximum or minimum prices – price ceilings or price floors. A maximum price for bread was understood as a means to protect the poorest from starvation and the maximum price for house rents to protect them from becoming homeless. The minimum wage – the price floor for labor – was seen as a guarantee to prevent unskilled workers from falling below a minimum living standard.

Nonetheless, many economists are skeptical about these mechanisms because they interfere with the natural operation of the market and distort the pattern of resource allocation. Additional objections sound not in utilitarianism but in moralism. By changing the prices that emerge from the free interaction of the participants on commercial exchanges, price controls pervert the relationship between price and worth. According to the moral objections, the former should reflect the latter for there to be a just exchange. Moreover, according to the objectors, price ceilings will, by definition, cause shortages, and price floors will lead to surpluses, therefore ending up penalizing precisely the groups that price controls were intended to protect. As such, the imposition of price controls, apart from having unintended consequences, appears to violate the principle of justice in economic transactions.

Price controls have been extensively discussed throughout the centuries, not only by economists, but by all sectors in society. In this chapter, we approach the question of price controls using a Christian framework, analyzing the arguments employed by recognized authors from various denominations. After a brief introduction, Section 10.2 explores the sources and origins of Christian thought on price controls and market economies, with a special emphasis on the medieval legacy, and in particular the thought and work of St. Thomas Aquinas. Section 10.3 discusses the main topic according to subsequent developments in Catholic thought, focusing mainly on late scholasticism, which was crucial in shaping Catholic views on economic issues in the transition to modernity. Section 10.4 approaches prices controls from the point of view of Protestant thought distinguishing between the perspective of three political economists – Pufendorf, Hutcheson, and Smith – and the perspective of Martin Luther. Finally, Section 10.5 concludes the argument, with an attempt to synthesize (at least to the extent common ground can be found) a general Christian position on price controls and market economies.

## 10.2 SOURCES AND ORIGINS OF CHRISTIAN THOUGHT ON PRICE CONTROLS AND MARKET ECONOMIES: THE MEDIEVAL LEGACY

Concerns about the justice of prices practiced in markets are not new. They may ultimately be traced back to antiquity, when the first forms of economic exchange emerge. Christian thought on price controls and market economies traditionally drew on two major sources. The first was, of course, the biblical texts from which divine law was ascertained and interpreted. The second was the Aristotelian tradition, particularly the framework for dealing with justice in exchange relationships set up in Aristotle's *Nicomachean Ethics*. As noted by the historian of medieval economic thought, Diana Wood:

> In his Nicomachean Ethics (v, v) Aristotle set up a model of justice in exchange which is fundamental to the idea of the just price. He did not discuss the just wage as such, because the society in which he lived was based largely on slavery, but his model generated ideas amongst later commentators which were applicable to both subjects. Aristotle's real concern was to apply justice to exchange. In its widest sense he saw justice as a state of mind which disposed someone to act rightly. It was righteousness itself, and as such it was the epitome of all virtue. "Justice . . . is not a part of virtue, but virtue entire." For him virtue consisted in a mean. The just or virtuous person was one who avoided all extremes, and whose disposition led him to apply the mean, or moderation, to his behaviour. Justice in the sense of righteousness was a universal quality. When he discussed justice in exchange, however, his concern was with "particular" rather than universal justice – justice as applied to relationships between people.[1]

[1] Diana Wood, *Medieval Economic Thought* (Cambridge: Cambridge University Press, 2002), p. 133.

It was during the Middle Ages, when economic life developed significantly, that the doctrine of just price became a principal concern for medieval writers.

According to John Baldwin, the encapsulation of the medieval economy's doctrine of just price was that "the just price was essentially determined by the cost of production ... [and] consisted of the sum total of material costs necessary for producing goods plus a reasonable wage to maintain the craftsman or merchant in his appropriate station of life."[2] As such, the reward for the effort put forth by craftsmen or merchants in the production of goods was differentiated by and directly associated with their position in the social hierarchy. It was possible to make these distinctions because the medieval economy was organized within the guild system; it was generally static, consisting of local and small markets, a limited number of buyers, and a level of goods supply that was either elastic or known to all participants on economic exchanges. Guilds, Raymond de Roover clarifies, consisted of "welfare agencies which prevented unfair competition, protected consumers against deceit and exploitation, created equal opportunities for their members, and secured them a modest but decent living in keeping with traditional standards."[3]

Nonetheless, the quick and substantial progress in trade that took place between the eleventh and the thirteenth centuries – and which meant not only an increased number of commercial transactions but also the development of new financial tools – revived the debate about the *justum pretium*. And in the normative analysis of this economic question, three groups of medieval authors stood out: the Canon lawyers, the Roman lawyers, and the theologians.

Classical Roman law evidently influenced medieval Roman lawyers, and, for that reason, the principle of freedom of bargaining played a fundamental role for them in the question of price determination. According to the free-bargain principle, as explained by Odofredus in his Lectura,[4] sellers and buyers were free to negotiate and to offer different prices before agreeing upon a certain price. To complement this process, medieval Roman lawyers also revived and generalized a device from the Justinian Code known as *laesio*

[2] John W. Baldwin, "The Medieval Theories of the Just Price: Romanists, Canonists, and Theologians in the Twelfth and Thirteenth Centuries," *Transactions of the American Philosophical Society*, vol. 49, no. 47 (1959), p. 7.

[3] Raymond de Roover, "The Concept of the Just Price: Theory and Economic Policy," *The Journal of Economic History*, vol. 18, no. 4 (December 1958), p. 418.

[4] Quoted in Baldwin, "The Medieval Theories of the Just Price," p. 21.

*enormis*, which established that the price could be rectified if it was below one-half of the just price.[5]

On the other hand, discussion among Canon lawyers was dominated by the important concept of usury, which the Carolingian economic legislation defined as "when more is demanded back than what is given."[6] Early Canonists[7] rejected any possibility of price profiteering and favored price regulation as a mechanism to protect both sellers and buyers from the abusive practice of usury. However, a few centuries later, the Decretists' interpretations of the Decretum of Gratian introduced an important difference between profit – *honestus questus*, which resulted from labor and the expenses of craftsmanship and was necessary for self-support – and usury, *turpe lucrum*, which resulted from speculative sale and greed. William of Rennes later confirmed this, arguing in favor of a moderate profit (*lucrum moderatum*) and clarifying that gains were only sinful if conducted out of greed (*cupiditas*):

> Although business can scarcely be conducted without sin, merchants may receive a moderate profit from their ware for the maintenance of themselves and their families. Since they work for all and perform a kind of common business by transporting merchandise back and forth between fairs, they should not be held to pay their own wages. From the merchandise itself they can accept a moderate profit, which is regulated by the judgement of a good man, because the amount of profit permitted cannot be exactly determined in shillings, pounds, or pennies.[8]

But Romanists and Canonists were neighbors in Bologna, the center of the two legal systems at the time, and neither was immune to the influence of the other. Popes Alexander III and Innocent III introduced the device of laesio enormis into Canon law. For both systems, the just price was the current price; the price that goods currently fetched at a specific time and place. For this reason, the *justum pretium* resulted from a common estimation and

5 In its original form, *laesio enormis* was developed to protect sellers, but during the Middle Ages, Roman lawyers extended its benefits to buyers as well. As explained by Baldwin, this development can be seen as "a revolution which deposed the seller from his place of privilege and elevated the buyer to at least an equal position" (ibid., p. 27).

6 Ibid., p. 32. In this point, it is possible to identify the general suspicion toward merchants and mercantile activity that was inherited from the ancient Church Fathers, who believed that commercial activity was always a "morally risky business" (ibid., p. 14) because money enhances the chances of fraudulent and deceitful attitudes by all participants in the exchange.

7 Referring to the period of the late eighth and ninth centuries and including the laws and canons of the Carolingian Empire.

8 Quoted in ibid., p. 48.

fluctuated according to different localities or moments.[9] There was also a coincident view of the problem of fraud (*dolus*), which was considered to be a deliberate misrepresentation of the quality or quantity of goods.

Theologians did not seriously consider the question of just price until the thirteenth century; nonetheless, their intellectual accomplishments were even more remarkable than those achieved by medieval legists.[10] Although not the first theologian advocating a just price of economic goods, Thomas Aquinas is often referred to as the father of the theory of just price because of his thorough exposition of the topic. His careful analysis of the subject can be found in Question 77: "By Sins Committed in Buying and Selling" of *Secunda-secundae* of his *Summa Theologica*. Reflecting the prevailing view that economics was part of justice, Aquinas' objective was normative – to give a theoretical justification for the ethical character of prices.

In his first article, Aquinas asserts that it is sinful to sell a thing for more than the just price. Doing so is a form of deceit and of injury to the other party involved in the transaction. He proceeds to distinguish two different ways of buying and selling: the first that tends to be advantageous for both parties and the second that tends to the advantage of one party and the disadvantage of the other. Explaining the former type of transaction, Aquinas asserts that all contracts "should not be more of a burden to one party than to another, and consequently all contracts between them should observe equality of thing and thing."[11] For this reason, when the price exceeds the quality of the thing or the quality exceeds the price, there is no equality of justice, and the sale is unjust and unlawful. In this case, "to fulfil the demands of equitable justice the contract price and the true economic value of goods must be equivalent."[12] It is by focusing merely on passages similar to these that some authors have

9 Romanists developed a manual for *estimatores*, those who were responsible for determining the just price of goods. The manual defined their duties to include "the determination of obligations between debtors and creditors, the appraisal of landed properties and their boundaries, the division among partners of things held in common, and the adjudicating of the right of way" (ibid., p. 28). Additionally, in his *Lectura*, Odofredus also established four standards for this estimation, the first and most important of which referred to the price that was "observed commonly," in contrast to the price that arose "from the whim or needs of single individuals" (ibid., p. 28). Following the same methods, Canonists emphasized the importance of leaving individual affections aside from the estimation of just price, which should be the result of a common estimation. Bernard of Botone left the influence by Romanists very clear when he stated the formula "a thing is worth as much as it can be sold for" as being the Canonist definition of just price (ibid., 54).

10 Ibid., p. 58.

11 St. Thomas Aquinas, *The Summa Theologica*, trans. Fathers of the English Dominican Province (Cincinnati: Benziger Bros., 1947), II, II, q. 77, art. 1, ad resp.

12 Baldwin, "The Medieval Theories of the Just Price," p. 72.

concluded that Aquinas follows Marxian dialectics and establishes a theory of value in line with Karl Marx. This theory, however, is deconstructed by Roover, who accuses these authors of "selecting those passages favorable to their thesis"[13] and of ignoring other statements that completely contradict this theory, especially in the last article of Question 77.

Aquinas's second method of buying and selling, on the other hand, refers to those accidental situations "when a man has great need of a certain thing, while another man will suffer if he be without it."[14] Here, the just price will be defined not only by the economic value of the thing sold, but also by the loss imposed on the seller. For it is thus possible "to sell a thing for more than it is worth in itself,"[15] but never for more than it is worth for the seller.[16] Before concluding the article, Aquinas separates human law from divine law and clarifies that, according to the latter, there should be compensation for those who suffer loss from unlawful contracts.

Defects in the thing sold are the main topic of Aquinas's next two questions, with a three-part classification – the fault may regard the thing's substance, its quantity, or its quality. In any case, Aquinas is very straightforward in affirming that if a sale is made with awareness of a fault, it is fraudulent and unlawful. But the same does not apply if the seller is not aware of the fault: "if any of the foregoing defects be in the thing sold, and he knows nothing about this, the seller does not sin."[17] Nevertheless, the buyer always has the right to be compensated for the loss caused, even if the seller only learns of the defect after the sale is made. Another relevant point regarding the sale of faulty things respects the obligation of the seller to state the defects of the thing to be sold. If the seller acts otherwise, he would be giving someone "an occasion of danger or loss" and the contract would be fraudulent.[18]

In the last article of the question, Aquinas addresses those situations where it is acceptable to sell a thing dearer than what the seller paid for it – the mark-up question. According to the author, exchange can be seen in two different ways, one by natural necessity – which he considers "commendable" – and

[13] Roover, "The Concept of Just Price," p. 421.

[14] Aquinas, *The Summa Theologica*, II, II, q. 77, art. 1, ad resp.

[15] Ibid.

[16] On this point, Aquinas introduces two remarks that are important to understand the overall theory. If one person greatly benefits of the thing to be sold and if the seller does not suffer any loss by selling it, then the price shall not be raised, even though it is for the advantage of one party. Moreover, if a man buys something he considers to be to his great advantage, he may pay the seller a higher price for it; but the gesture belongs only to his honesty.

[17] Ibid., art. 2, ad resp.

[18] The author explains, however, that if the defects are too obvious, there is no need to inform the buyer.

the other one by profit, which he considers "deserving of blame." Gains considered in themselves, in their nature, are neither virtuous nor sinful; it is the final objective of trading that determines their justness:

> Thus, for instance, a man may intend the moderate gain which he seeks to acquire by trading for the upkeep of his household, or for the assistance of the needy; or again, a man may take to trade for some public advantage, for instance, lest his country lack the necessaries of life, and seek gain, not as an end, but as payment for his labor.[19]

In this point, Aquinas approaches the ideas of Aristotle, considering that, apart from reflecting the factors of labor and expenses, the economic value of a thing also reflects the concept of human want or need. Differences of value "were due, first of all, to the abilities of goods to satisfy need, and, secondly to the amounts of labour and expenses expended in their production."[20] Also in his comments on Aristotle, the theologian argues that "arts and crafts would be doomed to destruction if the producer did not recover his outlays in the sale of his product," thus arguing that "the market price could not fall permanently below cost."[21] Therefore, for Aquinas, the just price cannot be determined with mathematical precision, being instead an estimate that takes into account the economic value of goods relative to a specific time and place. Moreover, the just price also enjoys some elasticity to "vary within a certain range, so that minor deviations do not involve any injustice."[22] The example given to illustrate this argument can be found in Question 77, Article 3, Objection 4. Here, Aquinas tells a story about a merchant who arrives with wheat in a place that faces starvation. The merchant knows that other merchants are coming after him with more wheat. Is this merchant able to sell the wheat at a higher price due to the scarcity of the good or is he bound to tell the truth and to sell the wheat at a lower price than its prevailing price? According to Aquinas, the seller "does not seem to act contrary to justice through not stating what is going to happen,"[23] even though he would act virtuously if he chose to do so and lowered the price accordingly.

As a theologian, Thomas Aquinas understood the just price as justice entering the world of commerce, and, probably for that reason, in his thought the just price takes precedence over the concept of *laesio enormis* as a limit to the free bargaining of contracts. The concept had traditionally acted as a

[19] Ibid., art. 4, ad resp.

[20] Baldwin, "The Medieval Theories of the Just Price," p. 74.

[21] Roover, "The Concept of Just Price," p. 422.

[22] Ibid., p. 422.

[23] Aquinas, *The Summa Theologica*, II, II, q. 77, art. 3, ad resp.

limitation on the enforcement of agreements that would be deemed to result in abnormal harm (*laesio enormis*) inflicted on one of the parties. But for Aquinas, despite allowing for small deviations from the just price without resulting in a fraudulent sale, the integral just price (and not any stipulated fraction of it such as half or two-thirds) was regarded as the central concept for evaluating the justice of transactions. An implication of this is that, of course, computation of the just price then becomes a central issue for determining the proper role and scope of economic regulation and price controls. For this purpose, as explored in the next section, the notion of "common estimation" will play a key role.

Two additional points unanimously made by medieval authors are the rejection of any form of price discrimination to maintain a social hierarchy and the understanding of monopoly as "a deleterious practice, inimical to the commonweal."[24] All practices adverse to competition were considered to be of a criminal nature and "those who escaped conviction in the secular courts were still punishable *in foro conscientiae*,"[25] because monopoly profits corresponded to *turpe lucrum*, for which restitution was always required.

## 10.3 CATHOLIC THOUGHT ON PRICE CONTROLS AFTER THE REFORMATION

While Christian thought on price controls and market economies naturally had many variants, it is safe to say that the Thomistic framework explained in the previous section of this chapter was the dominant approach at least until the Protestant Reformation. From the Catholic side, the period of the Counter-Reformation was marked by some notable developments in economic theory as well as by important developments in the application of normative concepts of justice to prices and their regulation.

In this period, the work of the late scholastics – particularly those of the School of Salamanca – had a central and long-lasting influence in shaping Catholic views on prices, the operation of the market economy, and its relationship with state controls and regulation.[26] The designation "School of

24 Roover, "The Concept of Just Price," p. 426.

25 Ibid., p. 429.

26 For an overview of the economic contributions of the late scholastics, see Alejandro A. Chafuen, *Faith and Liberty: The Economic Thought of the Late Scholastics* (Lanham: Lexington Books, 2003). Specifically about the School of Salamanca, see Marjorie Grice-Hutchison, *The School of Salamanca: Readings in Spanish Monetary Theory 1544–1605* (Oxford: Clarendon Press, 1952) and André A. Alves and José M. Moreira, *The Salamanca School* (New York: Bloomsbury, 2013).

Salamanca" refers to a distinct group of Iberian scholars of the sixteenth and early seventeenth centuries who followed in the footsteps of Francisco de Vitoria (c. 1483–1546). These authors – mostly Dominicans and, later, Jesuits – employed and expanded the earlier Thomistic framework in order to deal with the new economic and political problems that arose in a time of rapid growth of business activity and European expansion into the "New World."

While for the most part their emphasis is on continuity with earlier Christian economic thinking, the Salamanca School combines a more elaborate understanding of the functioning of market economies and the role of prices with greater practical skepticism about government intervention in general and price controls in particular. As emphasized by Alves and Moreira:[27]

> One of the key distinguishing features of the Salamanca School – and perhaps the most important characteristic of its economic thought – is its sophisticated understanding of the operation of the market economy. While the late Iberian scholastics did not, in most areas, offer a radical break with the past, they often put forth a more benevolent view of the functioning of the market economy than other earlier and contemporary thinkers. This view was also associated with a greater awareness of the dangers associated with undue political intervention in the market, which raised a broad scope of ethical concerns.

The late scholastics, to a greater extent than anyone before, incorporated into the idea of just price notions of supply and demand, as well as what can be regarded as an early understanding of the subjective theory of value (which was only explicitly and fully defined in economic theory in the second half of the nineteenth century).Thus, the founder of the Salamanca School, Francisco de Vitoria, describes the operation of market economies and the important role played by prices and their relationship with common estimation in the following manner:

> It follows from this principle that wherever there is a marketable good for which there are many buyers, neither the nature of the good nor the price for which it was bought, that is today, how expensive it was, nor the toil and trouble it was to get it should be taken into account. When Peter sells wheat, the buyer need not consider the money Peter spent nor his work but, rather, the common estimation of how much wheat is worth. If, according to

[27] André A. Alves and José M. Moreira, "Business Ethics in the School of Salamanca," in *Handbook of the Philosophical Foundations of Business Ethics*, ed. Christoph Luetge (Dordrecht: Springer, 2013), p. 216.

> commons estimation, the bushel of wheat is worth four silver pieces and somebody buys it for three, this would constitute an injustice to the seller because the common estimation of a bushel of wheat is four silver pieces. In the same way, if that seller were to sell at a higher price, taking into account his expenses and his work, he would selling unjustly, because he should sell it according to the common estimation of the market.[28]

Reinforcing his emphasis on the centrality of common estimation achieved through voluntary action in the context of the market, Vitoria then immediately goes on to clarify that other considerations used to deduce the just price and value of a good are only valid until the price has been established through common estimation, which should then be respected as the just price. In line with Vitoria, Domingo de Soto, another towering figure of the School of Salamanca, explains the notion of prices and their connection with utility, anticipating (although not in a fully consistent way) developments in economic theory that would only materialize again in an explicit form much later with the so-called marginalist revolution in the nineteenth century:

> The price of things should not be calculated by their nature, but by the utility they serve to men. The reason for this conclusion is natural; because as the world and everything in it has been made for man, the things in common estimation ought to be worth as much as they serve men.[29]

Or, in the words of another important representative of the school, Diego de Covarrubias y Leyva:

> The value of an article does not depend on its essential nature but on the estimation of men, even if that estimation be foolish. Thus, in the Indies wheat is dearer than in Spain because men esteem it more highly, though the nature of the wheat is the same in both places.[30]

In line with the earlier Christian doctrine on the just price, it was deemed to include both the *natural price* (associated with common estimation in the market in the absence of coercion, fraud, monopoly, or monopsony) and the *legal price* (fixed by a legitimate authority, but not arbitrarily, since the price was restricted by the need to be in line with the pursuit of the common good).

Also in line with the earlier doctrine, exceptions were allowed for price controls. But distrust was on the rise about the potential ill effects of these

[28] Quoted in Chafuen, *Faith and Liberty*, pp. 82–83.

[29] Domingo de Soto, *De iustitia et iure* – facsimile of the 1556 Latin edition accompanied with a Spanish translation (Madrid: Instituto de Estúdios Políticos, 1968 [1556]), book vi, q. ii, a. iii.

[30] Quoted in Marjorie Grice-Hutchison, *Early Economic Thought in Spain 1177–1740* (London: George Allen & Unwin), p. 100.

interventions and detrimental unintended consequences of regulation that jeopardized the common good. This inspired leading Catholic thinkers of the period to issue strong warnings about these risks. While legal prices that shied away from common estimation were admitted as valid in principle, skepticism about them grew deeper and geared Catholic economic thought in a direction that was more receptive to the operation of market economies (in the absence of coercion, fraud, monopoly, or monopsony)[31] than in earlier periods.

Elegido offers a useful synthesis of the prevalent views of the School of Salamanca on prices and market economies:

> In my view the leading authors of the Salamanca School can contribute three key ideas to a modern discussion of justice in pricing. They used a substantive standard for assessing the justice of exchanges; they claimed that the fundamental standard of commutative justice is equivalence in value; and, finally, they argued that the best indicator of the value of a good is the price that it fetches in an open market.[32]

The inclination of the late scholastics (and particularly within the School of Salamanca) to be skeptical about government intervention in the market and particularly about the imposition of price controls even led Raymond de Roover, in his highly influential article on the concept of the just price, to consider it a weakness on their part:

> One weakness of the scholastic doctors was that they were interested only in laying down principles and tended to overlook practical difficulties, which, they claimed, did not concern the theologians but were the province of the "politicians." An extreme position was taken by Martin Azpilcueta (1493–1587), better known as Navarrus, who opposed all price regulation because it was unnecessary in times of plenty and ineffective or harmful in times of dearth. Several others, among them Molina, looked upon price regulation with the same disfavor.[33]

A definitive judgment on whether this strong inclination on the part of Azpilcueta, Molina, and others ought to be considered a weakness or a strength of their analysis will, of course, be largely dependent upon one's

[31] These conditions may be seen as the central (although not exclusive) tenets of a business culture compatible with Catholic Social Teaching. See André Azevedo Alves, Philip Booth, and Barbara Fryzel, "Business Culture and Corporate Social Responsibility: An Analysis in the Light of Catholic Social Teaching with an Application to Whistle-Blowing," *The Heythrop Journal* (April 2016).

[32] Juan Manuel Elegido, "The Just Price: Three Insights from the Salamanca School," *Journal of Business Ethics*, vol. 90, no.1 (2009), p. 30.

[33] Roover, "The Concept of the Just Price," p. 426.

own contemporary view about the desirability and usefulness of price controls. But regardless of that judgment, it is fair to say that, in this period, Catholic views on the subject evolved toward a more favorable view of the operation of competitive and open market economies and toward a more skeptical position on the adoption of price controls, even if the Catholic thinkers continued to admit price controls as being legitimate in principle.[34] Although not unchallenged, this continues to be the prevailing view emerging from the Catholic tradition and an accurate description of other Christian perspectives on price controls and market economies.

## 10.4 PROTESTANT THOUGHT ON PRICE CONTROLS AFTER THE REFORMATION

### 10.4.1 The Protestant Reformation and Economic Thought

When the Protestant Reformation began in sixteenth-century Europe, the capitalist economic model was not excluded from its criticisms. As Thelma McCormack very well explains by referring to the arguments of R. H. Tawney and Émile Durkheim, capitalism in its initial form was seen by many as providing "economic growth at the expense of social purpose"[35] and as suffering from "a chronic debilitation of morale in terms of an ethical vacuum, an organic division of labour without a larger awareness of interdependency, economic activity without a guild ethic."[36]

In this context, and given the apparent inertia of the established Catholic Church to address these changes and its consequences, the Reformation started as a protest within the Church, with the main objective of trying to "bring order out of chaos by providing a new normative framework."[37] This modern norm – the Protestant ethic – favored the differentiation of roles in society and the interaction among them, this being fundamental to the definition of new roles for social participation and the division of labor.

[34] For a more detailed analysis of the late scholastics' views on price controls, see also Chafuen, *Faith and Liberty*, pp. 85–90.

[35] Thelma McCormack, "The Protestant Ethic and the Spirit of Socialism," *The British Journal of Sociology*, vol. 20, no. 3 (September 1969), p. 266.

[36] Ibid., p. 267. These considerations may be justified by the enormous changes capitalism brought, combined with not only the discovery of new routes of trade – which included not only the transformation of small villages into big cosmopolitan, urban towns and the growth of population with the increasing movement of people and goods – but also with important changes in the labor market that resulted in labor shortages and unemployment (Cf. ibid., pp. 269–270).

[37] Ibid., p. 270.

Furthermore, the Protestant ethic also carried a tradition of Natural Law. This combination began with Hugo Grotius in 1625, continued with Pufendorf, Hutcheson, and Adam Smith, and provided "the theoretical foundations of political economy," including "the nucleus of value and price theory."[38] (Note: For an exposition of Smith's, Pufendorf's, and Hutcheson's views in relation to antitrust, see Chapter 4 by Elzinga and Crane.)

### 10.4.2 Value and Price Theory in Pufendorf, Hutcheson, and Smith

The main common element concerning the definition of value among the authors of this tradition is the determination of just price by using a combination of a good's utility and the costs of labor expended in its production. In 1672, Samuel Pufendorf developed his influential theory of value and price in his *De Jure Naturae et Gentium*, where he defines price as being "a moral quality of things and actions in so far as they are understood to serve some purpose in common life."[39] Three elements can thus be distinguished in the process of defining a certain thing's price. The first element is subjective valuation. This reflects the usefulness of a certain thing for human life or the thing's ability to contribute to a more pleasant life.[40] Scarcity is the second element. It is perhaps the most important one when considering high prices, since there is a tendency for price to be lower when quantity is greater, even with things "which men are least able to do without."[41] The last element is the process of production, which reflects the complexity of the cost factors

[38] Jefrey T. Young, "Law and Economics in the Protestant Natural Law Tradition: Samuel Pufendorf, Francis Hutcheson, and Adam Smith," *Journal of the History of Economic Thought*, vol. 30, no.3 (September 2008), p. 283.

[39] Quoted in ibid., p. 284.

[40] In this point, however, Pufendorf recognizes that there are some things that, despite having no price, are extremely useful for human life, namely, things that "are and should be exempt from dominion" (e.g., the air and the open ocean), things that "are removed from commerce by law and/or custom" (e.g., sacred sites or articles), and things that "cannot be held separately, although they are accessory to things the price of which they influence" (e.g., a beautiful landscape) (quoted in ibid., p. 294). Following Pufendorf's rationale, Hutcheson also enumerates some objects for which prices cannot be determined, such as those things "naturally destined for community, or cannot come into commerce but as appendages of something else" (Francis Hutcheson, *Philosophiae moralis institution compendiaria, with A Short Introduction to Moral Philosophy* (Indianapolis, IN: Liberty Fund, 2007), p. 280, http://oll.libertyfund.org/title/2059).

[41] Quoted in Young, "Law and Economics in the Protestant Natural Law Tradition," p. 285. Adam Smith also associates the idea of scarcity with that of price and property when he recognizes that the air, the running water, and the sea cannot be owned because "they cannot be lessened or impaired by use, nor can anyone be injured by the use of them." Adam Smith, *Lectures on Justice, Police, Revenue and Arms* (Oxford: Clarendon Press, 1986), i.60.

involved in the making of the thing. These factors include, among others, the difficulty of the production, the quantity of workers needed, and the positions they occupy.

As for the contexts in which prices can be formed, Pufendorf explains that, in the state of nature, where transactions occur only occasionally, prices are agreed between the parts involved in the transaction. In organized states, however, prices can be set either by authorities or "by the general valuation and judgement of men, with the further consent of those who are the parties to bargain."[42] When the determination of the price follows a consented judgment of men, the established price is known as "common or natural price," which is taken as the *just price*. In this case, the merchant is allowed to reflect in the price the costs of labor and expenses borne to obtain the product, being thus able to sell more dearly and to profit from the sale of a product without violating the just price:

> But merchants can include in their estimation the time they have spent, the plans they have formed, and the troubles they have met in acquiring, preserving, or distributing their merchandise, as well as all necessary expenses for the labour of their servants . . . it would surely be inhuman, and likely to destroy the industry of men, to try to allow a man for his business, or any other sort of occupation, no more profit than barely permits him to meet his necessities by frugality and hardships.[43]

Some decades after Pufendorf developed his theory, Francis Hutcheson developed his own account of value and price in two of his works, *System of Moral Philosophy* (1747) and *A Short Introduction to Moral Philosophy* (1755), in which he recognized the contribution by Pufendorf. According to Hutcheson, prices are determined by an equal influence of the elements of demand and supply. The author places a special emphasis put on the latter, which he refers to as "difficulty." The supply that determines the price thus reflects effort expended and includes not only the quantity of the good, but also subjective factors such as the toil required for production, the genius or ingenuity of the producer, and even the life standards of the merchant:

> From what we said about the grounds of price, 'tis plain that in estimating the values of goods {in any place}, we are not only to compute the disbursement made in buying, importing, and keeping them safe, with the interest of money thus employed; but also the pains and care of the merchant; the value of which is to be estimated according to the reputable condition in

[42] Quoted in Young, "Law and Economics in the Protestant Natural Law Tradition," p. 285.
[43] Quoted in ibid., p. 285.

> which such men live, and to be added to the other charges upon the goods. This price of the merchant's labour <and care> is the foundation of the ordinary profit of merchants.[44]

For Adam Smith, an account of the theory of value and price can be found in his conception of justice. Under the designation of "natural price," Smith sees the just price as a combination of the utility of the good with all the aspects involved in its creation. In the beaver and deer story that the author tells in his *Wealth of Nations*, he introduces the notion of the right to the fruits of one's labor with the claim that the hunter shall receive something in return for his labor.[45] This right is also seen as a form of equity – another important concept presented by Smith in his *Lectures on Jurisprudence* – which is related to retributive justice, even being used synonymously with the concept of natural justice:

> Servants, labourers, and workmen of different kinds, make up the far greater part of every great political society. But what improves the circumstances of the greater part can never be regarded as an inconveniency to the whole. No society can surely be flourishing and happy, of which the far greater part of the members are poor and miserable. It is but equity, besides, that they who feed, cloath and lodge the whole body of the people, should have such a share of the produce of their own labour as to be themselves tolerably well fed, cloathed and lodged.[46]

Under the influence of and inspired by the notion of price as defined by Samuel Pufendorf and Francis Hutcheson,[47] Smith goes beyond those two authors and elaborates on situations where price controls should be implemented.

The most known example of this kind of mechanism can be found on the market for loans, where Smith clearly favors the imposition of a price ceiling on interest rates. This usury law – as it is commonly called – aimed mainly to reduce the flow of high-risk loans and increase the availability of money to be borrowed by "sober" and "prudent" men. According to Smith, the absence of

44 Hutcheson, *Philosophiae moralis*, p. 284.

45 In Adam Smith's own words: "the property which every man has in his own labour, as it is the original foundation of all other property, so it is the most sacred and inviolable" (Adam Smith, *An Inquiry into the Nature and Causes of the Wealth of Nations* (Indianapolis, IN: Liberty Fund, 1976): I.x.c.12).

46 Ibid., I.viii.36.

47 This influence is extensively explored by Andrew Skinner, "Pufendorf, Hutcheson and Adam Smith: Some Principles of Political Economy," *Scottish Journal of Political Economy*, vol. 42, no. 2 (May 1995), pp. 165–182, or by Enzo Pesciarelli, "Aspects of the Influence of Francis Hutcheson on Adam Smith," *History of Political Economy*, vol. 31, no. 3 (1999), pp. 525–545.

a legal rate ceiling would result in higher interest rates and would consequently concentrate loans in the hands of "prodigals and projectors," who would be likely to use it for speculative and unproductive investments. Following this rationale, Smith proposes the legal rate "to be somewhat above," but not "much above the lowest market rate," so as to have "a great part of the capital of the country . . . thrown into the hands in which it is most likely to be employed with advantage."[48] By defining the interest rate ceiling slightly above the market price, Smith's main intention was to reduce incentives for high-risk loans, since, with low interest rates, high-risk lenders would not receive the full risk premium of the loans required to make them feasible.[49]

Smith was also in favor of regulations in the banking sector. His main commentators justify this by reference to two events in Scotland that shaped Smith's economic thinking: The "small note mania" and the Ayr Bank Crisis.[50] Having recognized the dangers posed by those situations and wishing to prevent them from occurring in the future, Adam Smith suggested two main regulating tools. The first corresponded to the real bills doctrine, according to which banks should only issue money in exchange for short-term real bills. The second consisted of a prohibition of small notes – for Smith considered this practice to have a speculative character and that it penalized poor people.[51]

Smith himself recognized that these kinds of controls were exceptions to his main theory of natural liberty and *laissez faire*, but he considered them necessary for assuring a greater good:

48 Smith, *Wealth of Nations*, II.iv.15.

49 Adam Smith's perspective on the market for loans and on usury laws is thoroughly analyzed by Joseph M. Jadlow, "Adam Smith on Usury Laws," *The Journal of Finance*, vol. 32, no. 4 (September 1977), pp. 1195–1200.

50 As explained by Hugh Rockoff, "Adam Smith on Money, Banking, and the Price Level," in *The Oxford Handbook of Adam Smith*, eds. Christopher J. Berry, Maria Pia Paganelli, and Craig Smith (Oxford: Oxford University Press, 2013), pp. 307–332, these two shocks had a significant impact on the Scottish banking system, as well as repercussions on international financial institutions, having resulted in a "V-shape" economic recession. The "small notes mania" was characterized by the issuing of "redeemable notes for very small sums of money," while the Ayr Bank Crisis refers to a financial crisis in 1772 – "the first modern banking panic faced by the Bank of England" – on which Ayr Bank was "at the very epicentre of the boom, and was the trigger of the subsequent crash" that was the result of bad investment decisions made by the bank (ibid., pp. 310–315).

51 "Where the issuing of bank notes for such very small sums is allowed and commonly practised, many mean people are both enabled and encouraged to become bankers. . .. But the frequent bankruptcies to which such beggarly bankers must be liable, may occasion a very considerable inconveniency, and sometimes even a very great calamity to many poor people who had received their notes in payment" (Smith, *Wealth of Nations*, II.ii.90).

> Such regulations may, no doubt, be considered as in some respects a violation of natural liberty. But those exertions of the natural liberty of a few individuals, which might endanger the security of the whole society, are, and ought to be, restrained by the laws of all governments, of the most free as well as of the most despotical. The obligation of building party walls, in order to prevent the communication of fire, is a violation of natural liberty exactly of the same kind with the regulations of the banking trade which are here proposed.[52]

## 10.5 LUTHER AND PRICE THEORY

Martin Luther is a prominent figure in Protestant thought. His importance and influence in European history during the sixteenth and seventeenth centuries is undeniable, with his intellectual impact lasting well into the present day through Protestantism. His economic theory is founded on the Christian virtue of charity, with a particular emphasis given to the seventh commandment – *you shall not steal* – "which extends that subject from regular theft to the idea of relieving a person of his property against his will by furtive practices in the marketplace."[53] Despite recognizing its necessary character, Luther had an ambiguous attitude regarding trade. He considered that buying and selling would always turn people into victims of greed, "for businessmen will cheat and lie."[54] Given this inevitability, Luther believed that the only solution for the greedy disposition of merchants was to have prices determined by the estimation of wise and honest men appointed by temporal authorities. According to this theory, developed in *On Trade and Usury*, the just price would be based on the real cost of the product, combined with the necessary profit for the merchant to continue his economic activity and sustain his family. In the absence of fixed prices, the just price would be the one decided in the common market:

> It is fair and right that a merchant make as much profit on his wares as will cover his cost and pay him for his trouble, his labor, and his risk . . . one can truly give you no instructions but leave it to your conscience to be careful not to overcharge your neighbor by your greed but seek your modest living.[55]

[52] Ibid., II.i.94.

[53] Odd Langholm, "Martin Luther's Doctrine on Trade and Price in Its Literary Context," *History of Political Economy*, vol. 41, no. 1 (2009), p. 92.

[54] Ibid., p. 94.

[55] Quoted in ibid., p. 96.

Influenced by pre-Reformation Catholic ideas, Luther also condemned the practices of fraud, understood as "fooling the opposite party,"[56] and economic coercion, seen as "exploiting the *need* of the opposite party in order to obtain more favorable terms of exchange."[57] As for collusion and monopoly, the critique is absolute. Luther considers that those who engage in trade just to control the supply or price of certain goods and to make money in that manner are "un-Christian," practice "selfish business," and "should not be tolerated."[58]

In general, the Protestant tradition's theory of value and price defends the just price as an arrangement that combines cost estimates with a fair profit for merchants. Furthermore, the claims for compensation associated with cost elements are grounded in the account of natural property rights and markets. And the exchange of goods is understood as "embedded in social institutions" and as "a form of human interaction and cooperation," which is essential for men to live in a peaceful society.[59]

Within this Protestant natural-law tradition, it becomes possible to distinguish the perspective of the political economists (including Samuel Pufendorf, Francis Hutcheson, and Adam Smith) from Martin Luther's point of view. While the former have a more positive view of the market economy, the latter aligns with a more restrictive and distrustful vision of commercial exchanges.

## 10.6 CONCLUSION

As one would expect, contemporary Christians' views on mechanisms of price control are largely shaped by the positions developed centuries ago, with a special emphasis on the Thomist framework and its contribution of the definition of the *justum pretium*.

In the more heterogeneous context of Protestant denominations, there is naturally a greater variety of positions regarding this theme. Some have a more positive perspective of the market economy, while others argue in favor of greater restrictions and take a more skeptical opinion about commercial transactions. A detailed analysis of this heterogeneity would go vastly beyond

56 According to Luther, the most common forms of fraud included: "using false weights, measures or coins; overestimating merchandise; overcharging customers; selling false or bad merchandise; taking advantage of customers by nimbleness, queer finances, or dexterous tricks" (quoted in ibid., p. 98).

57 Ibid., p. 92.

58 Quoted in ibid., p. 103.

59 Young, "Law and Economics in the Protestant Natural Law Tradition," p. 288.

the scope and possibilities of this chapter, but we should nevertheless acknowledge it.

Although there are various Catholic views on price controls, Catholic positions on the subject have a more easily discernible central core. This is not only because there is greater unity and centralization in the Catholic Church but also because of the orientations provided by the Catechism. The general framework of the idea of price controls and market economies is built upon earlier advances in Catholic thought. It can be found in John Paul II's encyclical letter *Centesimus Annus*, 32: "A person who produces something other than for his own use generally does so in order that others may use it after they have paid a just price, mutually agreed upon through free bargaining." Additionally, one of the most significant references appears in the discussion of the seventh commandment:

> The seventh commandment forbids theft, that is, usurping another's property against the reasonable will of the owner.[60]
>
> Even if it does not contradict the provisions of civil law, any form of unjustly taking and keeping the property of others is against the seventh commandment: thus, deliberate retention of goods lent or of objects lost; business fraud; paying unjust wages; forcing up prices by taking advantage of the ignorance or hardship of another. The following are also morally illicit: speculation in which one contrives to manipulate the price of goods artificially in order to gain an advantage to the detriment of others; [. . .].[61]

In *Centesimus Annus*, it is also possible to identify certain specific circumstances where the regulation of prices appears to be suggested, even though it does not necessarily imply price controls imposed by the state:

> The State, however, has the task of determining the juridical framework within which economic affairs are to be conducted, and thus of safeguarding the prerequisites of a free economy, which presumes a certain equality between the parties, such that one party would not be so powerful as practically to reduce the other to subservience.[62]

These specific circumstances, however, cannot be defined *a priori* and are not independent of judgment on economic theory, as they will be fundamental to evaluate implications of both prices and regulation on the common good.

[60] *Catechism of the Catholic Church*, p. 2408.
[61] Ibid., p. 2409.
[62] *Centesimus Annus*, p. 15.

In order to analyze these particular cases that may justify some sort of intervention, more detailed and in-depth studies and analyses are necessary.[63]

Perhaps the best way to synthesize the Christian position on price controls (to the extent a common Christian position can be ascertained) is in terms of a general inclination to respect the just price. The just price is mostly understood in contemporary terms as the free market price voluntarily agreed upon by the parties in the absence of fraud, coercion, or situations of extreme need. This implicitly recommends against any form of controls on prices that respect those basic conditions. At the same time, there is a recognition that in certain relatively exceptional situations, the prices set by private actors may be in violation of the seventh commandment and, for that reason, may justify (or even require) the regulation of prices.

[63] A good example is Debra Wilson, "Price Gouging, Construction Cartels or Repair Monopolies? Competition Law Issues Following Natural Disasters," *Canterbury Law Review*, vol. 20 (2014), pp. 53–90.

# Index

For EU product safety concerns, contact us at Calle de José Abascal, 56–1°,
28003 Madrid, Spain or eugpsr@cambridge.org.

www.ingramcontent.com/pod-product-compliance
Ingram Content Group UK Ltd.
Pitfield, Milton Keynes, MK11 3LW, UK
UKHW020946040526
470679UK00007B/31
* 9 7 8 1 1 0 8 4 9 5 1 0 3 *